Gadamer's Path to Plato

Gadamer's Path to Plato

*A Response to Heidegger
and a Rejoinder by Stanley Rosen*

Andrew Fuyarchuk

WIPF & STOCK · Eugene, Oregon

GADAMER'S PATH TO PLATO
A Response to Heidegger and a Rejoinder by Stanley Rosen

Copyright © 2010 Andrew Fuyarchuk. All rights reserved. Except for brief quotations in critical publications or reviews, no part of this book may be reproduced in any manner without prior written permission from the publisher. Write: Permissions, Wipf and Stock Publishers, 199 W. 8th Ave., Suite 3, Eugene, OR 97401.

Wipf & Stock
An Imprint of Wipf and Stock Publishers
199 W. 8th Ave., Suite 3
Eugene, OR 97401
www.wipfandstock.com

ISBN 13: 978-1-60608-772-5

Manufactured in the U.S.A.

To my mother, Ruth Evelyn

Contents

Acknowledgments ix
Key to Abbreviations xi
Introduction xiii

Part I: Heidegger and Gadamer
    Introduction 1
  1 Heidegger's Plato 5
  2 Provocation and Inspiration 21

Part II: Gadamer's Correction of Heidegger
    Introduction 31
  3 Counterarguments 35
  4 Heidegger's False Modernism 43
  5 Heidegger's Aristotelianism: The Production Thesis 60
  6 Hermeneutical Situations 76

Part III: Gadamer's Plato
    Introduction 83
  7 Truth as Unconcealment 87
  8 Physics 93
  9 The Good 96

Part IV: Stanley Rosen's Rejoinder
    Introduction 103
  10 Gadamer's Dialectic: Hegel, Tübingen, and Klein 107
  11 Incongruity of Speech and Deed 115
  12 Plato's Dialectic Reconsidered 123

Part V: The Politics of Exclusion
    Introduction 137
  13 Gadamer's Interpretation of the *Republic* 141
  14 Rosen's Interpretation of the *Republic* 155
  15 Human Nature 169
  16 The Politics of Inclusion 183

Appendix 195
Bibliography 199

Acknowledgments

*Thank you to Debbie Sawczak for editing the manuscript,
to Cathy Ding for patience and support,*

*and to the staff at the Angus Glen Community Library,
where much of the book was written.*

*Thanks to the staff at Wipf and Stock
for making this book possible
and especially to Tina Campbell Owens
for the finishing touches.*

Key to Abbreviations

WORKS BY MARTIN HEIDEGGER
(INCLUDING EDITED COLLECTIONS)

BPP	*Basic Problems of Phenomenology*
BH	*Becoming Heidegger*
BT	*Being and Time*
GBT	*The Genesis of Heidegger's Being and Time*
IM	*Introduction to Metaphysics*
PDT	*Plato's Doctrine of Truth*
QCT	*The Question Concerning Technology and Other Essays*

WORKS BY HANS-GEORG GADAMER

DD	*Dialogue and Dialectic*
GR	*The Gadamer Reader*
HD	*Hegel's Dialectic*
IG	*Idea of the Good in Platonic-Aristotelian Philosophy*
PA	*Philosophical Apprenticeships*
PH	*Philosophical Hermeneutics*
PDE	*Plato's Dialectical Ethics*
TM	*Truth and Method*

WORKS BY STANLEY ROSEN

PR	*Plato's Republic*

Introduction

DESPITE EFFORTS TO PROJECT a neutral or impersonal attitude toward the history of philosophy, the past is invariably used by scholars to justify one course of action or another. In North America liberal democracy has in many instances become a hidden standard against which to gauge Plato's teachings. The result is a foregone conclusion: he is a conservative, which has been construed by some to entail capitalist, militant, and elitist values that hold social justice in contempt. No one in the history of thought could be a greater threat to the values of individual liberty, the right to private property, and equality enshrined in the American constitution than the apologist for a philosopher-king, noble lies, and propertyless guardian class. When teachers conflate ideology and philosophy, or use a publicly funded university to consolidate a definable set of values among like-minded persons, it goes without saying that the possibility of recognizing limitations and prejudices is compromised. If history is little more than material to be recast to justify what persons already believe—for example, an abstract notion of right that avoids recognizing the contingency of its historical origins by identifying itself with a universal natural law—then there is simply no point in talking about history, or in doing philosophy for that matter. This is why the work of Martin Heidegger, Hans-Georg Gadamer, and Stanley Rosen is so fascinating: they aim for a creative retrieval of Plato's thought for the purpose of thinking critically about present times.

There is a conversation about Plato between Heidegger, Gadamer, and Rosen that is worth investigating for its own sake. But any investigation so undertaken is not without political ramifications. A quest for understanding alone, in fact, translates into the most politically subversive of lives; Socrates is a case in point. The philosophers among whom I have created a conversation are speculative thinkers, but they also point toward what needs to be done concretely in their respective circumstances. At one time Heidegger argued for the end of the tradition of philosophy, or what he called Platonism, in order to justify a new era of thinking that took its bearings from Aristotle's alleged authentic grasp of pre-Socratic philosophy. Given the overall despair in Europe in the aftermath of World War I, his project spoke to people's aspirations and hopes for renewal in the future. Howevermuch Plato's thought entered into German idealism, modern science and technology and for that reason needed to be questioned in the early twentieth century, insodoing Heidegger also set in motion a rupture with the tradition that was itself forgetful of origins.

While modern projects toward renewal might encourage the pursuit of an unknown yet hoped for future, Gadamer's encouraging the formation of self-understanding in dialogue with the tradition cultivates humility and moderation, sources of restraint on political zealotry and religious enthusiasm. In terms of Plato's philosophy, rather than foster an antithetical relationship to him, Gadamer builds common ground between Plato and Aristotle on the basis of Socrates's method of inquiry that foregrounds the question of the meaning of what something is, respect for the other as other and recognition of their situation. Accordingly, demands are not made upon the tradition to justify itself before spokespersons of a new age but rather, it is contemporary thought that is interrogated by the wisdom of the ancients. Gadamer thus reminds Heidegger that understanding the end of the tradition entails a dialogue with it, and that it is not the tradition or Platonism but his own thinking that ought to be called into question.

Plato's dialogue form was the basis for the development of Gadamer's hermeneutical philosophy. This is refreshing to know because the image of Plato that Heidegger set in motion continues to define the course of Western philosophy. That Heidegger admitted he was wrong to have read Plato as the father of metaphysics, and thanked Gadamer for the correction of that view, seems not to have made any difference to postmodernism, which continues to associate Plato and metaphysics with the end of philosophy. This indicates that Gadamer still has, and likely will always have, a contribution to make; the impulse toward new beginnings and futures seems endemic to the human condition. But at the same time, the image of Plato to which Gadamer directs us might not have the same critical bite today as it had (or should have had) on the German intellectual culture during the 1930s and 1940s.

From the time Rosen was introduced to Gadamer by Leo Strauss in 1963, he initiated an indirect criticism of Gadamer's studies of Plato.[1] Contra Gadamer, who attributed to Plato a dialectical theory of Being, an intersubjective notion of truth, and a society of philosopher-citizens, Rosen defends a notion of Being in Plato that is transcendent to human beings and a personal erotic experience of the Good. The alternative he suggests to Gadamer's idea of political association consists of philosophers remaining aloof from public life, contemplating truth and justice amongst themselves apart from the *hoi poloi*. Such a contrast goes a long way toward understanding differences. But then the question surfaces as to which view can best be used to criticize contemporary trends of thought?

A critical appraisal of Gadamer's reading of Plato's *Republic* by Stanley Rosen reveals a bias toward a mathematical approach to philosophy that privileges a community of rational discourse. Gadamer's hermeneutical philosophy grounded in Plato's dialogue form is not as inclusive as it seems. Underlying it is a decision about what humans essentially are and desire to become. Those who who have no interest in dialogue, consider it foolish, or experience a notion of truth not revealed through intersubjective agreement, are excluded from Gadamer's idea of political association; moreover, there is no way to include them except by turning them into procedural rationalists.

Rosen could not facilitate an understanding of Gadamer's bias were he not attuned to another dimension of existence. While the idea of the apolitical contemplative life is a powerful current in his thinking, his

---

1. Rosen provides what Plato did not: a coherent theory of the ideas. He writes, "No single Idea is visible or intelligible in and through itself alone; each Idea, as an expression of intelligibility, not merely implies but exhibits the Whole (like Leibniz' monads), or Intelligibility as the totality of its moments, as the sum of Ideas." "Ideas," 422. Rosen also examines the problem of the one and the many in this essay, which is essential to Gadamer's understanding of Plato's dialectical theory of Being. Five years later, as if in reply to Rosen, Gadamer writes in "Plato's Unwritten Doctrine," "Plato can hardly be said to have subordinated the realm of ideas to a divine mind like Leibniz's central monad, in which everything is present which is, everything which can be true. And that he did not have any such thing in mind seems to me to be exactly what is implied in Plato's so-called doctrine of 'principles' as well as in the kaleidoscopic play of assertions in his dialogues." *DD*, 154. Rosen's argument in "The Role of Eros in Plato's *Republic*" (1965) takes on a "Hegelian" reading of Plato where *logos* is divested of *eros*, which is Gadamer's contention, and his commentary on the *Republic* is rich in arguments against Gadamer's interpretation of the dialogue in *Idea of the Good*. Their conversation through these and other works is undertaken in the second half of this book.

interpretation of the *Republic* demonstrates, in contrast to Gadamer's, that the formation of a just society includes the views of such miscreants as Thrasymachus and of such innocuous elders as Cephalus, albeit with modifications. This is because a love of the Good constrained by the moderation (mathematical proportion) recommended by Gadamer enables recognition of the other as other—which is precisely what Gadamer purports to advocate but actively denies by assuming that everyone is the same. There is something about keeping the idea of the Good out of the cave that facilitates recognition of substantive differences between persons, a recognition that is required in order to respect people's dignity and include them in a conversation about justice.

OUTLINE

Part One, "Heidegger and Gadamer," distinguishes three readings of Plato within Heidegger's philosophical development. During the 1920s at Marburg University, Heidegger's fascination with Aristotle's phenomenology as a way of legitimizing faith philosophically brought him into a critical relationship with the tradition of Neoplatonism. Although purged of its religious underpinnings, this antipathy became more pronounced after the publication of *Being and Time* (1928), when Nietzsche became a catalyst for his project to overcome the history of forgetfulness of Being (that is, nihilism), originating in Plato's metaphysics. While Gadamer was inspired by Heidegger's phenomenological and hermeneutical method of interpretation, he was disconcerted by Heidegger's first contrasting Plato with Aristotle at Marburg and then associating Plato with metaphysics at Freiburg University in the 1930s. The first part of this book outlines the changes in Heidegger's understanding of Plato, which were not unidimensional, and the ways in which Heidegger both inspired and provoked Gadamer's own study of Plato.

Part Two concerns "Gadamer's Correction of Heidegger". Jean Grondin reports, "Published letters by Heidegger indicate that he prized Gadamer's studies of Plato from the 1970s, hoping that they would correct his own understanding of Plato."[2] The book Heidegger hoped Gadamer would write on Plato did not come to fruition.[3] Nevertheless,

---

2. Grondin, *Hans-Georg Gadamer*, 293.

3. While reflecting upon the process of composing *Truth and Method*, Gadamer writes, "Indeed, I began asking myself whether philosophy could still be placed under the rubric of such a synthetic task at all. Indeed, for the continuation of hermeneu-

towards the end of his life Heidegger thanked Gadamer for correcting his understanding of Plato and also expressed regret for having accepted Nietzsche's position on the history of philosophy. Since Gadamer, for the most part, did not challenge Heidegger directly, the exact arguments that convinced Heidegger he had made a mistake cannot be known for certain; nevertheless, insofar as Gadamer refuted him indirectly, that is to say through both reinterpretations of Plato's dialogues and scholars with whom Heidegger's thinking has an affinity, including Jaeger and Natorp, it is possible to discern what may have been relevant to such a refutation up to and including work in the 1970s. The result is a reconstruction of a conversation with Heidegger that might have some historiographical credibility, but which is above all of philosophical import for understanding the limits of Heidegger's view of Plato that justify an alternative approach to studying the history of ideas.

In Part Three, Gadamer's view of Plato is developed from Heidegger's teachings with the aim of finding common ground between Plato and Aristotle in matters of ethics, truth, metaphysics, and physics. This is significant since it is largely on the basis of Aristotle that Heidegger builds his understanding of Plato's philosophy. By demonstrating, for instance, that Plato is an Aristotelian in matters of ethics, and Aristotle a Platonist in matters of physics, Gadamer undermines the antithesis Heidegger creates between them. The common ground thus established is Gadamer's primary achievement in *The Idea of the Good in Platonic-Aristotelian Philosophy* (1978).

Part Four, "Stanley Rosen's Rejoinder," investigates Gadamer's understanding of Plato's dialectic, and Part Five, "Politics of Exclusion," his reading of the *Republic* in order to discern the unarticulated doctrine in his Plato studies. While Gadamer's hermeneutical philosophy is designed to leave the meaning of Being undecided or open, his interpretation of the meaning of dialectic for Plato indicates that a decision about this meaning has already been made. This is indicated by the self-referential incoherence of Gadamer's reasoning. Although he intends to take into consideration the dramatic elements of Plato's dialogues in his interpretation of dialectic, Gadamer in fact suppresses them be-

---

tical experiences, must not philosophy hold itself open, captivated by what remains always evident to it, and use its powers to oppose all redarkening of what it has seen? Philosophy is enlightenment, but precisely also enlightenment with regard to its own dogmatism." "Autobiographical Reflections" in *GR*, 20.

cause, according to Rosen, he privileges a mathematical path toward philosophy. This mathematical approach, anonymous and focused on universal structures of reasoning, that compels Gadamer to bypass the literary aspects of the dialogues in an interpretation of Plato's philosophy, is commensurate with the view of human nature he attributes to Plato in the *Republic*. A close examination of Gadamer's reading of that dialogue reveals his belief that, for Plato, human beings are by nature rational agents, hence nonrational persons, or those without any interest in philosophy so understood, are excluded from his version of Plato's just state. For Rosen, this is precisely what the *Republic* was written to warn against; namely, the attempt to institute a perfectly just regime for everyone, because the result is profoundly unjust and brutal toward people most of whom, thankfully, have no interest in philosophy. In contrast to Gadamer, Rosen understands Plato to be recommending a state fit for both philosophers and nonphilosophers while at the same time maintaining a distinction between them. In contrast to Gadamer, who subtly recommends measuring people's lives according to the same standard of mathematical equality that suppresses differences, Rosen argues for a pluralist society in which differences of character and desire are recognized. This is relevant to Heidegger's reading of Plato because Rosen is a metaphysician who believes that the meaning of Being is to be sought higher up in the transcendent pure and simple, yet whose political theory, unlike that of either Gadamer or Heidegger, is inclusive of the other as other.

Part I

Heidegger and Gadamer

Introduction

GADAMER'S PATH TO PLATO developed in reply to Heidegger's claim in the late 1920s to early 1930s that Plato was responsible for the forgetting of the meaning of Being by the West.[1] Gadamer explains to Leo Strauss in 1961 that his "point of departure is not the complete forgetfulness of Being, the 'night of Being,' rather, on the contrary—I say this against Heidegger and Buber—the unreality of such an assertion."[2] The belief that Being is forgotten is unrealistic for Gadamer because forgetting is a precondition for a mode of remembering (*a-lethia*). Since this is a position Gadamer had learned from Heidegger during the Marburg years (as well as from Hegel) there is a sense in which Gadamer's challenge to Heidegger's understanding of Plato reminds Heidegger of himself. It is thus not surprising to find that Heidegger's relation to Plato is more complex and variable than we might otherwise gather from Gadamer's emphasis upon the claim about Plato as a metaphysician. Some of Heidegger's lectures during the 1920s prefigure and provide justification for Gadamer's argument that Plato and Aristotle share common ground. Outlining the development and changing character of Heidegger's Plato does not, however, vitiate the relevance of Gadamer's criticisms. Despite having two dimensions, Heidegger's view of Plato the metaphysician has remained constant for over forty years. Moreover, it is primarily as a metaphysician that Heidegger's Plato has been granted to us, giving rise to antimetaphysical movements including

---

1. *IG*, 5.
2. Quoted from Wachterhauser, *Beyond Being*, 14.

phenomenology, existentialism, and postmodernism.[3] In other words, Gadamer's image of Heidegger's Plato is relevant insofar as it continues to define the character of Western philosophy, a character about which Gadamer would have been understandably ambivalent insofar as it is based upon an unreflective relationship to the history of thought. Since Heidegger justified this orientation with an argument for the end of philosophy, yet during the Marburg years (1924–1928) provided Gadamer with the conceptual tools for resisting it, Gadamer was both provoked and inspired by him.

OUTLINE

Part I is an introduction to the evolution of Heidegger's understanding of Plato and how it was received by Gadamer when he studied under Heidegger in the 1920s at Marburg University. Chapter 1, "Heidegger's Plato," sketches three portraits of Plato based on different dimensions and stages of Heidegger's philosophical development. The first, "Plato: Metaphysics 1909–1920," argues that Heidegger was initially a metaphysical realist in the sense of striving to achieve a better grasp of things-in-themselves. Although relatively indifferent to Plato during this time, he was nevertheless averse to the notion of universal and first causes. This aversion becomes pronounced when he turns to Aristotle's phenomenology for purposes of developing a philosophical justification for faith. The obstacle to that goal is, for Heidegger, the legacy of Neoplatonic concepts within a Christian understanding of existence. This is discussed in "Aristotle and Destruction."

"Plato II: Platonism" argues that Heidegger enters a new phase in his philosophical development, a shift from identifying with the task of metaphysics (though not Plato) to overcoming metaphysics (Plato). In this famed "turn" Heidegger, on account of a renewed interest in Nietzsche, associates Plato with Platonism. This is also the portrait of which Gadamer is critical.

"Plato III: Appropriating Plato" investigates evidence throughout Heidegger's philosophical development for a more charitable interpretation of Plato. This is a dimension of Heidegger's philosophy that anticipates Gadamer's project to correct him. "Plato III," then, brings

---

3. I have in mind Jean-Luc Marion, Michel Henry, Jean-Louis Chrétien, Jean-Yves Lacoste, Jean Paul Sartre and Jacques Derrida.

into question the accuracy of Gadamer's view of Heidegger's Plato, but as mentioned, neither its critical relevance to Heidegger nor trends in contemporary thought that remain in the grip of Plato the metaphysician who forgets the meaning of Being.

Chapter 2, "Provocation and Inspiration," investigates both Gadamer's admiration for and ambivalence about Heidegger's teachings during the Marburg years: while Gadamer was inspired by Heidegger's phenomenology and hermeneutics because of the way they revivified the past in an incisive criticism of Marburg's neo-Kantian and scientific intellectual culture, he was also troubled by Heidegger's antipathy toward Plato and by his juxtaposition of Plato with Aristotle.

1

Heidegger's Plato

1. PLATO I: METAPHYSICS (1909–1920)

Among Heidegger's earliest intellectual influences were the works of Husserl (*Ideas*, published 1913, and *Logical Investigations*, published 1900) and Aristotle. Before he became Husserl's teaching assistant in 1916, Heidegger had been alerted by Franz Brentano in 1907 to the many ways in which beings become manifest, and by Carl Braig in 1909 to the question of their unity in Aristotle's philosophy. From the outset of his philosophical development, Heidegger had an ambivalent relationship to Plato's theory that Being transcends beings. Rather than resort to a ground of meaning independent of the cohesion of everyday life, Heidegger sought to uncover a sense of meaning intrinsic to a given state of affairs. In his 1915 lecture "The Concept of Time in the History of Philosophy," he says that metaphysics posits hidden qualities as a cause in order to explain phenomena, cites Plato's notion of hypothesis to illustrate what he means by metaphysics, and suggests an equivalence between metaphysics and Galileo's quantitative science.[1] He indicates that the causes Galileo identifies, while visible and measurable, are comparable to Plato's in that scientific causes are, to the same extent as metaphysical ones, hypotheses; that is, they are a subject matter placed under discussion. Metaphysics, according to Heidegger at this time, concerns intelligible principles that are not independent of a linguistic context, but rather, like scientific hypotheses, are ways of making sense of the world. Metaphysics is another language about reality, with no greater corner on truth than the language spoken by scientists and epistemologists.

---

1. *BH*, 61–64. The lecture contrasts time in physics with time in history, the former being homogeneous and linear, the latter being heterogeneous and nonlinear.

This assessment of the "Queen of the sciences" is an invitation for Heidegger to develop a general theory. The general theory for which he aims is metaphysical, as Dostal reports, but not in a conventional sense.[2] "Being" for Heidegger is not a supersensible cause grasped by reason alone. On the contrary, after having been schooled in the transcendental phenomenology of Edmund Husserl, Heidegger partook of a movement that was challenging the legacy of Greek rationality in the modern age. Even before the devastation of World War I, when disillusion with scientific rationality and progress reached a new pitch in Europe and the phenomenological movement in Germany gained momentum (Max Scheler, Martin Buber), Heidegger was challenging scientism, although from a confessional standpoint. While science, i.e., Greek concepts, abstracted from and thereby obscured the authentic experience of faith, Heidegger sought unadulterated access to religious experience. From 1909 to 1913 he "published a series of articles in the antimodernist Catholic journal *Akademiker*" in what John van Buren names Heidegger's "Catholic Neo-Catholic and Anti-modernist Phase,"[3] and identified with the mystical experiences of Augustine, Søren Kierkegaard, Martin Luther, Meister Eckhart, Bonaventura, Bernard of Clairvaux, and Tauler. Heidegger passed through two more early Freiburg stages before 1919, yet they share a common ground in the valorization of the mystical and primordial experience of Christianity. Contra the "Greekification" of thought in which Edmund Husserl was implicated by equating knowing with intuitive seeing, Heidegger was a metaphysical realist in the sense of seeking an encounter with reality that is unmediated and not subject to interpretation.[4] His confessional turn to Protestantism from Catholicism in 1917 was similarly motivated.

---

2. According to Robert Dostal, the stages in the development of Heidegger's thought are as follows: (1) an identification with the task of metaphysics; (2) a call to overcome metaphysics; and (3) a claim to being finished or done with metaphysics. Dostal, "Gadamer's Continuous Challenge," 289.

3. John van Buren outlines three stages in Heidegger's development after WW I: (1) "The Catholic Neo-Scholastic and Anti-modernist Phase" of 1909 to 1913, marked by Heidegger's study of theology and plans to enter the priesthood; (2) "The Neo-Neo-Scholastic Phase" of 1913 to 1916, marked by an interest in reviving a new scholasticism and medieval mysticism; and (3) "The Protestant and Mystical Phase," beginning around 1917 and marked by a growing interest in Schleiermacher and a confessional turn to Protestantism. Van Buren, "Martin Heidegger, Martin Luther," 160.

4. *GBT*, 229. Husserl unearthed the idea that the truth of judgments is not solely a question of validity (the "logical prejudice") but in addition, "presupposes a deeper

2. ARISTOTLE AND DECONSTRUCTION (1920–1928)

In the 1920s Heidegger's relation to Greek philosophy underwent a dramatic shift that had significant implications with regard to Aristotle, but not Plato, whose metaphysical ideals remained an obstacle to what Heidegger thought needed to be concretely done. Marlene Zarander observes that between 1923 and 1928 Heidegger's relation to the Greeks exhibited two dimensions. She writes, "To conclude: the status of the Greeks, in the course of these years at Marburg, is ambiguous. But it is the Greeks, as a whole, who are both solicited and criticized at one and the same time."[5] Zarander is referring to Heidegger's method of "phenomenological destruction" whereby the essential elements of traditional concepts are dissected and analyzed in order to effect a truly radical and authentic reconstruction. The germination of this method is accounted for in sources unavailable to Zarander in the mid 1990s: Heidegger's Freiburg and Marburg lectures.[6] While the first indications of the method are in his *Habilitationsschrift* entitled *Duns Scotus's Theory of Categories and Meaning* (1915), it was not until the lectures at the close of his course in the winter semester of 1919–1920 that Heidegger adopted the term "destruction".[7] Even so, the method was not well developed until after lectures delivered in summer to autumn of 1920 were compiled and crafted into the essay "Critical Comments on Karl Jaspers's Psychology of Worldviews." Heidegger writes, "The task of destruction is

---

notion of truth as identity of what is meant (judged) with what is intuited (perceived)." With this thought Husserl, as Dahlstrom points out, makes a significant step beyond propositional truth yet retains the husk of a correspondence theory. The result is that the ontology of truth (hermeneutic-as-structure) remains hidden. Dahlstrom, *Heidegger's Concept of Truth*, 175–176. Among the earliest criticisms of Husserl, although indirect, is the passage in "Critical Comments on Karl Jaspers's Psychology of Worldviews" (*BH*, 110–149), where Heidegger suggests that Husserl does not acknowledge the methodological assumptions or interpretive character of his investigations. See Carmen Taylor, *Heidegger's Analytic*, 55.

5. Zarander, "Mirror," 10.

6. In the mid 1990s when Marlene Zarander was formulating her thesis, as she observes, the Marburg lectures were just becoming available. Ibid., 24 n9.

7. The earliest evidence of this "destruction" is in his *Habilitationsschrift*. He points out that the "scholastic mode of thought" conceals phenomenological observations with metaphysical speculations. Poggeler, *Heidegger's Path*, 15. It may have been inspired by Luther's primal quest for primitive Christianity, or a theology of the cross, through a devastating criticism of a theology of glory. Van Buren, "Martin Heidegger, Martin Luther," 172.

equivalent to the explication of the original motive-giving situation from which the basic experiences of philosophy have arisen."[8] Heidegger's articulation of this method of uncovering the "original motive-giving situation" coincided with his immersion in Aristotle's phenomenology.

Heidegger's investigation of Aristotle had two sides, the epistemological and the religious, from which the genuine Aristotle was retrieved by applying the method of phenomenological destruction. On the one hand, Heidegger observes that Aristotle had been implicated in the tradition on the basis of *Metaphysics* X, where he locates truth in judgments verified by the correctness of a representation.[9] At the same time, however, he frees Aristotle from this association by asserting that Aristotle does not discuss truth in the passages about judgment. Instead, suggests Heidegger, Aristotle refers to a correspondence theory of truth only as something commonsensical, i.e., "vulgar," and hence disapproved; such a theory of truth, says Heidegger, is precisely what Aristotle was criticizing with the notion of truth as unconcealment (*aletheia*).[10] Whereas the tradition had unqualifiedly attributed to Aristotle a belief in a permanent and eternal being on the basis of *Metaphysics* VII,[11] Heidegger argues that Aristotle is asking a question about the meaning of *ousia*, which Heidegger translates as beingness (*Seiendheit*). Although *ousia* included an idea of constancy and familiarity (since it also means possessions or real estate), Heidegger distinguishes from the latter an idea of becoming-present that harks back to the early Greek notion of *physis*.[12] While *logos* implies an eternal and divine word that stands on its own

---

8. *BH*, 118. Plato is mentioned parenthetically alongside Aristotle for continuing to shape the sense of theory.

9. *Metaphysics* X, chapter 10, 1051b.

10. According to Heidegger, the tradition of philosophy arrives at three conclusions regarding truth that it attributes to Aristotle: (1) truth belongs to judgments; (2) truth is a correspondence of thinking with reality; and (3) the correspondence theory of truth most agrees with common sense. *BH*, 220, repeated in *BT*, 198. (*aletheia*). Dahlstrom has an excellent discussion of Aristotle's understanding of truth and Heidegger's interpretation of it in his book *Heidegger's Concept of Truth*, 175–222.

11. Aristotle writes, "Indeed, that which always, both now and long ago, is sought after and which is always a source of puzzlement, i.e., the question, What is being?, is really the question, What is primary being? [*ousia*] . . . So we too must, most of all, primarily, and so to speak exclusively, investigate about that which is being in this way [i.e., that which is being in the primary way]: what is it?" *Metaphysics*, 1028b2–7.

12. This is a paraphrase of Carol J. White's argument in "Heidegger and the Greeks," 137–138.

independent of time, Heidegger argues that for Aristotle, (1) this immutable order is expressed in *legein* or everyday speech; and (2) the speech that reveals beings from out of hiddenness is dependent upon "the basic comportment of being-true that *Dasein* is."[13] In short, Heidegger deconstructs traditional notions of truth, time, and rational discourse (*logos*) attributed to Aristotle in order to reveal a sense of those terms that is remarkably subversive of their conventional meanings. At the broadest level, Heidegger argues against severing *logos* from *physis* by showing how, according to Aristotle, human temporal existence is implicated in knowledge of truth.

On the other hand, Heidegger was drawn to Aristotle for religious reasons. The development of a "phenomenological destruction" in the years 1919–1920 was coordinate with Heidegger's shift from Freiburg to Marburg, from Kierkegaard and Christian mysticism to Aristotle, and from a project to grasp Being in its unity in ultimate metaphysical principles to a phenomenology of factic (actual) life articulated by Aristotle.[14] Part of Heidegger's reason for profiling Aristotle in his lectures was to craft an essay that would earn him a teaching assignment at Marburg University.[15] Yet Heidegger was obviously more than a pragmatist; he was deeply involved in the questions he posed.[16] Aristotelian scholasticism, in which he had been trained in preparation for entering the Catholic priesthood (1909–1911), did not open Christianity to him, but rather closed a door to it. He detected the same shortcoming in his students in 1920, who he thought lacked a theological training on account of "Greekification."[17] His 1920–21 lecture course "Augustine and

13. In "Being-There, Being-True," Heidegger uses *Nicomachean Ethics* VI to argue that Aristotle understood how *logos* reveals beings from out of hiddenness because he understood this kind of *logos* as the "basic comportment of being-true that human *Dasein* is." There are five ways of "being-true" (ways in which the soul disposes over truth) including *episteme, techne, phronesis, sophia,* and *nous.* BH, 224–226.

14. Poggeler, *Heidegger's Path*, 17. "Factic life" was first referred to by Heidegger in "Introduction to Phenomenology of Religion," and means, in the words of Poggeler, that grasping blissful life in historical performance matters more than content. Ibid., 24.

15. The essay in question is "Phenomenological Interpretations with Respect to Aristotle," which was given to Natorp and shown by him to Gadamer the same year, 1922.

16. Gadamer reports that Heidegger was also attempting to give up the Aristotle of scholasticism in order to "become a Christian" in the early 1920s. Van Buren, "Martin Heidegger, Martin Luther," 173.

17. The "Greekification" of early Christian thought and Scripture was argued by

Neoplatonism" was thus designed to demonstrate how Augustine was separated from union with God by a Neoplatonic category of Being. According to Heidegger, the latter abstracts from the toil and travail of existence, the temporal struggle with pride and temptation. Otto Poggeler explains of the 1920 course on Augustine and Neoplatonism, "Augustine lives and thinks starting from the unrest belonging to factical life; nevertheless, in the quietism of the *fruito Dei* which stems from Neoplatonism he misses the factical life-experience of primordial Christianity and becomes untrue to himself."[18] By finding refuge and solace in eternity Augustine closed down, or escaped from, the possibility of a genuine experience of God in time that Heidegger believed Aristotle's phenomenology could open up.

In the early 1920s Heidegger thought that Aristotle's philosophy provided the conceptual tools with which to understand Christian factic life, or Pauline kairological time; for example, in *Nicomachean Ethics* VI Heidegger finds four compartments or virtues (*hexis*) that reveal different aspects of phenomena, of which he believes the most significant for making sense of Christian factic life is *phronesis*.[19] If an experience of Eternity or God can be worked out of *Dasein*'s way of existing, then time in general has an "eminent relation to 'soul' and 'spirit.'"[20] If time has a relation to the soul, then Aristotle was on the verge of grasping that the meaning of Being was temporality. Heidegger adds a footnote from Aristotle's *Physics* to this effect in *Being and Time*.[21] This is perhaps

---

Harnack and Dilthey, whom Heidegger likely had in mind. GBT, 228.

18. Poggeler, *Heidegger's Path*, 27.

19. Kisiel writes, "In his reading of Aristotle's account of the different kinds of truth in *Nicomachean Ethics* VI, Heidegger thought he also found an original experience of *kairos* paralleling that of primitive Christianity." GBT, 229. The different kinds of truth to which Kisiel is referring are four kinds of perception that Heidegger equates with "a specific disposition (*Befindlichkeit*)" (BH, 226): *sophia, episteme, techne,* and *phronesis*. Heidegger associates the "original experience of *kairos*" with *phronetic* insight of *phronesis*, which is distinct from yet also related to *sophia*. Whereas *sophia* relates to that which always is, *phronesis* relates to that which could be otherwise than it is. But the two virtues are not mutually exclusive. Just as *episteme* includes *techne*, *sophia* includes *phronesis*. That the latter are concomitants is captured in Plato's term for *phronesis* in the *Republic* IV: *sophrosune* (soph- + phron-). For kairological time see Romans 13:11 and 1 Thess 4–5, where Paul speaks of Christian hope and uses kairotic time to refer to the advent of Christ.

20. BT, 391.

21. Heidegger cites *Physics* IV, 223a25; 11, 218b29–219a1, 219a4–6 and quotes Aristotle as follows: "But if nothing other than the soul or the soul's mind were natu-

why Heidegger turned to him: to understand the existential structures of Pauline kairological time that Augustine bypassed, and thereby to clarify a religious experience phenomenologically.

Dostal thus observes that during the Marburg period, despite frequent references in his lectures and notes to the classical phrase *epekeina tes ousias* (beyond beings), Heidegger pays little attention to Plato.[22] To the extent that he does, Plato is for the most part subsumed under an Aristotelian and modern agenda; for instance, although Heidegger refers to the *Statesman* and *Protagoras* in the winter semester of 1921–22, he does so in order to highlight notions of practical wisdom, i.e., Aristotle's ethic of *phronesis*.[23] In the early-to-mid 1920s Heidegger consistently conflates Plato's dialectic with Hegel's (e.g., in the *Sophist* lectures of 1923–1924)) and argues that dialectic, being constrained by language, is inferior to the *theoria* of Aristotle.[24] Overall, in the 1920s Heidegger reads both Augustine and Plato on time, desire, and God in terms of Aristotle; he does so in part, as Gonzalez points out, because of "the hermeneutical principle that we should always proceed from what is clear back to what is obscure,"[25] but also because Plato and Neoplatonism are implicated by Heidegger in the spirit of modern science.[26]

3. PLATO II: PLATONISM (1929–1935)

During his first period of identifying with the task of metaphysics, Heidegger had been relatively quiet about the practical ramifications of Plato's notion of Being, except insofar as it separated Augustine from

---

rally equipped for numbering, then if there were no soul, time would be impossible." *BT*, 416 n14. Heidegger explains that the temporal interpretation of ancient ontology reached its highest stage in Aristotle (*BT*, 23); that Aristotle understood the unity of transcendental universals as the unity by analogy, and so placed the problem of Being on a new foundation wherein an understanding of Being is always already contained in everything we apprehend in being (*BT*, 2 and 79 n). Quoting Aristotle, he writes, "The soul (of the human being) is in a certain way beings. The 'soul' which constitutes the being of human being discovers in its way to be—*aisthesis* and *noesis*—all beings with regard to their thatness and whatness, that is to say, always also in their being." *BT*, 12.

22. Dostal, "Beyond Being," 82–83.
23. Van Buren, *Young Heidegger*, 233.
24. See Gonzalez, "Dialectic."
25. Ibid., 365.
26. For a more detailed discussion of Heidegger's relation to Aristotle during these years see Van Buren, *Young Heidegger*, especially the chapter "Aristotle."

God. However, in the late '20s to early '30s he thinks of Plato's idea of the Good along the lines of any other idea of human consciousness, aligning Plato with the history of Christendom and, after World War II, with twentieth-century technology. In his 1942 essay "Plato's Doctrine of Truth," he holds Plato responsible for transforming the early Greek experience of truth (*aletheia*) and Being (*physis*) into correctness of representation and idea respectively. By equating Being with an idea (human perspective) and paying little attention to the movement proper to Being as *physis* (emergence-withdrawal), Plato lays the foundation for the Western metaphysical tradition's forgetfulness of the meaning of Being, which fades into a technological rage against nature.[27] Ideas from Nietzsche, Natorp, Jaeger, and Aristotle coalesce to support the new direction taken by Heidegger after *Being and Time*, announced in *An Introduction to Metaphysics* (1935), to overcome metaphysics;[28] this tight web of ideas cannot be untangled here, but will be the subject of discussion in Part II. Suffice it to say that Nietzsche (together with Holderlin) is the catalyst for combining their views into an argument that Plato is the founder of the tradition of metaphysics.[29]

Although Heidegger had written about Nietzsche in his *Habilitationsschrift* and studied him with Rickert (1911–1915), he did not recognize Nietzsche's significance for the history of philosophy until after *Being and Time* (1928).[30] It would seem that he was led to Nietzsche by way of the National Socialist German Worker's Party (NSDAP), which had identified Nietzsche as its intellectual forebear. Even if this could be established, however, Heidegger's alleged support for the National Socialists in 1933–1934 is not unambiguous. He seems to have been hoping for a "spiritual change" in the movement from "within," and thus

---

27. Heidegger's interpretation of the early Greek notions of Being and truth and how Plato transforms them from *physis* and *aletheia* to idea and *orthotes* is discussed in the Appendix.

28. Natorp fueled Heidegger's belief that Plato was an idealist, Jaeger his conclusion that Aristotle had matured beyond Plato, and Aristotle his understanding that for Plato Being is a permanent idea. See Part II.

29. Charles Bambach writes, paraphrasing Hölderlin, "In an age where 'the gods have fled, where the presence of the sacred no longer evoked a response in the human soul, it would be no easy task to recover the dormant power of the Greek gods hidden within the earth." Bambach, *Heidegger's Roots*, 51. See also Hölderlin, "Germania," 210–211.

30. Poggeler, *Heidegger's Path*, 3.

covertly criticized the regime by refusing to dismiss persons from office as requested by the Party and associating the Nazi state with other technological monoliths such as the United States and Russia.[31] Something other than a political ideology drew Heidegger to Nietzsche. Notably, there are three ways in which the two cross paths on Plato: (1) Plato is a Christian in that he valorizes the supersensible at the expense of the sensible realm; (2) the history of Platonism is over; and (3) the pre-Socratics are decisive for reversing the Platonic-Christian tradition.[32]

First, Nietzsche's belief that Christianity is Platonism appears in the Preface to *Beyond Good and Evil*, where he asserts that Christianity is "Platonism for the people."[33] Their identification hinges upon equating existence and meaning with supersensible ideas, i.e., a perfect, "otherworldly" idea of the Good and God. Heidegger reaches the same conclusion in *The Basic Problems of Phenomenology*, stating that Plato's ideas were tailor-made for the Judeo-Christian worldview,[34] and writes similarly in *An Introduction to Metaphysics* that "Nietzsche was right in saying that Christianity is Platonism for the people."[35] The rationale for these judgments is Plato's alleged dualist ontology, which Nietzsche associates with the "afterworld" in Christianity. This is represented in the following interpretation of Plato's ideas by Heidegger in 1935:

> It was in the Sophists and in Plato that appearance was declared to be mere appearance and thus degraded. At the same time being, as idea, was exalted to a suprasensory realm. A chasm, *chorismos*, was created between the merely apparent essent here below and real being somewhere on high.[36]

---

31. This is the argument of W. J. Korab-Karpowicz in "Heidegger's Hidden Path."

32. Gregory Fried says that Heidegger accepts from Nietzsche (1) the notion that nihilism begins with Plato; (2) Plato's otherworldliness; and (3) the claim that morality is subsumed by Christian theology and ethics. Fried, "Back to the Cave," 173 n4.

33. See also "How the 'Real World' at Last Became a Myth," 40, and "The Madman," 181, in Nietzsche's *Gay Science*. See also Heidegger's "Word of Nietzsche" in *QCT*, 53–114.

34. In *BPP*, quoting from Dostal, "Beyond Being," 86.

35. *IM*, 106.

36. Ibid.

In the 1947 lecture on Nietzsche, Heidegger repeats that formulation:

> For Platonism, the Idea, the supersensuous, is the true being. In contrast, the sensuous is *me on*. The latter suggests, not nonbeing pure and simple, *ouk on*, but *me* – what may not be addressed as being even thought is not simply nothing. Insofar as, and to the extent that, it may be called being, the sensuous must be measured upon the supersensuous; nonbeing possesses the shadow and the residues of Being which fall from true being.[37]

Heidegger and Nietzsche agree that Plato is a metaphysician because his theory of ideas devalues the sensible realm.

Second, both Nietzsche and Heidegger agree that the history of philosophy has ended. For Nietzsche, this is connected to an elevation of the lowest values to the rank of the highest; that is, the declining will to live is the norm in the modern era, marking the triumph of Platonism-Christianity. But this victory is also a defeat since, for Nietzsche, it is by plumbing the depths that one is exalted, and hence the age of nihilism is ripe for the redeeming work of Zarathustra, the bringer of life-affirming values. Heidegger seems to affirm Nietzsche's view of the history of thought during the opening of his 1923/24 course, "Introduction to Phenomenological Research," asserting, "It is my conviction that philosophy is at an end."[38] However, it is more likely that with these words he is thinking of Husserl's diagnosis of a crisis in the European sciences, including philosophy, after World War I. A somewhat more Nietzschean language is evident in the following words by Heidegger: "And if indeed our unique *Dasein* itself stands before a great journey, if what Friedrich Nietzsche, the last German philosopher who passionately seeks God, says is true: 'God is dead' – if we must put into practice this abandonment of contemporary man in the midst of beings ..."[39] Nietzsche's contempt for bourgeois contentment resonated with Heidegger's antimodernism. For both, the mediocrity or "leveling down" of human beings signaled that the spirit of the times had exhausted itself or worked out all its possibilities. Heidegger made sense of that exhaustion in terms slightly different from Nietzsche's. For Heidegger, history is over because the internal logic of Being as an idea (Plato) has fulfilled itself in an intoxi-

---

37. Heidegger, *Nietzsche*, 154.
38. Bambach, *Heidegger's Roots*, 100.
39. Poggeler, *Heidegger's Path*, 83.

cated rage against non-Being, i.e., the coming-to-be of beings (*physis*); for Nietzsche, history is over because the highest values have devalued themselves, that is, the best have become the most pitiable and ugliest of priests. Nevertheless, Heidegger's and Nietzsche's mutual disdain for reason and science is a thread between them initially spun in *The Birth of Tragedy*.

Third, both Nietzsche and Heidegger are inspired by the pre-Socratics. Both regarded the pre-Socratics as "pure" (because pre-Christian) and in some sense able to provide the inspiration and conceptual resources to plot a new destiny for the West. Nietzsche looks to the pre-Homeric Greeks and Heidegger to Aristotle, whom he credits with understanding better than the early Greeks the very notions of Being (*physis*) and truth (unconcealment) that they experienced.

In short, Nietzsche was decidedly significant for Heidegger's endeavor to "overcome" metaphysics. If, as Nietzsche says, Christianity is Platonism, then an overcoming of Platonism is not to be found in theology, but rather in the historical origins of metaphysics in Plato's philosophy, i.e., in an epochal break from the original pre-Socratic experience of *aletheia* grasped by Aristotle.

Yet Heidegger also distinguishes himself from Nietzsche. However much their projects resemble one another in historical scope and values, Heidegger argues that Nietzsche is himself a metaphysician. He quotes Nietzsche from *The Will to Power*: "My philosophy is an inverted Platonism: the farther removed from true being, the purer, the finer, the better it is. Living in semblance as goal."[40] Heidegger argues that Nietzsche elevates the sensible to the status accorded the supersensible by Plato, with the result that Nietzsche is indeed an inverted Platonist as he calls himself—but a Platonist nevertheless. It is not Nietzsche, therefore, who marks the end of history, but Heidegger; and he thereby displaces Zarathustra as the prophet of a new age.

4. PLATO III: APPROPRIATING PLATO

Gadamer considers Heidegger to have insisted upon a rupture in the history of philosophy between the pre-Socratics and Plato, between Platonism and himself. Yet this is by no means the only attitude Heidegger

---

40. Heidegger, *Nietzsche*, 154. See also "Word of Nietzsche" in *QCT*, 53–114, which is based on lectures given in 1936–1940.

exhibits in relation to the past, a fact which in turn explains variations in his understanding of Plato. Robert Bernasconi argues that when Heidegger said philosophy had ended, he meant not that the tradition no longer has anything to say to us, but that it speaks to us in a different way; on account of our being historically situated there is no ultimate notion of metaphysics to speak of, only a way in which metaphysics is granted to us.[41]

In support of this position Bernasconi cites evidence from *Being and Time* and *On the Way to Language*. In the former, Heidegger argues that although the history of ontology is over, it includes an appropriation of what had been thought.[42] In *On The Way to Language* Bernasconi reports on Heidegger's behalf that the tradition remains rich in truth.[43] In addition, in a lecture "The Basic Problems of Phenomenology," Heidegger writes of the phenomenological destruction, "And this is not a negation of the tradition or a condemnation of it as worthless; quite the reverse, it signifies precisely a positive appropriation of tradition."[44] Rather than advocating historical discontinuity or a clear break from the tradition, Heidegger's view of the end of philosophy includes an original repetition of the history of philosophy from which new possibilities for thought are uncovered.

From Bernasconi's standpoint it is possible for Heidegger's Plato to be the father both of forgetting and of remembering the meaning of existence, since any theory about the end entails a reflection upon beginnings. Heidegger therefore revisits Plato's philosophy in the years before *Being and Time*, as well as in conversation with Gadamer throughout his life, and modifies his interpretations. In "Plato's Doctrine of Truth" Heidegger argues that Plato is a humanist, but also exempts him from the moderns; he writes in that essay, "the contemporary notion of value

---

41. The history of philosophy is therefore over because we remember it, in which case, another beginning is inseparable from the past. This argument on behalf of Heidegger, challenging Gadamer's emphasis on discontinuity in Heidegger's thinking, is made by Bernasconi in "Bridging the Abyss," 1–24.

42. Heidegger writes, "The elaboration of the question of being must therefore receive its directive to inquire into its own history from the most proper ontological sense of the inquiry itself, as a historical one; that means to become historical in a disciplined way in order to come to the positive appropriation of the past, to come to full possession of its most proper possibilities of inquiry." *BT*, 18.

43. Bernasconi, "Bridging the Abyss," 9.

44. *BPP*, 23.

(*Wert*) is not at all appropriate to the Platonic notion of the good (*to agathon*)."[45] Similarly, although he argues that Plato transforms the early Greek notion of truth, Heidegger retracts this in the "End of Philosophy and the Task for Thinking" (1966), where he writes that "the assertion about the essential transformation of truth [in Plato] . . . from unconcealment to correctness . . . is untenable."[46] In "The Question Concerning Technology" (lecture, 1955) Heidegger suggests that Plato cannot be held responsible for the history of metaphysics, writing, "But man does not have control over unconcealment itself, in which at any given time the real shows itself or withdraws. The fact that the real has been showing itself in the light of Ideas ever since the time of Plato, Plato did not bring about. The thinker only responded to what addressed itself to him."[47] In a reversal of his characterization of seeing as that which tends to stabilize meaning in a form that conceals movement as movement, Heidegger argues that the theoretical attitude "is that kind of praxis in which the human being can be authentically human."[48] Heidegger even "credits Plato with getting into view what in *Being and Time* is called primordial temporality."[49] He identifies with the aim of Plato's Academy, to make of students "scientifically oriented human beings with a conscience in their respective disciplines" (1924);[50] in a letter to Edmund Husserl (1929), he quotes with approval from Plato's *Seventh Letter* (341c) on what is a philosopher;[51] and in his course in the winter semester of 1921–1922, after comparing the kairological moment to making music in Plato's *Phaedo* (61a), Heidegger distinguishes him from the Sophists. In contrast to them, Heidegger asserts, "Plato would never define philosophy

45. Dostal, "Beyond Being," 79. Heidegger explains in *Being and Time*, with reference to Plato, that "Thinking remains bound to the tradition of the epochs of the destiny of Being, even when and especially when it recalls in what way and from what source Being itself receives its appropriate determination, from the 'there is, It gives Being.' The giving showed itself as sending." In other words, Plato's identification of Being with an idea is the way in which Being was sent to him historically and cannot on that basis be causally implicated in humanism or modern technology. *BT*, 9–10.

46. Dostal, "Beyond Being," 71.

47. *QCT*, 18.

48. Bambach, *Heidegger's Roots*, 100.

49. Fritsche, "Kairos before the Kehre," 156.

50. Heidegger, "Wilhelm Dilthey's Research." In *BH*, 257.

51. Heidegger explains that the philosophers' way of being is to be "open to dialogue with the powers at work in the whole of human existence," a characterization which he likens to the passage in Plato's *Letter*. "Husserl and Heidegger." In *BH*, 420.

as *techne*."⁵² Finally, "Thus if we had taken our starting point from Plato's Allegory of the Cave, philosophy could have been more originally described as 'illuminative' rather than 'cognitive' comportment." The illuminative comportment represented by Plato's Socrates, says Heidegger, "more readily comprehends . . . the authentic horizon of factic life."⁵³ The clearing in which beings are disclosed to *Dasein*, and which *Dasein* is, is the light of the Good (*lumen naturale*), i.e., the *kairos* in *phronesis*.⁵⁴

Heidegger both criticizes Plato for obscuring crucial dimensions of existence and also, in the words of Zarander, solicits him for new possibilities; in this way his Plato is similar to his Aristotle. This double movement characterizes the warp and woof of *Being and Time*, where drawing near to the matter in question creates distance. When such a pattern of reasoning is transposed into the relation of Plato to Aristotle, they are both far apart and near.⁵⁵ We thus find, alongside Heidegger's repetition of Aristotle's ontological criticism of Plato, evidence of his finding agreement between them. In his lecture on the *Theaetetus* (1931–32), Heidegger points out that Plato is as limited as Aristotle in that he breaks with the pre-Socratics by equating Being with the present-at-hand. But at the same time, he teaches that both Plato and Aristotle are on the right track in terms of interpreting phenomena and developing solutions—that they begin to philosophize from what is better known to us, avoid the subject-object dichotomy characteristic of modern thought, and ground an understanding of phenomena in

---

52. Van Buren, *Young Heidegger*, 239.

53. *GBT*, 238 and 235, and *BPP*, 283–284, where Heidegger writes, "Only if we stand in this light do we cognize beings and understand being." He also argues for creating distance from the Marburg School's tendency to interpret Plato subjectively or in a modern sense (*BPP*, 73), and writes in "On the Essence of Truth" (*BH*, 279): "Plato discovered that even non-being is, that even the evil, untrue, and bad are. Although he at first resisted it, he had to become the murderer of his father [Parmenides] and revise the thesis that being is and non-being is not. But what does that imply? Nothing less than that the goddess led Parmenides into untruth, or more precisely put, that she concealed from him that even the untruth as non-being is and that she herself as truth is at the same time the possibility of untruth."

54. For a fuller analysis of Heidegger's search for a philosophical legitimation of faith using Plato and Aristotle see van Buren, *Young Heidegger*, 233–234.

55. This is to be contrasted with Gonzalez, "Dialectic," 364. He argues that in the *Sophist* lectures Heidegger finds Plato "confused" about practically every major philosophical issue.

the soul (care).⁵⁶ In his course in the winter semester of 1924 on Plato's *Sophist* and *Philebus*, and his 1927 summer lecture "Basic Problems of Phenomenology," Heidegger explains that both Plato and Aristotle saw that the principal character of assertion is *apophanesis*, the "exhibiting of something from its own self".⁵⁷ But if something can exhibit itself, then it can also not exhibit itself—in which case, as Heidegger goes on to point out, Plato discovered the self-evident fact that the false and apparent is also being, that falsity occurs when something is lacking or is not as it is supposed to be. Truth, for Heidegger's Plato, includes untruth. Finally, Gadamer's thesis on the *Philebus*, supervised by Heidegger in 1928, is an Aristotelian reading of the dialogue that demonstrates how the idea of the Good was understood by Plato to include a concrete human good (*praxis*). Heidegger was clearly aware of the possibility of reading Plato and Aristotle in terms of one another, in a mutually complementary manner. Johannes Fritsche concludes that, prior to the Nazi seizure of power in 1933, "Plato was for Heidegger the sort of phenomenologist as which Heidegger understood himself during this time."⁵⁸

CONCLUSION

Heidegger's relation to Plato has two sides that coincide with the conditions of factic life: remembering and forgetting. Something positive about Plato's philosophy is revealed in the very act of criticizing it; privation includes possibility, forgetting includes remembering, the end includes the beginning. Heidegger's relation to Plato is dialectical.

But this is not the image of Plato that has been bequeathed to the history of philosophy. Instead, it is the phenomenological side of Heidegger's thinking—fueled by Luther's invectives against "the whore reason," Aristotle's criticism of Plato, and Husserl's phenomenology—that is propagated and contrasted with Plato's metaphysics, logocentrism, metanarrative, rationalism, Cartesianism, instrumental reason, positivism, and so on.⁵⁹ The catalyst for the focus on a nondialectical

56. Fritsche, "Kairos before the Kehre," 155–156.
57. BPP, 209.
58. Fritsche, "Kairos before the Kehre," 141.
59. Other influences on Heidegger that are impossible to discount include Kierkegaard and Augustine, the former occupying the work of Stephen Mulhall, *Philosophical Myths*, and the latter the research of Craig de Paulo (editor), *Augustine's Influence on Heidegger*.

relationship to Plato is Nietzsche, to whom Heidegger turned while experimenting with German Fascism. This is also the image of Plato about which Gadamer is critical, but not through Nietzsche. When Gadamer writes that it "is indicative of a complete misunderstanding to attribute to Heidegger a position sympathetic to Nietzsche," he may be indicating that Heidegger's resistance to Plato has more to do with Aristotle than with Nietzsche.[60] Regardless of the degree to which Nietzsche was a catalyst and inspiration for Heidegger's "turn," his poetry is not sufficiently rigorous to support Heidegger's analysis of *Dasein*'s existential situation, a theory about Plato's theory of Being, and a history of ontology. Nietzsche's Plato is indeed Heidegger's, but the conceptual foundations for this identity are in the lectures Heidegger gave at Marburg while reflecting upon classical philosophy. These lectures both provoked and inspired Gadamer.

---

60. Wachterhauser, *Beyond Being*, 210 n21.

2

Provocation and Inspiration

INTRODUCTION

After reporting that Heidegger motivated him to study both Plato and Hegel's notion of dialectic in greater depth (and in such a way as to distinguish them where Heidegger did not), Gadamer writes, "But in the background was the continuous challenge posed for me by the path Heidegger's own thought took, and especially by his interpretation of Plato as the decisive step toward 'metaphysical thought's' obliviousness to being (*Sein*)."[1] In his 1931 essay "Plato's Doctrine of Truth" Heidegger takes a definitive stand against Plato's metaphysics, but the rudiments of the thesis were developed throughout his years of teaching at Marburg (1924–1928), the years during which Gadamer was his student.[2] Although the young apprentice was inspired by Heidegger's hermeneutics, phenomenology, and lectures on Plato, the dynamic intellectual culture in which he had been schooled at the university had fostered an image of Plato considerably different from Heidegger's. Reconstructing the climate of thought at Marburg between the wars, Heidegger's approach to Plato and Gadamer's prior training help explain why Heidegger both provoked and inspired Gadamer.[3]

---

1. *IG*, 5.
2. Gadamer's formal and private studies with Heidegger began in April 1923 in Freiburg.
3. For a study of the history of the German interpretations of Plato during the early twentieth century, see Tigerstedt, *Interpreting Plato*.

1. PROVOCATION

When Heidegger arrived at Marburg in the 1920s, the university was undergoing an immense change that was part of a wider sociopolitical shift. Gadamer recalls, "The collapse of the empire, the founding of the new republic, and the weakness of Weimar provided the backdrop for the distinctly frantic search for orientation that confronted the young people of the time."[4] The turmoil of the nation was felt at the university and became a catalyst for creativity as Marburg sought to redefine itself no less than the troubled nation of Germany. Gadamer relates, "When we look back today on the time between the wars, we can see that this pause within the turbulent events of our century represents a period of extraordinary creativity."[5]

The period between the wars was extremely creative because Marburg was undergoing the end of one tradition and the birth pangs of another that centered upon its relation to Plato.[6] The prewar Marburg school had interpreted Plato as a precursor to mathematical natural sciences.[7] This was reflected in Natorp, whose 1923 book on Plato "had raised a furor over its provocative thesis that at bottom Plato's ideas embodied nothing but scientific laws."[8] Yet this view of Plato, congruent with Kantianism in the sense that Plato's ideas were interpreted to prefigure Newtonian categories, began to unravel with the defeat of Germany in 1918 and the emergence of the phenomenological movement. The progressive nature of science in which the scholars had invested their hopes had unleashed a torrent of technological violence, and postwar Marburg was swept into the crisis of having to chart a new direction. The overall upheaval, including the collapse of the empire, the founding of a new republic, and then the weakness of Weimar,[9] intensified the sense of urgency. Alongside the social and political challenges to the Marburg school's prewar orientation was the challenge posed by the new phenomenological movement led by Heidegger, Martin Buber, and Max Scheler. These challenges diversified Gadamer's intellectual environment and charged it with a sense of change and creativity.

4. *PA*, 7.
5. *PH*, 213.
6. The prestige of the university in neo-Kantianism was also being challenged by the phenomenology of Edmund Husserl, Max Scheler, and Martin Buber.
7. Grondin, *Hans-Georg Gadamer*, 90.
8. Ibid., 79.
9. As reported by Gadamer in *PA*, 7.

Three Plato scholars were at the forefront of the University of Marburg's redefinition. During the 1920s Paul Friedlander wrote his seminal two-volume study of Plato's dialogues, Hartmann came out "in opposition to Natorp's system-oriented idealistic style,"[10] and Natorp himself departed from neo-Kantian idealism upon discovering the mysticism of Plato's philosophy. When his 1923 book was published, Natorp acknowledged the mystical side of Plato that, separated from the scientific side as he suggested, "in a concealed manner," was the genuine Plato.[11] Having studied with Friedlander, Natorp, and Hartmann and written his doctoral dissertation on "The Nature of Pleasure according to Plato's Dialogues" (1922) under Natorp, Gadamer was schooled in some of the most original German scholarship on Plato. These were scholars who, in contrast to their prewar predecessors, were far less concerned with establishing any doctrine of Plato's than with the dialogical character of Plato's dialogues.[12] Their work included the methods of "*Formanalyse*" that had originated with Schleiermacher and Schlegel, the political understanding of Plato that took into account the significance of the *Seventh Letter* for interpreting the dialogues (Wilamowitz, Kurt Singer, Paul Friedlander, Nicolai Hartmann).[13] When one considers their contribution in the formation of Gadamer's thought, it becomes obvious that he could only have responded to Heidegger's Plato with a good deal of trepidation. Although a follower of Heidegger, Gadamer writes in a letter to Richard Bernstein that he was, ". . . already well prepared for his confrontation with Heidegger's 1923 lectures by his earlier acquaintance with the writings of Kierkegaard, the poetry of Stefan George, and the provocative figure of the Platonic Socrates."[14] In short, the Plato being tabled by Heidegger was the Plato on which prewar Marburg was fo-

10. "Autobiographical Reflections" in *GR*, 9.

11. Grondin, *Hans-Georg Gadamer*, 79–80. Grondin's reading does not quite square with that of Gadamer, who writes of the later Natorp that he "no longer maintained the separation of the logician Plato from the mystic Plato, something the early Natorp had carried to extremes." *PA*, 26.

12. As reported by Gadamer in *DD*, 125.

13. Paul Friedlander and Kurt Singer were part of the Stephan George Circle, which rejected the world and evoked a life of dreams and the secret presence of death in everything nature does. They had a religious and apolitical outlook. Other members of the secret circle included Karl Reinhardt, Heinrich Friedemann, and Heinrich Barth. Grondin, *Hans-Georg Gadamer*, 47–48. Gadamer relates that Stephan George's poetry was "electrical."

14. Sullivan, "Translator's Introduction," ix.

cused, i.e., the doctrinal thinker. Gadamer's literary background and his enthusiasm for the new ground being broken in Plato studies prepared him for a confrontation with Heidegger's belief—crystallized under the influence of Nietzsche—that Plato is the first metaphysician.

2. INSPIRATION

In the "preface to the recently published sketch of Heidegger's 1922 Aristotle project," Gadamer writes, "When I today once again read this first part of the introduction to Heidegger's studies of Aristotle . . . it is as though I have rediscovered the clue to my own philosophical development."[15] What precisely is the "clue" to which Gadamer is referring?

At the turn of the century Marburg University was dominated by a Hegelian intellectual milieu. Robert Sullivan depicts the Hegelians as follows:

> Their achievement, if one can call it that, was to fabricate enormous systems of thought that clearly did more to smother than to encourage independent thinking. The basic premise of this epigonal work was the existence of an objective truth in terms of which the world could be seen as an "expression" by the systematic philosopher. This tendency can rightly be called "scientism."[16]

The Hegelian approach to philosophy attempted to create an objective system of thought and thereby instantiate the aims of "scientism." Traces of this tradition persisted at Marburg into the early 1920s.[17] Gadamer observes generally about the intellectual climate, "To be sure, there was a concealed, unacknowledged Hegelianism behind the neo-Kantian interpretations of Plato in Cohen and Natorp and their successors Cassirer, N. Hartmann, Honigswald, and Stenzel."[18] The traces of the Hegelian tradition to which Gadamer is referring include a progressive view of history and the privileging an objective and impersonal relationship to philosophy.

---

15. Zuckert, "Hermeneutics in Practice," 222.

16. Sullivan, "Translator's Introduction," x.

17. *GR*, 17. The Marburg School "was a school of neo-Kantian philosophy represented by the Marburg philosophers Hermann Cohen (1842–1918) and Paul Natorp (1854–1924), as well as Nicolai Hartmann (1882–1950) and Ernst Cassirer (1874–1945)." Ibid., 434 n7.

18. *IG*, 2.

The Hegelian influence on classical studies at Marburg was carried forward by the Wilamowitz school. Sullivan describes it as follows:

> The tradition laid emphasis on constructing philology as a science that did not make value judgments on Greek thinkers, assuming instead that they and their thought had been fully systematized by the methods of modern historicism and critical analysis. This attitude made classical philology into the handmaiden of academic philosophical research.[19]

Gadamer concurs that the Wilamowitz school refused to make value judgments, preferring critical analysis. It was imperative for his teachers at Marburg to see the Greeks as they were "in themselves," independently of modern biases, to be loyal to this "being-other." Friedlander and classical scholarship in general was dedicated, Gadamer reports, to "becoming aware of the otherness of the Greeks." The outcome of this approach was, again in Gadamer's words, "Natorp's construction of encompassing systems, and the naïve objectivism of Hartmann's categorical research."[20] The framework for scholarship was defined by the imperatives of a scientific approach that culminated in Wilamowitz's book on Plato.

Given the Hegelian setting for philosophical inquiry, Heidegger's seminars in 1923 could only have been refreshing.[21] He fused the art of detailed analysis with artistic dramatizations. Gadamer writes of his mentor's appropriation of Edmund Husserl's conceptual method:

> Heidegger worked his way through both the Catholic Aristotelian and neo-Kantian traditions, and in appropriating Husserl's minutely detailed art of conceptualization, he had steeled the endurance and power of intuition, which are indispensible for doing philosophy with Aristotle.[22]

In addition to a refined sense for making clear distinctions, honed through Edmund Husserl's supervision, Heidegger displayed a remarkable power for intuition. With these rarely combined capacities, the *esprit géométrique* and *esprit de finesse*, Heidegger's instruction broke

---

19. Sullivan, "Translator's Introduction," xiii.

20. GR, 10.

21. For a list of courses Heidegger taught at Freiburg and then at Marburg 1923–1926, see Heidegger, *Supplements*.

22. IG, 3–4.

through the "otherness" of the Greeks propagated at Marburg by appearing "like an *Aristoteles redivivus* [Aristotle brought back to life]."[23] Reflecting upon the impact of Heidegger at Marburg, Gadamer writes:

> The remarkable phenomenological power of intuition Heidegger brought to his interpretation liberated the original Aristotelian text so profoundly and strikingly from the sedimentations of the scholastic tradition and from the lamentably distorted image of Aristotle contained in the criticism of the time (Cohen loved to say, 'Aristotle was an apothecary') that it began to speak in an unexpected way.[24]

The 1922 essay on Aristotle's *Physics* that liberated the Peripatetic from "the sedimentations of the scholastic tradition" was congruent with Heidegger's pedagogy. The personification of Aristotle assumed by Heidegger during seminars enacted the "hermeneutical situation."

The "hermeneutical situation" presupposes a breach with a text.[25] The disparity between an ancient text and modern times presents seemingly insurmountable challenges to recovering the original compelling validity of the ancients. In response to this dilemma of the distance between the present and the past, Heidegger in his essay on Aristotle demonstrates that it is incumbent "on each 'time' and generation of philosophers to appropriate its own past (i.e., the history of philosophy) through radical interrogation out of the hermeneutical situation of its own living present by first making its temporally particularized prepositional structure as transparent as possible."[26] The hermeneutical situation of the living present is shaped by an historically affected consciousness. We belong to history and hence engage the past from out of a prior understanding of the way in which Being has been disclosed to us—a given horizon. Thus "separated" from the past, we cannot know what Aristotle really meant. Nevertheless, the questions he raised may still be reconstructed by making our prior understanding of Being—the understanding that belongs to us as we belong to history—as transparent as possible.[27] In recovering Aristotle's philosophy, therefore, it is not

23. *GR*, 13.
24. *PH*, 201.
25. Gadamer observes that the art of translation was first required when Homer's intended audience, a noble society, was replaced by a democracy. *GR*, 46.
26. *BH*, 152. (Editor's introduction to Heidegger's essay "Phenomenological Interpretations.")
27. Gadamer cites Plato's *Sophist* 246d in support of "the Platonic axiom" to make

first and foremost Aristotle who is interrogated, but ourselves: our self-understanding and the horizon of meaning in which we dwell.[28] When we ourselves are called into question, we are more likely to be open to Aristotle's situation and to appropriate his philosophy in a manner that speaks to us today. As we become aware of the "hermeneutical situation," of "the question and the intellectual resistance with which we confront Aristotle,"[29] Gadamer explains, Aristotle is brought near in an "original repetition" that speaks to the present.[30]

Heidegger's articulation of the "hermeneutical situation" created the conditions for an engagement between the present condition of human self-understanding and the ancients that resonated with Gadamer's fascination with, and education in, the philosophy of antiquity. What impressed Gadamer about Heidegger's 1922 essay on Aristotle was the way he "went back to the thought of the Greeks, brought them to speak in a primordial unheard of way, so that the Greeks were made relevant to present-day philosophical research yet also pointed the way to the future."[31] In contrast to the tendency at Marburg to interpret the classics at a distance that Gadamer felt disengaged the students, he recalls the "tremendous power emanating from Heidegger's creative energies in the early 1920s," and writes:

> The distance separating our historical consciousness from the tradition seemed to be nonexistent. The calm and confident aloofness with which the Neo-Kantian "history of philosophical problems" was accustomed to deal with the tradition, and the whole of contemporary thought that came from the academic rostrum, now suddenly seemed to be mere child's play.[32]

And again:

> It is impossible to exaggerate the drama of Heidegger's appearance in Marburg. Not that he was out for sensation. His appearance in the lecture hall certainly had something of a guaranteed

---

the opponent's position stronger. *PH*, 201.

28. Gadamer asks, "For what else is interpretation in philosophy but coming to terms with the truth of the text and risking oneself by exposure to it?" *PH*, 201.

29. *PH*, 200.

30. I have glossed Heidegger's discussion in "Phenomenological Interpretations" in *BH*, 155–157.

31. Grondin, *Philosophy of Gadamer*, 94.

32. *PH*, 230. See also *PDE*, xxxii.

effectiveness to it, but the unique thing about his person and his teaching lay in the fact that he identified himself fully with his work and radiated from that work. Because of him the lecture format became something totally new. It was no longer the "lesson presentation" of a professor who put his essential energy into research and publication.[33]

Far from being calm and aloof and focused on research and publications, Heidegger directed his energies during his seminars toward a reenactment and creative interplay with ancient thought. He was unique among the neo-Kantians with their preoccupation with the history of problems. Gadamer says of Heidegger's overall influence, "Heidegger's appearance as a young teacher at Freiberg University in the years just after World War I created a profound sensation."[34] Heidegger "seemed to sweep along the generation of students returning from WWI or just beginning studies."[35] The spark that Heidegger ignited in Gadamer, the "flash of lightning" that was "the clue to his own philosophical development," was the discovery of a "method" that unleashed the critical potential of antiquity. That potential struck at the industrial rationalism of prewar Germany. Writes Gadamer:

> The contemporary reader of Heidegger's first systematic work was seized by the vehemence of its passionate protest against the secured cultural world of the older generation and the leveling of all individual forms of life by industrial society, with its ever stronger uniformities and its techniques of communication and public relations that manipulated everything.[36]

Heidegger's capacity to bring Aristotle's teachings to life cut against the grain both of the academy and of twentieth-century industrial society generally. Given Gadamer's passion for the arts, Shakespeare, and modern art, as well as his antipathy toward modern industrial society,[37] Heidegger's

---

33. *PA*, 48. Also, Gadamer writes, "Heidegger's mode consisted in making the interpretation of a text as convincing as possible, to a point where we risked losing ourselves to it. That is how things went for us in Heidegger's lectures, and this was especially the case for me with reference to Plato and Aristotle, so that all criticism was lost on me." Ibid., 38–39. "What Heidegger put into words was revolutionary for our consciousness at this time, because his thinking went back to primordial experiences of existence in such a way as to replace the workings of science with radical philosophical reflection." Ibid., 62.

34. *PH*, 214.

35. Ibid., 229.

36. Ibid., 214–215.

37. Gadamer writes, "I loved Shakespeare and the ancient Greeks just as much as

performance in 1922 touched Gadamer's philological and classical education in a way that was politically and socially meaningful.[38]

CONCLUSION TO PART ONE

After having read Heidegger's manuscript "Phenomenological Interpretations with Respect to Aristotle" in 1922, Gadamer went to Freiburg for a year to study with Heidegger before returning to Marburg and studying with him until 1928. Heidegger was on the committee that certified Gadamer to teach classical philology in 1927. He also supervised Gadamer's *Habilitationsschrift* in 1928 on Plato's *Philebus*. These were profoundly formative years in Heidegger's study of Plato that both provoked and inspired Gadamer; the fact that they did so speaks to the complexity of Heidegger's thinking—broadly speaking, to his method of phenomenological destruction that sought to solicit possibilities from out of deficiencies. Gadamer pulls on the positive side of Heidegger's thought. He reports that during private conversations Heidegger brought to his

---

the classical German writers." *PA*, 3.

38. Of the students closest to Heidegger in the 1920s—Gadamer, Gerhard Kruger, and Karl Lowith—Gadamer seemed the least auspicious. Karl Lowith was Gadamer's senior by three years, the first to habilitate, and the first to receive a teaching appointment at the University of Marburg. (Gadamer recalls of Karl Lowith, "Lowith's brilliant style of delivery, his art of interlacing original quotations into the contemplative progression of his lectures in such a way that they worked like a strengthening of his own voice, the certainty of his appearance, the immovability of his face, his sarcasm and his sometimes hardly audible irony—these qualities drew in many listeners. Among the theologians it was customary to say of him: 'Lowith, my sweet poison.'" *PA*, 70-71). Gerhard Kruger distinguished himself during seminars with exceptionally well-articulated constructions. Gadamer recalls that he "... was a born teacher, clear and consistent in the construction of his lectures, strict and superior in his seminars" *PA*, 71. He also attracted more students than Gadamer while they were Privatdozents. Grondin, *Hans-Georg Gadamer*, 130-131. Gadamer suggests why: "Among the students at Marburg, that is how it stood with Kruger and me: from Kruger one learns what is right about everything, from Gadamer how little we know what is right." Grondin, *Hans-Georg Gadamer*, 134. Gadamer recalls that "A joking observer, a student of Lowith, once expressed it as follows: With Kruger everything would be laid out clearly; with Gadamer everything would once again be confused." *PA*, 7. In comparison to Lowith's accelerated progress in the university and Kruger's adroit presence in the classroom, Gadamer seems to have paled. His academic advancement seemed to lag behind that of his peers; he was consigned to the status of a Dozent in Marburg for ten years. He did not distinguish himself with a formidable philosophical work, *Truth and Method*, until his sixtieth year. Even within his own métier of Platonic studies, Gadamer would seem to have been superseded. Other philosophers in their own right had developed concise and incisive criticisms of Heidegger's interpretation of Plato, including Paul Friedlander, Gerhard Kruger, and Stanley Rosen.

attention "that Aristotle stood on the same ground of the *logos* which Plato had prepared in his discipleship to Socrates."[39] The very dialectical relationship that Gadamer weaves between Plato and Aristotle through Socrates is in debt to Heidegger.

But so too is his resistance. The rupture with the tradition instigated by Heidegger's "proof" that philosophy had ended is precisely the space in which a hermeneutical philosophy is most relevant. By purporting to have transcended history, Heidegger reveals something deeply historical about his thought. In reply, Gadamer recalls in reference to this period of Heidegger's life (the turn) that he had sought to use hermeneutics to describe self-understanding "coming up against its limits."[40] The method Heidegger used to retrieve Aristotle from the sediment of scholasticism, Gadamer used in turn to retrieve Plato from Heidegger. Gadamer thus relates in his 1982 Preface to *Plato's Dialectical Ethics* that, despite already having done his PhD under Natorp on the subject of pleasure in Plato's dialogues (1922),[41] he had become again a first reader of Plato due to the "decisive influence that Martin Heidegger's teaching during his years in Marburg had on me."[42] Although Heidegger provoked Gadamer to resist an interpretation of Plato that juxtaposes his reputed idealism with Aristotle's phenomenology, it is also fair to say that Gadamer's correction amounts to a reminder to Heidegger that during his famous turn from roughly 1929 to 1935 he misunderstood himself. This is why Gadamer prefers to describe Heidegger's overcoming of metaphysics with the term *Verwinden* rather than *Kehre*. *Verwinden* suggests that metaphysics remains with us.[43]

---

39. Gadamer, "Reflections," 10.

40. Ibid., 21.

41. The title of Gadamer's PhD dissertation is "The Essence of Desire According to the Platonic Dialogues."

42. *PDE*, xxxii.

43. Gadamer argues in "Hegel and Heidegger" that, for Heidegger, overcoming metaphysics always implies coming to grips with the whole tradition. *HD*, 100–101. This is the line of argument developed by Bernasconi in reply to Gadamer's emphasis upon the Heidegger who focuses upon a rupture with the past.

PART II

Gadamer's Correction of Heidegger

Introduction

GADAMER AGREES WITH HEIDEGGER that Plato's thought defines the course of Western philosophy. He concurs that by focusing on *eidos*, the what-of-Being, Plato grounds the meaning of knowledge in *logos*, represented by Aristotle in *Metaphysics* X,[1] and states summarily, "with his doctrine of ideas, his dialectic of ideas, his mathematization of physics, and his intellectualization of what we would call ethics," Plato "laid the foundation for the metaphysical conceptualization of our tradition."[2] Consequently, as noted by P. Christopher Smith and Jean Grondin, in *Truth and Method* Part III Gadamer "shadows" Heidegger when he argues that in the *Cratylus* Plato abstracts from natural language,[3] and that "Plato's discovery of the ideas conceals the true nature of language even more than the theories of the sophists."[4] Gadamer's agreement with Heidegger that Plato founded the tradition of metaphysics must, however, be understood within the context described by Heidegger in

---

1. Gadamer, "Greeks," 84.

2. *PA*, 184.

3. Smith writes, "In Part III of *WM* Gadamer takes Heidegger's line of argument and focuses it specifically on the problem of language in Plato, something which Heidegger, though he certainly acknowledges the primacy of language in any experience of the world, largely omits from his discussion of the allegory of the 'cave.'" Smith, "Gadamer's Heideggerian Interpretation," 212. Grondin writes, "It is not difficult to sense the shadow of Heidegger lingering throughout this chapter of *Truth and Method*. Plato becomes, due to his *logocentric* or '*eidocentric*' conception of language, the forefather of the *caracteristica universalis* and of a metaphysics of domination." Grondin, "Universality of Hermeneutics," 327.

4. *TM*, 408.

1924;[5] namely, that Plato strove to lodge meaning in permanent ideas in response to the sophists who had scrambled conventional wisdom about justice.[6] The responsibility for the metaphysical tradition cannot be laid squarely at Plato's doorstep alone. The primary progenitor of that tradition is Heidegger in the late 1920s and early 1930s.

It might be countered that Heidegger was interested in Plato*nism*, i.e., the way in which Plato had been received and had defined the destiny of the Western metaphysical tradition until the twentieth century, and not in Plato *per se*.[7] But at the same time, Platonism is an image of Plato, and true only to the extent that it bears a resemblance to his philosophy. Moreover, there is little evidence that Heidegger believed his account, in "Plato's Doctrine of Truth," (1942) of Plato's transformation of the meaning of the early Greek notion of truth (*aletheia*) to correctness (*orthotes*) to be anything but a philosophically credible story. However concerned Heidegger may have been with Platonism or Plato's shaping of the tradition, unless Plato truly is the first metaphysician by virtue of having identified Being with a permanently present idea, the tradition is not Platonic. And in that case, Heidegger can neither claim to have overcome it for the sake of a pre-Socratic truth, announced in *Introduction to Metaphysics* (1935),[8] nor to have finished altogether with the tradition and replaced Nietzsche's Zarathustra as the prophet of a new age. On the contrary, Gadamer demonstrates that Heidegger is in

---

5. *BH*, 224.

6. Along the lines of Heidegger's 1924 Cologne address, "Being-There, Being-True According to Aristotle," Gadamer points out that Plato was aggravated by the sophists who corrupted the conventional understanding of virtue by dividing meaning from the word. Once this step is taken it is possible not only to interrogate the meaning of words, but to twist them to suit unjust ends. That which the Athenians had thought was a good and happy life the sophists argued was unhappy and even unjust (e.g., Thrasymachus and Callicles). Plato's answer was inspired by Socrates. Despite the breakdown of tradition and the verbal gymnastics of the sophists he remained steadfast. His very demeanor suggested to Plato a ground that transcended the word and was not pliable but permanent and unchanging. Plato thus came to associate ideas with universal and eternal ideal numbers.

7. Gregory Fried makes this observation in "Back to the Cave," 174 n5.

8. Heidegger explains that the Greeks are a "higher type of Hottentot, whom modern science has left far behind" and that the greatness of the great beginnings of philosophy with the Greeks ended in greatness with Aristotle (*IM*, 15). Heidegger intends to recover that greatness at the moment of its greatest forgetting, which Gadamer suggests is a Hegelian dialectical reversal (*HD*, 109), although Heidegger attributed the notion of the greatest danger harboring the greatest saving power to Hölderlin in *QCT*, 28.

the grip of his times, that underlying his interpretation of Plato are the very scientific and idealist movements from which he claims to have dissociated himself.

OUTLINE

Chapter Three, "Counterarguments" is a review of the essays pertinent to understanding Gadamer's criticism of Heidegger's Plato. From his first book in 1928 to the mid-1970s, Gadamer presents a Plato that is considerably different from that of Heidegger in the areas of ethics, politics, and metaphysics (theory of ideas). While the chapter might, therefore, be considered a guide to Gadamer's criticisms, it is also cursory and the aforementioned themes do not by themselves constitute the core of Gadamer's refutation. It is above all Aristotle that Heidegger privileges in his denunciation of Plato, neo-Platonism, and its legacy in German idealism and modern science; the most effective thrust against Heidegger is against Aristotle's reading of Plato. Chapter 1 is thus an historical survey of Gadamer's Plato studies that are critical of Heidegger but whose criticism is without foundation because they do not take Aristotle's stand into account.

The next two chapters demonstrate Gadamer's indirect method of criticizing Heidegger from two angles. Chapter Four, "Heidegger's False Modernism," argues that however earnestly Heidegger attempts to extricate himself from history, his interpretation of Plato is shaped by the developmental design argument of Werner Jaeger and the neo-Kantian version of Plato's ideas tabled by Paul Natorp. Given the affinities between Heidegger's thesis and their thoughts, Gadamer's refutation of Jaeger and Natorp is tantamount to a refutation of Heidegger. Chapter Five, "Heidegger's Aristotelianism," represents Gadamer's second indirect criticism of Heidegger through Aristotle. Since Heidegger recapitulates Aristotle's criticism of Plato, Gadamer's argument that Aristotle did not in fact attribute to Plato an identification between ideas and Pythagorean numbers constitutes a criticism of Heidegger's belief that Plato's metaphysics is fulfilled in modern technology (or twentieth-century mathematical physics).

Chapter Six, "Hermeneutic Situations," is a criticism of Heidegger's literalist understanding of Aristotle. The proposal that Aristotle could have misunderstood his teacher after twenty years at the Academy, Gadamer contends, is incredible. To account then for Aristotle's misrepresentation of Plato, repeated by Heidegger, Gadamer returns to the respective hermeneutical situations of the two ancients in order to better understand their differences. A return to these situations is a reminder to Heidegger of the pretheoretical origins of thought that he had investigated during the Marburg years, and is also a significant step toward discovering the common territory between Plato and Aristotle. This territory is investigated in Part III, "Gadamer's Plato."[9]

---

9. Wachterhauser points out, in *Beyond Being*, 170, that Gadamer is closer to the early Heidegger, who wanted to dismantle and reconstitute the metaphysical tradition in order to infuse it with new life. Gadamer recalls his first learning of the method in "Reflections," 21.

3

Counterarguments

In the 1982 Preface to *Plato's Dialectical Ethics*, Gadamer writes of his first book:

> It sought, with conscious one-sidedness, to stand out against the patterns recommended by its predecessors and teachers. Scholars like Paul Natorp, Nicolai Hartmann, and Julius Stenzel and classical philologists like Werner Jaeger, Karl Reinhardt, and Paul Friedlander stand behind this first attempt, although it does not expressly connect up with them.[1]

Under the aforementioned instructors Gadamer had become versed in Greek history, language, philosophy, and art.[2] Lommatzsch, Paul Friedlander, and Heidegger certified him to teach classical philology in July, 1927. Yet as the passage above makes clear, in spite of this indebtedness, Gadamer's first book was intended "to stand out against the patterns recommended by its predecessors and teachers." Gadamer could "stand out against" their patterns of reasoning because he was attuned to prejudices, and hence to avenues of thought that reached beyond them. Sullivan reports that Gadamer's instructors were "conditions of an apprenticeship, which is nothing other than a productive discourse," and continues: "Therefore—because he did not take the prejudices of his teachers to be the final outcomes of discursive learning—Gadamer was able to move on from a first apprenticeship with Paul Natorp to

---

1. *PDE*, xxxi–xxxii.
2. But these three were not the only mentors from whom Gadamer drew inspiration. He reflects upon the significance of Hartmann and of French and English intellectuals to his philosophical development: "Nicolai Hartmann's dissociation of himself from neo-Kantian idealism stimulated me to try to penetrate Aristotle's thought, and the French and English research—of Robin, Taylor, Ross, Hardie, and, above all, the incomparable Hicks—proved most helpful in my endeavors." *IG*, 3.

second and third apprenticeships with Martin Heidegger and Rudolf Bultmann."[3]

No less than with his teachers at Marburg, Gadamer was intent on a productive discourse with Heidegger. In his 1928 *Habilitationsschrift* on Plato's *Philebus*, written under Heidegger's supervision, Gadamer argues that the Good is not irrelevant to practical ethics as Aristotle argues at the outset of his three ethical treatises—a criticism Heidegger repeats.[4] Instead, argues Gadamer, while the Good is noetically distinct or separable from a concrete good, it is also visible in the latter through a mixture. In the *Philebus*, the fact that the Good is constitutive of all things is conveyed to Protarchus in just this way: in terms of a mixture of limit and indeterminacy.[5] By publishing his book in the same year as Heidegger's essay on Plato's transformation of the early Greek notion of truth (1931), Gadamer announces a departure from and challenge to his teacher's thesis that Plato's Good is, practically speaking, irrelevant. Perhaps as a result of having supervised Gadamer's work on Plato's *Philebus*, Heidegger reconsidered and retracted his plans to deliver a lecture on the said dialogue.

During the rise of the National Socialists, from 1933 to 1937, Gadamer broke off his relations with Heidegger.[6] During this period of time and the following years of war, Gadamer kept a low profile by immersing himself in the seemingly politically innocuous classical philosophy. Dostal reports of these years (1939–1945) that Gadamer "stayed, for the most part, within the realm of Greek philosophy. His published efforts included work in classical Greek atom theory, on Plato on the poets and on education, on Hegel and historical spirit (*Geist*), and on 'People (*Volk*) and History in the Thought of Herder.'" Gadamer's

---

3. Sullivan, "Translator's Introduction," vii–viii.

4. Aristotle's three ethical treatises are *Nicomachean Ethics*, *Eudaimonian Ethics*, and *Magna Moralia*.

5. I have relied on Zuckert, "Hermeneutics in Practice," 217.

6. Dostal writes, "When Heidegger assumed the rectorship of Freiburg University in 1933 and became a public and official advocate for National Socialism, Gadamer broke off his contact with Heidegger. He renewed his relationship with Heidegger in the late 1930s, years after Heidegger had given up the rectorship and any public political role, and continued to remain in contact with him until Heidegger's death in 1976." Dostal, "Gadamer's Relation to Heidegger," 249. Grondin reports that Gadamer traveled to Frankfurt for Heidegger's lectures on the "Origin of the Work of Art" in November 1936, but did not meet with him. Grondin, *Hans-Georg Gadamer*, 348.

lectures in this period were almost exclusively on Greek philosophy or German idealism (Schelling, Hegel)." Dostal continues and explains that during the war years Gadamer planned a book on Plato's politics.[7] Although this plan did not come to fruition, Gadamer's work from this period, including "Plato and the Poets" (1934) and "Plato's Educational State," (1942) stand out as a criticism of both the times and Heidegger's response to them.[8]

Germany was undergoing a period of disaffection and social transformation in the form of the Third Reich, and Heidegger was swept into the confusion. He felt that the Germans under the Nazis could save the world from the rootless global economies of the U.S. and U.S.S.R.[9] and, like many intellectuals, he found company with Plato. Plato's simile of the cave had been used by German philologists and philosophers throughout the 1920s and 1930s to react against neo-Kantianism and the Weimar Republic; Hans Heyse, Carl Vering, Ernst Krieck, and Werner Jaeger had inaugurated a tradition of arguing for a quintessential Greek and German spirit. The context was thus set for Heidegger to invoke Plato in a similar way. He began lecturing on Plato's Allegory of the Cave in the summer semester of 1928/1929 in his course "Introduction to Academic Studies."[10] These lectures were used by Heidegger in his essay "Plato's Doctrine of Truth,"[11] and are the background to his Freiburg address on the occasion of being inaugurated as Rector of the University, a post he held from April 1933 to April 1934. Kisiel comments, "A topic of his courses [Allegory] since 1927, a central focus since 1929, this Platonic parable is undoubtedly one of the clues to the interpretation of the tripartite structure of Plato's Republic into the Rector's address."[12] The tripartite structure refers to the division of classes into workers, guardians, and philosophers, who are related to one another through a love of their *Volk*.[13] Heidegger repeats this in his speech "Self-Assertion of the

---

7. Ibid., 19–20.

8. So I am not convinced by the arguments of Teresa Orozco in "Art of Allusion" that suggest Gadamer supported the National Socialists. These arguments were refuted by Catherine Zuckert.

9. From Dreyfus and Hall, *Heidegger*, 15.

10. Kisiel, *Heidegger's Way of Thought*, 34.

11. Partenie and Rockmore, *Heidegger and Plato*, xix.

12. Kisiel, *Heidegger's Way of Thought*, 34.

13. Fritsche, "Kairos before the Kehre," 153.

German University;" labor and the military service, he says, are bound with students through the mystic notion of the people.[14] By referring to this class structure as laid out in the *Republic*, Heidegger was implicitly urging that the German classes—intellectuals and workers—become galvanized into one by the militant state, presided over by a Führer whom he urged his students to follow.[15]

Gadamer also returned to Plato and the *Republic*, but drew from them a spirit contrary to that of the National Socialists. While Heidegger's Freiburg address praised the division of labor in Plato's utopia for contributing to the good of the state, Gadamer in "Plato's Educational State" emphasized that persons in Plato's notion of a just society are not measured by their capacity to contribute to an economy of goods external to themselves, but rather by a standard internal to themselves, namely, self-understanding. In contrast to Heidegger's prioritizing the state, Gadamer prioritizes the individual and the capacity of the individual to be self-determining; this capacity, he says, is available to everyone in Plato's *Republic*. Whereas Heidegger urged his students to follow Hitler, and in the Freiburg address aimed to vitalize the spirit of the German nation and language, Gadamer argued in "Plato and the Poets" that poets who urge the imitation of models of perfection external to the self alienate persons from the order of their soul. Plato, he says, thus challenged the poets (above all, the militant Homer) for forgetting the meaning of Being (as self-understanding).

Thus the very dialogue Heidegger used to indirectly praise the Nazi regime and accelerate the momentum toward societal transformation and revolution, Gadamer used to recommend a conservative ethos and sober deliberation. It is not the revolutionary and utopian character of the dialogue that interests Gadamer, but the education it offers in the virtues of moderation and self-control. Heidegger, at the end of his 1927 lecture "Basic Problems of Phenomenology," expresses disagreement with Kant and says that he would prefer to separate Plato the "man of letters" (an allusion to the autobiographical *Seventh Letter*) from Plato the enthusiast, who, like modern science, attempted to exceed the limits

---

14. Heidegger, "Self-Assertion," 35.

15. Heidegger told his students, "Let not theories and 'ideas' be the rules of your being. The Führer himself and he alone is German reality and its law, today and for the future." Sheehan, "Heidegger and the Nazis," 38.

of knowing by crowning a philosopher King.[16] By contrast, Gadamer grounds his interpretation of Plato in the Athenian cultural context, as it is portrayed in the *Seventh Letter*, and begins his interpretation of the *Republic* in "Plato's Educational State" with reference to the political circumstances Plato was answering. Whereas Heidegger propagated the myth of the Germans having rich spiritual roots in ancient Greece, Gadamer emphasized the pairing of their fractured cultures: it was not the reputed glory of the Greeks, but rather the dissolution of their culture that he saw reflected in Nazi-era Germany.[17] While Heidegger opened his Rectoral address in 1933 by sounding a note of agreement with the revolutionary character of the times, calling upon the University to provide leadership, Gadamer introduces his 1934 essay "Plato and the Poets" with a quotation from Goethe that urges philosophizing against the norms then prevailing in Germany.[18] Gadamer comments on that quotation, "[S]uch a motto signaled to the perceptive reader at a time of ideological conformism the assertion of a differential stance."[19] No less than Heidegger, Gadamer's philosophy was motivated by the climate of change in Germany, yet clearly their attitudes to this change diverge. In reply to Robert Sullivan's theorizing about his political theory, Gadamer writes that "Plato and the Poets" "was ultimately sustained by faith in culture or the cultural hopes of the intellectual class of the Weimar Republic."[20]

16. *BPP*, 329.

17. Fred Dallmayer quotes Gadamer from a 1930 essay on Greek ethics: "Classical Greek philosophizing occurred in the midst of a pervasive crisis of culture. How in the dissolution of the old this philosophy seeks to preserve tradition, how in the midst of divisiveness and discord [*Entzweiung*] it attempts a reconciliation with an old way of life—this aspect is congenial and intelligible to us due to the divisiveness of our own moral condition." Dallmayer, "Hermeneutics and Justice," 94.

18. "Difficult though it might be to detect it, a certain polemical thread runs through any philosophical writing. He who philosophizes is not at one with the previous and contemporary world's ways of thinking of things. Thus Plato's discussions are often not only directed to something but also directed against it." *DD*, 39.

19. Dallmayr, "Hermeneutics and Justice," 108 n6.

20. Gadamer, "Reply to Sullivan," 256. In "Gadamer's Early and Distinctively Political Hermeneutics" Robert Sullivan argues that in "Plato and the Poets" Gadamer conveys the "modern political condition" by (1) dissolving the *sensus communus* (Plato symbolically destroys Greek culture when he burns his tragedies); (2) making the individual responsible for creating a meaningful life, i.e., assuming the atomized individual of either Hobbes's or Locke's state of nature; and (3) responding to this modern condition with a political education that would mend, through poetry (Plato's *Republic*), the rift between

Following World War II Gadamer takes a more pronounced stand against Heidegger. He reports that the philosophical hermeneutics of *Truth and Method* (1960) was a theoretical challenge to Heidegger's position that Plato was the first metaphysician.[21] Rather than propagate a rupture with the tradition of philosophy, as Gadamer evidently believed Heidegger was doing post *Being and Time* (1928),[22] Gadamer urges a constructive dialogue with the past for the sake of self-understanding. The theoretical justification for entering into a dialogue with the history of philosophy, rather than disposing of it as the history of ontotheology,[23] is paired by Gadamer with a "practical challenge" to Heidegger's Plato. Jean Grondin writes, "We can say that Gadamer invoked this Plato of finitude in all his works after *Truth and Method*, against the Heideggerian reading which makes the forgetfulness of being and finitude begin with Plato."[24] Contra Heidegger (although in an essay addressed to Jacques Derrida), Gadamer points out that Plato adopted an explicit critique of the logocentrism of metaphysics in the excursus to the *Seventh Letter*.[25] Gadamer is referring to his 1962 essay "Dialectic and Sophism in Plato's *Seventh Letter*"; according to this essay, Plato argues that having knowledge of the thing itself is uncertain because humans, and hence their means of knowing, are finite. But if so, then Plato understood non-Being as a concomitant of Being, suggesting that he is closer to both the early Greeks and Aristotle than Heidegger thought.

Six years later Gadamer embarked upon an effort to articulate the common ground between Aristotle and Plato in two essays: "Plato's Unwritten Dialectic" and "Amicus Plato Magis Amica Veritas" (1968). In the first he picks up on the thought that had concluded his 1942 es-

---

the gentle and bestial sides of the soul. The poetry to which Sullivan and Gadamer are referring is a play between question and answer whose performance forms the ethos of the community, i.e., "the play of shared language" that cultivates harmony in the soul and between self and others. Sullivan interprets this as a contribution to a liberal political ethic in which people are united in a quest for their respective personal good.

21. *IG*, 5.

22. See Bernasconi, "Bridging the Abyss," 1–24. He challenges Gadamer's reading of Heidegger's relation to history.

23. Joan Stambaugh, translator of Heidegger's *Identify and Difference*, explains in her Introduction (15) that metaphysics is ontology in that it thinks Being is the first and universal ground common to all beings, and theology in that it thinks Being is the highest ground above all beings.

24. Grondin, *Hans-Georg Gadamer*, 151.

25. *GR*, 379.

say, "Plato's Educational State"; namely, that understanding the unity of soul, state, knowledge, and world depends upon the law of the one and the many, of number and Being.[26] This law of the one and the many, according to Gadamer, is opened up by Aristotle in terms of the one and the dyad. For both Plato and Aristotle, unity is seen when contrary principles, e.g., the universal and particular, are thought together. The initial basis for cross-fertilization between Plato and Aristotle is thus carried beyond the realm of practical ethics and cosmic order, with which Gadamer had been concerned in his 1928 work *Plato's Dialectical Ethics*, beyond politics, as dealt with in "Plato's Educational State" in 1942, to the level of an unwritten mathematical doctrine, i.e., the dialectical structure of Being. The title "Amicus Plato Magis Amica Veritas" is reminiscent of the words Husserl had scrawled on the title page of *Being and Time* after having read it in the summer of 1929. The essay begins by observing that the perception of an antithesis between Plato and Aristotle, in marked contrast to ancient and medieval times when they were (despite Aristotle's criticism of Plato) thought to have been in agreement, is unique to the modern era. Gadamer explains that the natural scientific emphasis upon observation and mathematical hypotheses (Galileo), and subsequently Descartes's method of investigation that divested research of preconceptions (i.e., Aristotelian substantial forms), are responsible for the emergence of the said antithesis. Gadamer aims to reconcile the philosophies of Plato and Aristotle by explaining how their thinking germinates within the Socratic turn toward the *logoi* in the *Phaedo*. He explains that Aristotle's physics and Plato's mathematics both develop out of the dialectical structure of the Socratic dialogue form, and are investigating the same question—the question of what something is—from two different angles. With these two essays arguing for common ground, the first in a hidden number theory and the second in terms of how things are spoken about, Gadamer communicates to Heidegger what Husserl had intimated by quoting from *Nicomachean Ethics* Book I: truth is more important than friendship; or, in the words of Socrates, which Gadamer suggests Aristotle is mimicking, "To refute me is not difficult, to refute the *logos*, however, most difficult."

In "Plato" (1976) and "The Greeks" (1979), published after Heidegger's death (May 26, 1976) but likely representative of previous research and conversations, Gadamer challenges Heidegger on a number of fronts

---

26. DD, 92.

from his translation of Greek terms to Plato's notion of truth and practical philosophy. Yet the culmination of his Plato studies is in the 1974–1976 Heidelberg lectures and what he refers to as some smaller building blocks along the way, compiled in his 1978 book *The Idea of the Good in Platonic-Aristotelian Philosophy*. In this work Gadamer merges previous insights into Plato's ethics, politics, and metaphysics into a thesis that renders Plato an Aristotelian and Aristotle a Platonist. Their common ground, or what Gadamer calls their "unitary effect" (*Wirkungseinheit*), is represented by Plato's Socrates and Aristotle's conceptual grasp of Socratic *phronesis*. It is thus not so much the portrait of Plato that is being tabled in opposition to Heidegger in the 1970s, but rather the relation of Plato to Aristotle that Gadamer had investigated in the late 1960s. Robert Dostal observes of *The Idea of the Good* that Gadamer "comes to see more clearly this continuity [between Aristotle and Plato] as well as the limitation of Heidegger's approach to Plato and Aristotle."[27] For example, in "Polis and Knowledge of the Good" (in *Idea of the Good*), Gadamer demonstrates how Aristotle's notion of practical wisdom and Plato's idea of the Good converge and render the central teachings of the *Republic* intelligible. For Gadamer, reading Plato and Aristotle together removes the tension between philosophy and politics, theory and practice, such that Plato's ideal state consists solely of philosopher-citizens. Referring to knowledge of the Good in Plato's utopia, Gadamer writes: "In this state the very thing which made Socrates appear such an absurd exception in the Athens of his time becomes constitutive of its citizenry as a whole."[28] Gadamer's revisitation of the relation of Plato to Aristotle could not have failed to constitute a significant challenge to Heidegger's tendency to drive a wedge between them.

---

27. Dostal, "Gadamer's Continuous Challenge," 290.
28. *DD*, 201.

4

Heidegger's False Modernism

INTRODUCTION

Gadamer agrees with Heidegger that there has been a decisive break with the premodern era. As a result of the French Revolution, the splintering of national cultures, and the end of Christianity as a common tradition among the European states, the past has become distant—but (and in this he would disagree with Heidegger) not alien.[1] Contrary to Heidegger's claim that the history of metaphysics is over and that he is returning to a new, pre-Platonic beginning in the early Greeks, Gadamer writes, "It seems difficult to me to avoid the thought which forces itself upon us regarding Heidegger's historical justification of himself and his return to the question of Being, specifically, that such a return is not itself a beginning, but rather, that it is made possible by an end."[2] According to Gadamer, the claim to have begun again depends on the "end." An alleged rupture from the past is impossible without the very persistence of history, or traces of it, into the new age. This is not a strictly logical or conceptual argument. Gadamer's justification is not that a denial of tradition presupposes the idea of tradition. His argument depends upon a condition of temporal awareness. He writes, "There is no language of metaphysics," because there is no standpoint outside of time from which to make a judgment about the meaning of terms in metaphysics.[3] Consciousness is always already affected by history, and the content of metaphysical concepts is thus determined by

---

1. I am paraphrasing from Gadamer, "Hermeneutics," 329.
2. Bernasconi, "Bridging the Abyss," 16.
3. *GR*, 345.

use.[4] In short, Heidegger's decision about the end of an era cannot fail to be conditioned by history. One such condition to identify in this regard is political: Heidegger parrots the National Socialists, and ideologues in general, who revise history for the sake of a future unknown yet hoped for. In this case, the endless journey on the way toward Being, which slips away whenever it becomes a determinate object of consciousness, is conceivably a way of condoning perpetual revolution.

This characteristic of Heidegger's thinking may have something to do with his religious disposition.[5] Alternatively, Gadamer remarks of Heidegger's intellectual culture, "one must remember what these years were like, in which the greatest book success was Spengler's *The Decline of the West*."[6] We might add to this Edmund Husserl's belief, mentioned earlier, that the human sciences had entered a critical stage, and Nietzsche's belief that the Christian hegemony in philosophy had ended. In "Heidegger and the Language of Metaphysics" Gadamer initially distinguishes Heidegger from Hegel, since for Heidegger "there is nothing of that necessity of historical progress."[7] Yet he also points out that, regardless of the degree to which humans are temporally constituted, Heidegger still "raises the question of what is" and, indeed, legitimates it. But on what grounds? Gadamer answers by tracing the steps taken by thought in the West and then treating this as the wrong path.[8] Heidegger is then in this sense a Hegelian; his history of ontology justifies the advent of a new age, and this is why Gadamer describes Heidegger as claiming for himself an "eschatological consciousness."[9] However, there is another, more immediate route toward Heidegger's perspective on history, on historical finales and natalities. While there is scant evidence of Heidegger adopting either Werner Jaeger's or Paul Natorp's approach to the history of philosophy, there are convergences between his thinking and theirs whose explication is a prerequisite to understanding Gadamer's indirect criticism of Heidegger through them.

---

4. Gadamer, "Reflections," 48.

5. Gadamer writes: "About this I would say: his radicalism always bore the stamp of his religious background. For his whole life, his radicalism was driven by an endless search for God." *GR*, 425.

6. Ibid., 360.

7. Ibid., 348.

8. Ibid., 370.

9. Ibid., 348.

1. STENZEL, JAEGER, AND THE DEVELOPMENT THESIS 1

Gadamer suggests that Heidegger's view of Plato is coordinate with a developmental thesis argued for by Julius Stenzel in 1917 and then reinvigorated by the timely publication of Werner Jaeger's *Aristotle: Fundamentals of the History of his Development* (1923).[10] An overview of this developmental tradition constitutes the historical condition in which Heidegger's thought on Plato germinated.

Seventeen years before Jaeger's book, Stenzel argues in *Plato's Method of Dialectic* that Plato's theory of ideas was initially developed in response to a moral dilemma—namely, Socrates's inability to define the virtues—and that after the *Republic* Plato extended the principles of his moral ideals to epistemology and ontology, but then reached an impasse because he could not explain how the forms related to sensible phenomena. This is expressed in the difficulties set forth in the dialogue *Parmenides*, after which Plato was occupied with logical and nonmoral conceptual problems of dialectic (meaning *dihairesis* or the analysis and dissection of concepts in the *Sophist*, *Statesman*, and *Philebus*).[11] Gadamer adds that Stenzel's discussion with the neo-Kantian interpretation of Plato, focusing on the *Phaedo* and ideas as hypotheses, "led subsequently to the later Plato's dialectic of *dihairesis*. And this dialectic in turn, it is suggested, may have even evolved into the doctrine of ideal numbers,"[12] which points in the direction of Fichte or neo-Kantianism.[13] In this case, Plato's revised understanding of the Ideas—notably in the latter dialogues, *Sophist*, *Philebus*, and *Statesman*—prefigures the German idealists or, more simply, the separation of ideas from sensible things.

10. The Tübingen school of Wolfgang Schadewaldt, but above all Hans Joachim Kramer and Konrad Gaiser, it might be argued, contributed to the developmental thesis by using Aristotle, specifically the one and the dyad in *Metaphysics* and the virtue of *phronesis*, as clues to understanding Plato.

11. I am paraphrasing from Bluck, "View of Stenzel," 184–185.

12. *DD*, 128–129. Gadamer is referring to Julius Stenzel, *Studien zur Entwicklung der platonischen Dialektik von Sokrates zu Aristoteles* (Breslau, 1917). Gadamer observes, "This book has the revealing subtitle 'Arete and Dihairesis', which in itself is already an articulation of the 'development' hypothesis which the book will present." Kramer explains that Stenzel developed a picture of Plato "which led from 'arete' to 'diaeresis,' and finally, to the *atomon-eidos* in Aristotle." This in turn, he explains, made ample room for the indirect tradition in interpreting Plato's philosophy, focused upon ideal numbers. Kramer, *Plato*, 39–40.

13. Ibid., 157.

Gadamer objects to the idea of there being a development in Plato's thought from an attempt to define the virtues to the problem of separation and then the taking up of dialectic as *dihairesis*. On the one hand, drawing upon the Tübingen school's tradition of arguing for an esoteric oral teaching at the Academy that would overcome impasses represented in the dialogues, Gadamer takes Plato's works as an invitation to participate in and recreate that conversation. On the other hand, also drawing upon that school, specifically, Hans Kramer's thesis that Aristotle's virtue of *phronesis* is modeled after Plato's idea of the One, as well as the research of Jacob Klein on Greek number theory (discussed in Part IV), Gadamer argues that Plato's hidden teaching is an *arithmos* paradigm or the problem that the One is many and the many is One.[14] This teaching is then demonstrated by Gadamer to be present in Plato's works, from the earliest, such as the *Hippias*, to the latest, thus challenging the development thesis.

Nevertheless, it was Jaeger whose acclaimed book on Aristotle in 1923 entrenched the thesis, in the German intellectual culture of the early twentieth century, that Aristotle is an authority on the late development of Plato's thought. Jaeger employs a positivist theory of time and sequentially ordered categories to demonstrate the gradual unfolding of Aristotle's views from Plato's presuppositions. He argues that Aristotle evolves, in the words of Gadamer, from a Platonist into a critic of Plato and finally into an empiricist.[15] Jaeger writes of Aristotle, "Everywhere in his exposition he makes his own ideas appear as the direct consequences of his criticism of his predecessors; especially Plato and his school."[16] Plato may have been Aristotle's teacher for twenty years, but it is Aristotle who ultimately instructs Plato. Jaeger is for Gadamer the culmination of the design argument developed decades earlier by the Tübingen school.

To what degree does Heidegger's thinking about the relation of Plato to Aristotle resemble the intellectual culture of which Jaeger's work is the culmination? A year after the publication of Jaeger's book on Aristotle, Heidegger lectured on Plato's *Sophist* (winter 1924). In this course he

---

14. For detailed study of Gadamer's relation to the Tübingen school and other influences on the development of these points of view see Grondin, "Gadamer and the Tübingen School."

15. Gadamer characterizes Jaeger's thesis as a "simple schema . . . which gave us the outlines of Aristotle's development from Platonist to a critic of Plato's doctrine of ideas." *IG*, 7.

16. Jaeger, *Aristotle's Fundamentals*, 3.

makes arguments about the relation of Plato to Aristotle that resemble the developmental approach. Heidegger refers to the *Phaedrus*, saying that Plato's dialectic is completed by Aristotle; referring to the *Gorgias* he says that Plato laid the groundwork for a positive understanding of rhetoric later developed by Aristotle; and finally, in reference to the *Sophist*, he says that the idea of motion and *genos* or kind introduced by Plato is, in fact, Aristotle's contribution.[17] Heidegger inadvertently affirms Jaeger's thesis by drawing Aristotle into close proximity to Plato and then breaking away from this recognition to emphasize that what Plato indicates embryonically is developed in a positive and more radical direction by his student. In a 1924 lecture drafted during his first semester at Marburg, Heidegger thus acknowledges that Socrates and Plato were the first to challenge the ordinary speech of citizens in the Athenian *polis*, that is to say, the common ways of speaking characteristic of the public space or what Heidegger calls "Being-with-one-another."[18] Plato and Socrates understood that rhetoric was directed toward persuading and moving the audience rather than disclosing to them the truth of beings or "a pure showing of the things themselves."[19] However, as evinced already by his arguments about dialectic, rhetoric, and motion, Heidegger believes that the efforts of Plato and Socrates were incomplete, that even Plato "was not successful in actually breaking away completely." Plato remained within common speech, and thus obfuscated further the very matters into which he was inquiring. This was not the case for Aristotle, who, Heidegger says, understood things in terms of themselves—for example, movement as movement.[20] Overall, for Heidegger in the mid 1920s, the ideas bundled together by Plato are given conceptual clarity by Aristotle.[21] C. Partenie and T. Rockmore

---

17. I am paraphrasing Dostal in "Gadamer's Continuous Challenge," 293. Dostal observes that, as I have mentioned, Heidegger draws Aristotle in close proximity to Plato but then dogmatically breaks away from recognizing this. I have attempted to account for this pattern with Jaeger's thesis in mind.

18. *BH*, 224.

19. Ibid., 221.

20. Ibid., 224.

21. Heidegger explains in 1922 that "Plato bundled together the four kinds of knowing because he did not have the right guiding clue for truly seeing and distinguishing them . . . what they refer to" (*BH*, 227). He means to say that Plato tended not to distinguish the object of knowledge from the assertions about it, and thus never thought about the ways in which discourse discloses beings. Also, he writes, in 1927 that "The

conclude that Heidegger "straightforwardly claims that 'what Aristotle said is what Plato placed at his disposal, only it is said more radically and developed more scientifically.'"[22]

The foregoing seems to prove that Heidegger imitates Jaeger. That is not the point. Rather, the affinity between them means that a challenge to Jaeger on the evolution of Aristotle's empiricism from Plato's speculative science is tantamount to a refutation of Heidegger's tendency to read Plato in terms of Aristotle. Delving into the background of Jaeger's reading of Aristotle, primarily on the basis of a prior decision about what Jaeger thought needed to be concretely done, opens up a parallel avenue for understanding Heidegger's approach to Plato.

2. JAEGER AND THE DEVELOPMENT THESIS 2

Heidegger interprets Plato in terms of Aristotle, but a closer inspection of this method reveals that Aristotle is in turn the vehicle for a challenge to the spirit of modern science. The point at which to criticize Heidegger on this score is his approach to translation-interpretation. When the meanings of concepts are investigated independently of their context or origin, as Plato witnessed when Homer's epic poetry became alien to the Greeks, novel interpretations can take precedence that advance a private interest rather than the continuity of shared understanding. Insofar as Heidegger takes this tack in his Plato interpretation, that is to say, makes translations-interpretations that are indifferent to the time and place of the speaker, he may be revealing more about his own beliefs than about those of whom he speaks. Gadamer's hesitancy regarding Jaeger's work is a clue to this aspect of Heidegger's approach to Plato.

Robert Sullivan explains that Jaeger was chosen to succeed Wilamowitz as the chair of *Altphilologie* in Berlin 1919 both because he was a respected philologist and because he was in harmony with the preferences of bureaucrats at the Ministry of Education. Although Jaeger was well disposed to the *Bildung*'s tradition of Hölderlin and Humboldt, the methods and values preferred by the bureaucracy were crucial to the thesis in his book on Aristotle. He came out in support of the scientific methods of his predecessor Wilamowitz in the sense that he argued for

---

primary assertion is *apophansis*, a determination that Aristotle, and in principle Plato, too, already saw." *BPP*, 209.

22. Partenie and Rockmore, *Heidegger and Plato*, xx.

an evolution of Aristotle's thought from the naïve idealism of Plato—an interpretation reminiscent of the *Bildung*'s tradition—to a mature Aristotle pointing forward to positivist science. In the rivalry between the *Bildung*'s tradition and *Altertumswissenschaft* that had come to the fore again after World War I, Werner Jaeger's book on Aristotle (1923) sided with the scientific method and reaffirmed the values of the new industrializing Germany.[23] His book was as much a mask for educational and social reform as it was a contribution to classical scholarship. Sullivan concludes that Jaeger "could be read as a supporter of the established authorities, that is to say, state functionaries, professors, and the classical authors of texts."[24] As if to attest to the significance of Jaeger's trendsetting work, Gadamer reports that classical philology "had arrived at such a refinement of the sense of history that in Werner Jaeger's school in Berlin sureness of concepts in Aristotle's ethics and rhetoric were increasingly appearing untranslated in scholarly discussion—as though such mere taking-over guaranteed historical appropriateness."[25] Gadamer's point is that Jaeger's leaving Greek terms untranslated lends scholarship an aura of historical credibility while closing down important questions about how and when the terms were used.

In 1927 Gadamer thus challenged Jaeger's argument that Aristotle's *Protrepticus* is Platonic because its theory of ideas resembles the *Philebus*, away from which Aristotle allegedly evolved. Gadamer paraphrases and evaluates Jaeger as follows: "The picture looks even worse with regard to the 'development' in Aristotle's ethics. Aristotle's presumed evolution from a 'politics of the ideas' (in the *Protrepticus*) through a still hesitant distancing of himself from Plato in the *Eudemian Ethics* to the 'mature' and self-confident position of the *Nicomachean Ethics* is an arbitrary and contradictory construction of Jaeger's."[26] The basis for Jaeger's argument

---

23. Robert Sullivan muddies this picture of Jaeger. He explains that Jaeger's position is ambiguous because he was both a positivist thinker carrying on the *Altertumswissenschaft* tradition of August Block and Ulrich von Wilamowitz-Moellendorff as well as a *Bildung* philosophy in line with Humboldt, Hölderlin, Wolf and Schleiermacher. The latter partook of the position that it was the purpose of classical philology to capture the heroic spirit of the Greeks. Sullivan, *Political Hermeneutics*, 42–44.

24. Ibid., 63. As Gadamer says, Jaeger was swept up in the modern era to see Aristotle as the protectorate of the investigative mentality against the mathematical science of hypothesis. *DD*, 195.

25. *PDE*, xxxii.

26. *IG*, 9.

was an objective theory of ideas in the *Philebus*, an assessment Gadamer considered untenable for two reasons: (1) the *Philebus* is roughly contemporary with the *Protrepticus* and indicates that Plato is abandoning the theory of ideas typified by the *Phaedo*; and (2) meaning in the dialogues is negotiated through the contingencies characteristic of the spoken word.[27] By abstracting a doctrine from a living situation, Jaeger loosened meaning from its origins in an aural culture and replaced it with a notion of truth foreign to the *Protrepticus* or any other work by either Plato or Aristotle. Gadamer thus challenges Jaeger (and Waltzer), arguing that the shared terminology of Aristotle and Plato does not support a hypothesis of conceptual development, but instead indicates that "he [Aristotle] continues to live in the same word language as Plato's."[28] By returning to the context of a living conversation in which differences of perspective are negotiated, Gadamer refutes Jaeger's thesis that Aristotle's thought develops out of and improves upon Plato.

Can the same be said of Heidegger that has been said of Jaeger? Does he interpret Plato's and Aristotle's philosophy independently of their context? In his essay "Plato's Doctrine of Truth," Heidegger claimed to bring to light the underlying reality or original meaning contained in Plato's language, but Paul Friedlander points out that semantically similar words to *aletheia*, translated by Heidegger as "unconcealment," in fact mean accuracy or correctness—that Plato uses *aletheia* in the *Cratylus*, and Homer *orthotes*.[29] Gadamer similarly questions Heidegger's reading of classical texts. In "Heidegger and the Greeks" he explains that he was reluctant to accept Heidegger's etymologies and that there are two dozen mistakes in Heidegger's translation of the "Ode to Antigone."[30] In "The Greeks" he criticizes Heidegger's interpretation of *arche*, *dynamis*,

---

27. Sullivan, "Translator's Introduction," 61–62.

28. *IG*, 38.

29. Friedlander, *Plato*, 221–229. I have merely highlighted two aspects of his argument.

30. Gadamer criticizes Heidegger's translation of passages from Anaximander and Parmenides in "Greeks," 143–144. That he disputes Heidegger's translation of Antigone is from Dostal, "Gadamer's Relation to Heidegger," 265 n22. Paul Friedlander had also questioned Heidegger's etymological analyses in "Plato's Doctrine of Truth." Friedlander points out that, as early as Homer, *aletheia* "has all the essential aspects that come out more clearly in later literary language," i.e., Homer uses the word "truth" in connection with verbs of assertion. From Friedlander, *Plato*, 223.

physis, *eido*, *morphe*, and *metabole*.³¹ In *Idea of the Good* he questions Heidegger's identification of *eidos* with *idea* (discussed below in chapter 5) as well as his vague language.³² These criticisms by Friedlander and Gadamer suggest a different standard of interpretation from that used by Heidegger. At one level, Gadamer explains, Heidegger tended to "show from language the true lineage of concepts."³³ Heidegger thus relates that Plato's "disclosure of the Ideas takes its bearings from the soul's soliloquy (*logos*) with itself," and then suggests that this is what Aristotle has in mind with regard to "reason's assertoric knowledge," i.e., Descartes's *res cogitans* and Kant's notion of consciousness.³⁴ In another instance of the same tendency, Heidegger equates *eidos* with *Aussehen*, *das Fortwahrende* with *aei on* and *essentia* or *quidditas*, and *omoisis* with *adaequatio*. At another level, not unrelated to the first, he aims for a retrieval of Aristotle in order to effect a criticism of scholasticism, German idealism, and science. Just as Jaeger's scholarship aimed to justify the positive sciences then underlying Germany's public policy, Heidegger's preference, at the time of consolidating his perspective on Plato in the late 1920s or early 1930s, justified a retrieval of the early Greek notion of *physis*. Both Jaeger and Heidegger turned to Aristotle (although for precisely opposite reasons); but the prioritizing of Aristotle in either case speaks to a prior determination about the meaning of what is, i.e., a decision made independently of Aristotle's situation or the text in question.

Heidegger's method of interpretation has thus attracted the attention of such philosophers as Karl Jaspers, Stanley Rosen, and Gadamer on precisely the question of context. Jaspers writes, "H. treats Plato like a man with 'doctrines'—just like Zeller—a completely unPlatonic opinion [*Stimmung*]. No dialectic—no movement in real comprehending [*Nachvollzug*]—some phantasm—*nihil*—takes the place of existence-transcendence—Plato falsely characterized. Rather ridiculous blanket

---

31. Gadamer, "Greeks," 146–150.

32. In order to avoid the stabilization of meaning in concepts that stifle thinking (a process to which he believes Indo-European languages are prone), Heidegger had kept the meaning of such words as "hermeneutics" and "ontological difference" indefinite. Gadamer responds, "by using such terms Heidegger avoided sharpening the meaning of his terms too much . . ." and offers a more precise definition of these and other Heideggerian neologisms. *GR*, 358.

33. *GR*, 425.

34. *BH*, 307.

assertions [*Totalbehauptungen*]."[35] And Rosen comments on Heidegger's Plato:

> Like the most professorial of philologians, Heidegger normally ignores the dialectical context of those sentences which he abstracts for analysis, as though they were independent, technical propositions instead of the speech of irony. His procedure in this vein is also reminiscent of the way in which Rudolph Carnap casts positive scorn on one of Heidegger's negative utterances. Even when Heidegger seems to be aware of the dramatic context, as in *Platons Lehre von der Wahrheit*, he refers only to those aspects of it which seem to serve his purpose. He ignores the details even when insisting upon an individual nuance.[36]

Gadamer reiterates their concerns when he writes of Heidegger's lectures at Marburg, "Aristotle was forced on us in such a way that we temporarily lost all distance from him—never realizing that Heidegger was not identifying himself with Aristotle, but was ultimately aiming at developing his own agenda against metaphysics."[37] According to Gadamer, Heidegger was less interested in what Aristotle could teach him, or what Aristotle really meant, than in how his concepts (such as *physis*) could be used to undermine both German idealism and (as Gadamer goes on to say) the attack on nature by contemporary science. This clearly demands some creative reworking of the primary sources, especially in view of Heidegger's claim to have interpreted the "unsaid."

Attending to the "unsaid" in a thinker's work is not unique to Heidegger. In the *Critique of Pure Reason* Immanuel Kant voices an approach to interpretation that characterized German scholarship on Plato three hundred years later. He writes of Plato's "idea":

> I shall not engage here in any literary enquiry into the meaning which this illustrious philosopher attached to the expression. I need only remark that it is by no means unusual, upon comparing the thoughts which an author has expressed in regard to his subject, whether in ordinary conversation or in writing, to find that we understand him better than he understood himself. As

---

35. Gonzalez, "Dialectic," 382.
36. Rosen, "Heidegger's Interpretation of Plato," 57.
37. Gadamer, "Greeks," 141.

he has not sufficiently determined his concept, he has sometimes spoken, or even thought, in opposition to his own intention.[38]

Kant believes that what Plato really meant by an idea was not clear to him and that the reader can understand Plato better than Plato understood himself. In a similar vein the Tübingen school, in the words of Tom Rockmore, "turns to Aristotle to recover doctrines Plato allegedly communicated orally but did not record in written form."[39] The methods of this school prefigure Heidegger's approach to Plato. By equating *Lehre* or doctrine with what remains unsaid by Plato in the Allegory of the Cave, Heidegger perpetuates the same tradition.[40] But this is a dubious enterprise. Although Natorp claims to let Plato speak for himself,[41] the thesis Natorp sets forth cannot fail to conjure the thought that his prejudices about the importance of idealism to the destiny of Germany are being projected back into Plato's philosophy. Similarly, Jaeger's argument that Aristotle secretly criticizes Plato and then surpasses him is as much autobiography (with a tendency toward positivist values) as it is history. Dreyfus remarks of Heidegger:

> Heidegger cheerfully ignores, or violently reinterprets, lots of Plato and Nietzsche while presenting himself as respectfully listening to the voice of Being as it is heard in their words. But Heidegger knew what he wanted to hear in advance. He wanted to hear something which would make his own historical position decisive, by making his own historical epoch terminal.[42]

According to Dreyfus, although professing to hear something original, Heidegger knew what he wanted to hear in advance of interpreting what Plato really meant but did not say.[43] But what is the basis for the latter? Rosen points out that Heidegger does not so much attribute to-

---

38. Kant, *Critique of Pure Reason*, 314a.
39. Rockmore, "Heidegger's Uses of Plato," 197.
40. However, Leo Strauss stipulates that "reading between the lines" is "prohibited in all cases where it would be less exact than not doing so." *Persecution*, 30. Zuckert brought this passage to my attention. Zuckert, "Politics of Hermeneutics," 238.
41. Politis, *Paul Natorp*, 49.
42. Dreyfus, *Heidegger*, 225.
43. In "The Concept of Time in the Science of History" Heidegger's history of metaphysics bears out his own assessment of the science of history, wherein, according to Kisiel, "the selection of which past events will become 'historical' depends on their relatedness to certain present values." *BH*, 60.

Plato a secret doctrine "as he gives a kind of psychological interpretation of the actual motives and significance of that hypothesis.[44] By claiming to have uncovered these motives, Heidegger effectively foregrounds his own prejudices about what needs to be said and concretely done, here and now, in the language of authentic, primordial origins. Gadamer reiterates these concerns, writing, "To think the Greeks more Greeklike—does this challenge not lead to some hopeless hermeneutical difficulties, especially if attempted with one of Aristotle's pedagogic texts, such as his lectures on physics? . . . Does this not degenerate into an artificial archaism, like that which we come across with some of Heidegger's risky endeavors with the German language?"[45]

3. NATORP AND IDEALISM

Whereas Heidegger, during his first period of identifying with the task of metaphysics, had been relatively indifferent to the practical ramifications of Plato's notion of Being, in the 1920s he thinks of it along the lines of any other idea of human consciousness, aligning Plato with the devaluation of life in Christianity and, eventually, twentieth-century technology. In "Plato's Doctrine of Truth" Heidegger holds Plato responsible for transforming the early Greek experience of truth (*aletheia*) and Being (*physis*) into correctness of representation and idea respectively: according to Heidegger, by equating Being with an idea (human perspective) and paying little attention to the movement proper to Being as *physis* (emergence-withdrawal), Plato lays the foundation for the Western metaphysical tradition's forgetfulness of the meaning of Being. In contrast, then, to the years 1909 to 1920, when Heidegger considered Plato's metaphysics insignificant to the "life world," by 1929 to 1930 he is holding Plato responsible for the forgetting of Being and the denigration of "life," and after World War II calls Plato the definitive worker in the modern age.

Heidegger's argument depends, on the one hand, upon an Aristotelianization of what Plato means by "idea" (discussed in chapter 5) and, on the other hand, on the assumption that there is a continuous line of thinking about the meaning of Being from Plato to Nietzsche.

---

44. Rosen "Heidegger's Plato," 179.

45. Gadamer, "Greeks," 145. Gadamer points out that the methods used by Aristotle, including logic and dialectic, are foreign to the pre-Socratic period.

While this assumption of historical continuity in the history of Western metaphysics reflects the influence of Nietzsche on Heidegger, i.e., the identification of 2,000 years of Christianity as Platonism, it is also coordinate with Natorp's theory of the history of ideas wherein Plato is alleged to be a neo-Kantian.[46]

The groundwork for connecting Plato's ideas with human subjectivity in a project to revitalize culture was laid down by Paul Natorp and other scholars.[47] Natorp writes:

> The introduction to Plato is at the same time a training in philosophy, and the proper conception of philosophy originates here. But the conception of philosophy that arises in this strictly historical way is none other than idealism. To cast the exposition developed here of Plato's theory of ideas as an introduction to idealism is, therefore, not to import a foreign and unhistorical point of view into what is after all intended as a historical investigation. If Plato's theory of ideas is indeed the birth of idealism in the history of humanity, what better access to idealism could we desire than through reliving this very birth in the development of Plato's philosophy?[48]

Natorp felt that Germany had virtually lost sight of idealism and was entering into a crisis. His panacea was *Plato's Theory of Ideas* (1902).[49] Since Plato was the founder of idealism, studying his philosophy might reinvigorate the times.

Stepping back into antiquity for learned inspiration was not unique to Natorp. It harks back at least to the nineteenth-century *Bildung*'s move-

---

46. The neo-Kantians at Marburg included Hermann Cohen, Nicolai Hartmann, Paul Friedlander, and Paul Natorp.

47. Kant writes of Plato, "He knew that our reason naturally exalts itself to modes of knowledge which so far transcend the bounds of experience that no given empirical object can ever coincide with them, but which must none the less be recognized as having their own reality, and which are by no means mere fictions of the brain." Kant, *Critique of Pure Reason*, A 314. It stands to reason that Plato is thought, among the neo-Kantians, to have been the first idealist.

48. Politis, *Paul Natorp*, 48.

49. In the Preface to the first edition of *Plato's Theory of Ideas* (1902), Paul Natorp relates that the material for the book had been compiled fifteen years earlier and that Hermann Cohen and Eduard Zeller were his predecessors. Politis, *Paul Natorp*, 48. Zeller had argued that Plato's ideas are laws, and Cohen that the theory of ideas is the principle of idealism and "will remain nothing but the method-based principles of natural science." Ibid., 394.

ment led by Nietzsche, Humboldt, and Holderlin. Not unlike Richard Wagner's effort to create a new post-Christian religion on the basis of pagan myths, the *Bildung*'s movement challenged the dominating spirit of the times with a revival of classical thought. Heidegger sailed into the same current, seeking to transform the present by injecting some semblance of the archaic past—although, like those of the counterscientific movement, in a direction at odds with that being charted by Natorp in the early twentieth century.

Natorp in 1902 and Heidegger throughout the 1920s were wrapped up in a project to rebuild intellectual culture. While Natorp looked to Plato as a guide toward the revitalization of German idealism, signaled already by Kant in 1781, Heidegger targeted German idealism in the late 1920s as the plague, so to speak, of contemporary man.[50] Nevertheless, he shared with his erstwhile nemesis not only his overall method of reinvigorating contemporary culture, but also a certain view of Plato's ideas. Natorp writes, "We will see how he [Plato] in the *Theaetetus*, the *Phaedo*, the *Symposium*, and the *Republic* comes step by step closer to the overcoming of the transcendent on behalf of the transcendental, in order to achieve it in the *Parmenides*."[51] The ideas that Plato had argued are objective and independent of human subjectivity are (according to Natorp's genetic exposition of the dialogues) eventually located in the categories of understanding by Kant; Plato's philosophy of transcendent ideas is an immature or naïve grasping after Kant's *Critique of Pure Reason*. Although not interested in furthering the scientific spirit of the idealists, Heidegger could not have held an antithetical posture toward them without having something in common. In this case, it is Natorp's narrative that Plato is a proto-Kantian in matters of ideas. Heidegger's regard for Kant dates back to his *Habilitationsschrift*, where he found support for phenomenology in Kant's transcendental philosophy.[52] If the noumenal realm is beyond knowledge, then we are indeed left with what

---

50. Heidegger writes, "Plato's doctrine of 'truth' is therefore not something of the past. It is historically 'present,' but not as a historically recollected 'consequence' of a piece of didacticism, not even as revival, not even as imitation of antiquity, not even as mere preservation of the traditional. That change of the essence of truth is present as the slowly confirmed and still uncontested basic reality, a reality reigning through everything, the basic reality of the history of the world rolling on and on into its most modern modernity." *PDT*, 269.

51. Natorp, *Plato's Doctrine of Ideas*, quoted in Dostal, "Beyond Being," 76.

52. Poggeler, *Heidegger's Path*, 14–15.

is given to consciousness by the senses. In an endeavor to position phenomenology within the premoderns, in a lecture delivered in the summer semester of 1926 on the history of Greek philosophy from Thales to Aristotle, Heidegger stated that Kant was the first Greek philosopher since Aristotle.[53]

But this appropriation of Kant and transcendental philosophy into the phenomenological movement is not what aligns Heidegger with Natorp on Plato's ideas. This alignment only becomes visible in the early 1940s during the famed "turn," when, in "Plato's Doctrine of Truth," Heidegger reasons that "The beginning of metaphysics in the thought of Plato is at the same time the beginning of Humanism."[54] By equating Being with an idea, Plato is a Protagorean-humanist in that man becomes the measure of all things, seen and unseen, above and below the earth. Dostal concludes, "The early Heidegger understood the problem of interpreting Plato in precisely the terms set down by Natorp. Either the ideas reside in a place beyond the heavens or in transcendental subjectivity. Heidegger acknowledges in 'On the Essence of Ground' (1929), perhaps in deference to Natorp's interpretation, that the tendency toward the latter is prefigured (*vorgebildet*) in Plato."[55]

Dostal summarizes Gadamer's reply to Heidegger thus: "Gadamer shows us how Aristotle's thesis (and for that matter, Heidegger's as well) with his doctrine of the forms (*Ideenlehre*) mirrors Natorp's Plato of transcendental subjectivity and the categories. Neither is adequate to Plato's texts themselves."[56] In *Metaphysics* I, chapters 6 and 9, the ideas are said by Aristotle to be Pythagorean numbers, which set in motion a tradition of associating Plato with mathematical science (Galileo). Mathematics is the "language of nature" or scientific laws transposed by Kant into Newtonian categories of the understanding. Grondin writes, "Natorp's 1923 book on Plato had raised a furor over its provocative thesis that at bottom Plato's ideas embody nothing but scientific laws."[57] The mathematical Plato of Aristotle thus mirrors, because it is the deep origin of,

---

53. Fritsche, "Kairos before the Kehre," 164 n3.

54. *PDT*, 269.

55. Dostal, "Beyond Being," 76.

56. Dostal, "Gadamer's Continuous Challenge," 291.

57. Grondin, *Hans-Georg Gadamer*, 79. Dostal writes, "Plato's 'doctrine of ideas' is interpreted by way of Kant's categories and transcendental ideas." "Beyond Being," 75. See also *IG*, 2, 24.

Natorp's Plato of transcendental subjectivity. Since this mathematical-scientific image of Plato was being propagated by "Platorp,"[58] the most ardent of Platonists during Heidegger's time, Heidegger would have had good reason for accepting Aristotle's view of Plato's ideas. A numerological metaphysics in the fifth century BC is found to be the real beginning of mathematical physics in the twentieth century. Indeed, Heidegger traces the latter to Plato in "The Question Concerning Technology" and "Age of the World Picture."[59] But this thesis holds only insofar as Heidegger assumes, along with the neo-Kantians, that Plato is a "scientist."

The affinity between Natorp and Heidegger does not end with the interpretation of Plato according to a history of science that runs from Aristotle's Plato to Kant. Gadamer subtly suggests that Heidegger and Natorp are also in harmony on the production thesis. Gadamer writes of Natorp's "somewhat forced assimilation of Plato to Kant," on the "*eidos* of the best 'hypothesis'":

> To be sure, Natorp's interpretation was not lacking insight into the exceptional role of the good. For him the good was the principle of self-preservation. He saw hypothesizing the *eidos* as a procedure for knowing this principle, and in this way he came to identify "idea" with "natural law." What he had in mind, accordingly, was natural science. In its ascending hypotheses the latter does indeed move ever closer to the true order of the universe, and it is carried out in ongoing determinations of its object. For Natorp the "thing in itself" is nothing more than the infinite, "unending task."[60]

In this passage on Natorp's association of Plato's ideas with natural laws, the Good with the principle of self-preservation, and the "ongoing determinations" of objects in the universe with ascending hypotheses of the "thing in itself," we have the basic ingredients of Heidegger's linking of Plato's idea of the Good to the useful and thus to *techne*. If the ideas

---

58. "Platorp" was Natorp's nickname at the University of Marburg. Grondin, *Hans-Georg Gadamer*, 79.

59. Heidegger explains in "Age of the World Picture" (lecture, 1938) that, just as truth for Plato is correspondence between ideas and things, so too through mathematical physics is something "stipulated in advance as what is already known," and in "The Question Concerning Technology" (lecture, 1949) that the framing of modern technology that determines beings to be according to a mathematical standard of truth is heard already in Plato. QCT, 119.

60. *IG*, 24.

are, as the neo-Kantians held, scientific *a priori* laws (mathematical formulae), then an ontological dichotomy is established between those laws and the phenomenal world. This dichotomy in turn justifies knowing as making in the technical (productive or "present-at-hand") sense that is without limit, because in no way can that which is moving (nature) be rendered an absolute "standing-reserve." There is thus a crossing of paths by Natorp and Heidegger on Plato's concept of the Good and its advantages for us. But if Heidegger's Plato is Natorp's, then Heidegger does as much to reinvigorate the spirit of science and the conquest of nature as German idealism does.

5

Heidegger's Aristotelianism: The Production Thesis

INTRODUCTION

To recapitulate the result from the previous chapter: Heidegger aimed to overcome the history of metaphysics by returning to Aristotle, yet this very elevation of a phenomenological science over metaphysics is misplaced because it depends upon a pretheoretical context in twentieth-century German intellectual and social culture that Heidegger unreflectively mimics. In this chapter attention is directed toward Aristotle's view of Plato's ideas, repeated by Heidegger. Gadamer comments on Heidegger in the 1920's, "... in spite of the preponderance of Heidegger's ingenious discovery of ancient thought, in the end, I did not follow Heidegger's insistence on the superiority of Aristotle over the Platonic model."[1] Gadamer is pointing out Heidegger's belief, defended by Aristotle, that Plato's ideas are Pythagorean ideal numbers and hence universal entities separate from the physical realm without any intelligible basis for participation in it. On the basis of the separation of ideas and the thesis that they are categories of human consciousness (Natorp), Heidegger reasons that knowing for Plato is technical, a conclusion he may have gleaned from Descartes's *Regulae*, but which is prefigured in Aristotle's view of *episteme*.

In *Rules for the Direction of the Mind* Descartes writes, "Human knowledge receives no more diversity from them [forms] than does the light of the sun from the various things it illuminates."[2] Descartes is suggesting that the diversity of forms or objects of investigation is irrelevant to his method, which subsumes them to the same humanly constructed

---

1. Gadamer, "Reply to Dostal," 308.
2. Rosen, "Strauss and the Quarrel," 156.

rules through the force of the intellect's will. Yet this is *in nuce* a relation between human knowing and making that is mirrored in Heidegger's study of Aristotle in the mid 1920s. In his study of *Nicomachean Ethics* VI in 1924, Heidegger discovered four ways in which beings appear to human beings: *episteme, sophia, techne,* and *phronesis*. He reasons that *sophia* is related to that which never changes, e.g., rocks and the sea, and includes that which could be otherwise than it is, *phronesis*; *episteme* is related to an idea that includes *techne*. This "idea" is a human "look" projected in advance of the coming-to-be of beings; or, as he says in 1927, knowing consists of projecting, in advance of an appearance, the *eidos* or form/stamp of a thing by human seeing (*idea*).[3] Beings are thus determined, i.e., made to be, according to a human perspective characteristic of the craftsperson who models reality on the basis of a blueprint. Assuming that for Plato, the meaning of being *qua* being is a science (*episteme*), Heidegger is justified in attributing to Plato a convergence between knowing and technical making—illustrated, for instance, in his reasoning about the demiurge in the *Timaeus*. Heidegger states in *Basic Problems of Phenomenology* (1927) of the production thesis, "The idea [*tou*] *agathou* is nothing but the *demiurgos*, the producer pure and simple."[4]

Plato's demiurge is for Heidegger the elevation of a human perspective on beings to the rank of the divine or transcendent. This is another

---

3. *BH*, 227, 175. The connection between knowing and *techne* depends upon correctness. The standard for knowing, or that with which correct speech agrees, is "the aspect [*Aussehen*] (*eidos, idea*) for example, the Idea 'house.'" This Idea "remains permanently present [*das Fortwahrende*] (*aei on*)" and is thus juxtaposed to the sensible realm; or, as Heidegger says, "Particular real and possible houses, in contrast are changing and transitory derivatives of the Idea and thus belong to what does not endure" (*PDT*, 261). Nonetheless, that which is particular and changing is brought into agreement with the permanently present. *Episteme*, or knowing as correctness, involves *techne*. Heidegger writes, "From the earliest times until Plato the word *techne* is linked with the word *episteme*. Both words are names for knowing in the widest sense" (*QCT*, 13). But clearly, with the change in the sense of truth from *aletheia* to correctness (*orthotes*), the character of *techne*/making has also changed. In 1922 Heidegger explains that in contrast to pure beholding as existing (*phronesis*) and thus without speech, is *episteme* which "takes the spoken word as the point of departure." The "already is" to which *episteme* relates is a derivative notion of truth because it investigates an aspect of beings on the basis of what is commonly held to be valid (what is spoken about and repeated by everyone). *BH*, 230.

4. Dostal, "Beyond Being," 87. Heidegger writes, "What makes every idea useful to an idea is, Platonically expressed, the Idea of all ideas and consists therefore in making it possible for everything present to make its appearance in all its visibility (*Sichtsamkeit*)." *PDT*, 263.

way of asserting a two-world theory, a world bifurcated between intelligible forms and unintelligible phenomena.[5] It is also the background to the enframing of even human beings by their own technology.[6] If, as Aristotle says, Plato's ideas are Pythagorean numbers,[7] then a universal and unchanging mathematical structure objective to the world is the language of reality.[8] Heidegger thus explains in "Age of the World Picture" (lecture, 1938) that, just as truth for Plato is correspondence between ideas and things, so too through mathematical physics something is "stipulated in advance as what is already known,"[9] and in "The Question Concerning Technology" (lecture, 1949) that the enframing of modern technology that determines beings to be according to a mathematical standard of truth is already heard in Plato.[10] Given the rage of rationalism against nature during the modern era, Heidegger finds it all the more urgent to overcome the history of metaphysics by uncovering its origins in a human perspective, i.e., Plato's, and thereby return thinking to the early Greek notion of Being via Aristotle, a notion that might truly redefine the destiny of the West. Gadamer answers by investigating (a) Aristotle's sources; (b) Aristotle's Pythagorean reading of Plato; (c) *phronesis* in Plato; and (d) the role of the demiurge in the *Timaeus*.

---

5. "For Platonism, the Idea, the supersensuous, is the true being. In contrast, the sensuous is *me on*. The latter suggests, not nonbeing pure and simple, *ouk on*, but *me*—what may not be addressed as being even thought is not simply nothing. Insofar as, and to the extent that, it may be called being, the sensuous must be measured upon the supersensuous; nonbeing possesses the shadow and the residues of Being which fall from true being." Heidegger, *Nietzsche*, 154.

6. "Enframing means the gathering together of that setting-upon which sets upon man, i.e., challenges him forth, to reveal the real, in the mode of ordering, as standing reserve." QCT, 2.

7. *Metaphysics* I, chapters 6 and 9.

8. Heidegger explains that for Plato "Aspect (*idea*) names and is, also, that which constitutes the essence in the audible, the tasteable, the tactile, in everything that is in any way accessible." The ideas are thus the framework that penetrates into and determines even intimate experiences of eating and touching. Plato's ideas are thus analogous to enframing. QCT, 20.

9. QCT, 119. The lectures "The Question Concerning Technology" and "Age of the World Picture" were revised for publication in 1954.

10. This thesis appears in *An Introduction to Metaphysics* (1935) where he explains of *techne* sundered from *physis*, "Thus *techne* provides the basic trait of *deinon*, the violent; for violence is the use of power against the overpowering: through knowledge it wrests being from concealment into the manifest as the *essent*." *IM*, 160.

1. THE DIALOGUES

Heidegger recapitulates Aristotle's ontological criticism of Plato, but Gadamer demonstrates, on the basis of the Dialogues, that Aristotle errs in attributing "dualism" to Plato. According to Gadamer, Aristotle argues for the *choriston* in Plato on the basis of such later dialogues as the *Phaedo*, *Parmenides* and *Timaeus*.[11] In the *Phaedo* Socrates explains that insofar as the body partakes in reason, the soul is blemished (66b), that the intellect alone is fit to grasp the truth (66a), that reality is invariable and constant (77d). In the *Parmenides* Plato is presumed to be criticizing himself on the impossibility of participation with the "Third Man Argument" and complex and convoluted definitions of the one and the many. Gadamer comments:

> Even today the prevailing opinion is that the criticism in Plato's *Parmenides* which the head of the Parmenidean school directs at the young Socrates, i.e., that the latter had proposed the hypothesis of the ideas too soon, is in fact Plato's criticism of himself. According to this view the paradoxes displayed here in the "participation" of the particular in the universal are reflections of the crisis in Plato's doctrine of ideas.[12]

It seems that in the *Parmenides* Plato is arguing for the incoherence of the separation thesis, which in turn justifies a turn toward Aristotle's empiricism. Gadamer disagrees. He believes that the *choriston* is the first step in thinking about the ideas in a dialectical relationship to one another that includes participation. But he arrives at this insight by challenging the very sources used by Aristotle to suggest otherwise.

Gadamer argues that the aforementioned sources cannot be accepted without qualification as evidence of Plato's doctrine of ideas. The theory of ideas in the *Phaedo* is not, for Gadamer, a reliable guide for interpreting Plato's philosophy. The notion of ideas presented there, where Plato refers to them as *auto kath auto* (consisting in themselves) (66a, 78d, 100b), is according to Gadamer an early and undeveloped understanding of ideas configured so as to speak to the lapsed Pythagoreans,

---

11. "Aristotle cites the *Phaedo* just as readily as he does the *Parmenides* or *Timaeus* and seems not to have noticed at all that Plato himself ever placed his dogmatic theory of ideas in question." *IG*, 8–9. In *Metaphysics* (990b17, 1039a2, 1059b8, 1079a13), Aristotle refers to the "third man argument" in Plato's *Parmenides* (132a–b). In *Metaphysics* XII.6.1071b16–17 he rivals Plato's explanation for change in the *Timaeus*.

12. *DD*, 157.

Simmias, and Cebes.[13] By re-establishing the *chorismos* of the soul on analogy with self-consisting ideas, Plato is appealing to the dichotomy between perfect, unchanging numbers and the sensible sphere in order to lead Socrates's interlocutors from their fall into enlightened materialism back to their Pythagorean roots in mathematical idealism.[14] But by no means, for Gadamer, is this Plato's final position in the *Phaedo*. On the contrary, Socrates later explains that a direct apprehension of the ideas bedazzles the eye of the mind. As a result, he decides to study the ideas indirectly, in speech, which in turn changes the notion of idea from an intelligible form existing apart from language to a linguistic hypothesis.

Gadamer considers the *Parmenides* to be no more a reliable source for Plato's theory of ideas than the *Phaedo*. Rather than being a self-criticism about the impossibility of participation, the *Parmenides*, through the inappropriateness of the solution discussed in it, demonstrates—perhaps intentionally—the dogmatism implied in the question. Citing the "hardest *aporia*" at 133b, Gadamer argues that the problem of the one participating in the many indicates how absurd the separation theory is:

> The complete separation of a world of ideas from the world of appearances would be a crass absurdity. If Parmenides, in the dialogue of the same name, consciously pushes us in the direction of that complete separation, he does so, it seems to me, precisely in order to reduce such an understanding of the *chorismos* to absurdity (see *Parmenides* 133bff).[15]

Socrates had asked Parmenides to define the one and then the many independently of one another. The Eleatic philosopher replies by offering seven increasingly complex definitions of the one and the many without any intelligible result. Gadamer concludes, "The interweaving of the highest genera in the *Sophist* and, even more, the dialectical exercise which the young Socrates is put through by the elder Parmenides leads only to the negative insight that it is not possible to define an iso-

---

13. Gadamer is reiterating Natorp's criticism of Aristotle. According to Natorp, Plato's reference to the ideas as "*auto kath' auto*" is a Socratic formulation that Plato eventually surpassed but Aristotle hastily accepted because "he lacked the necessary dialectical perseverance." Dostal, "Beyond Being," 76 n17. Rather than follow Natorp and argue that Plato developed this early formulation into transcendental objects of knowledge, Gadamer argues that Plato turns toward the study of the forms in speech.

14. *IG*, 24.

15. *IG*, 16.

lated idea purely by itself . . ."[16] Contrary to what Aristotle argues when he repeats the third man argument, the *Parmenides* demonstrates that the one cannot be defined independently of the many. Aristotle (and Heidegger) thus arrives at precisely the conclusion that, according to Gadamer, Plato was trying to disprove in the dialogue. By reading Plato through Aristotle, Heidegger recapitulates the error.

In "Idea and Reality in Plato's *Timaeus*" (1974) Gadamer indicates that the emphasis upon Plato's identification of ideas with ideal numbers, which accounts for the two-world theory, is a modern perspective on Plato mediated by an unreflective acquiescence to Aristotle's criticism. Rather than reading Plato through Aristotle or according to scientific measures of validity, what is needed instead, says Gadamer, is a method of interpretation that establishes the philosophical significance of settings and the relation of the speaker to what is spoken.[17] Taking the latter into consideration yields the argument that the Pythagorean distinction between ideal numbers and reality, Being and becoming, is abandoned in the *Timaeus*. For Gadamer, the dialogue indicates precisely what Aristotle in the *Physics* thought impossible for Plato: how Being participates in becoming.

The key in the *Timaeus* to understanding participation, and ultimately change, is the *chora*. It is neither Being nor becoming, but rather a third genus beyond both: it is between them (different) yet also mediates them (the same) (*Timaeus*, 52b).[18] As such, the *chora* is a principle of generation or, as Gadamer says, space-granting. By mixing opposing principles, e.g., limited and unlimited, the *chora* grants space, or reveals order in the midst of disorder.[19] Yet this process, like the order of the cosmos, soul, and state is understood by Gadamer's Plato in terms of numbers. Gadamer explains the process of generation according to numbers as follows: "The numbers are units of ones. The principle of being one is generative in them. They all follow the principle of n+1. That they do is obviously the sole meaning of the being of the number one, just as the sole meaning of the one or unit of the world order is

16. Ibid.
17. *DD*, 159.
18. *GR*, 399–400.
19. Gadamer writes, "The consideration of the *chora* is motivated solely by the question of how within what is irrational and unreasonable, 'reason,' i.e., a logically understandable necessity, still prevails." *DD*, 179.

being that one order."[20] In this passage Gadamer reasons about creation as he understands Plato to have reasoned, in terms of a mathematical model. Just as the unit one is present to all numbers and generates them, so too does the world come into being from out of "one." Yet not only are numbers generated by one, they also strive for unity, which is to say, mathematical proportion (Gadamer, in *Sophist*, 251a, cites *logos*, which means mathematical proportion).[21] This same process of order emerging out of "one", the *chora*, is evident in the structure of creation in the *Timaeus*. Gadamer says that the mixing of contrary elements imparts reason to an otherwise formless or disordered material (earth/solid, water/liquid, fire/warmth, and air). This is represented by the geometrical forms, e.g., the pyramid for fire, the cube for earth, the icosahedron for water, that are derived from and therefore variations upon a single form (dodecahedron). Gadamer cautions that Plato ought not to be read literally; he reports that for Plato the idea of an underlying order of natural elements being geometrical, and striving for mathematical perfection, is a "likely story." Nevertheless, the *logos* he discerns in Plato's *mythos* challenges Heidegger's contention that Plato advances a two-world theory and cannot explain change. Heidegger's contention is thus challenged on the basis of the very dialogue that allegedly attests to the problem.

Yet another implication of Gadamer's rereading of the *Timaeus* pertains to Heidegger's understanding of the early Greek notion of *physis* as emerging-withdrawal. It is possible that this is not so much what the Greeks thought as a projection of Heidegger's thinking in terms of dialectical antitheses. While tracing the Hegelian influence on Heidegger, Gadamer highlights the antithesis between throwness and projection, authenticity and inauthenticity.[22] The same bivalent structure is evident in Heidegger's thinking about *physis* and *aletheia*. Gadamer challenges this pattern when he points out that in the *Timaeus*, and for Plato in general, whenever there is reason there is also life (psyche).[23] The com-

20. *IG*, 144. See also *Philebus*, 15b–16d and *Parmenides*, 131b cited in *IG*, 135–136. To Parmenides's reasoning that the one is separate from itself if it is also many, Socrates replies, "No it wouldn't. Not if it's like one and the same day. That is in many places at the same time and is none the less not separate from itself. If it's like that, each of the forms might be, at the same time, one and the same in all." *Parmenides*, 131b.

21. *IG*, 135.

22. *GR*, 348–349.

23. Gadamer points out that *psyche* or life is the essence of nature in the *Laws*, 892c (*DD*, 142). From Plato's *Laws*, the Athenian stranger explains to Clinias that the soul

bining of contraries by the demiurge therefore imparts life to the world, that is, order, symmetry, balance, beauty, and goodness. For Gadamer *physis* does not consist, as it does for the early Greeks, of an oscillation between revealing and concealing, a notion that Heidegger contends and Gadamer suggests is Hegelian in character; rather, *physis* is as self-regulating as the logic internal to number and hence is ordered movement. He writes, "the Greek concept of science is characterized by the scientific concept of *physis*, that is, the horizon of what points to itself from itself and exists in itself as a self-regulated order of things."[24]

2. THE PYTHAGOREANS

Dostal points out that in the lectures on the *Sophist* (1925) Heidegger accepts Aristotle's position that Plato follows the Pythagoreans and identifies ideas with the number concept.[25] If the idea is a number, then knowing consists in imitating the numbers as exemplified, for the Pythagoreans, in the cosmos and musical harmony. The background to Plato the Pythagorean is Aristotle's claim that although Plato used the word *methexis* instead of *mimesis*, as the Pythagoreans did, he meant the same thing by it.[26] As a result, Plato no less than the Pythagoreans had difficulty explaining both how ideas relate to, and how they participate in, sensible things and change.

---

is the first creation, "born long before physical things, and is the chief cause of all their alternations and transformations." To those who identify nature with the processes by which primary substances are created, which leads to supposing that nature is secondary to reason and art, the Athenian replies, "But if it can be shown that soul came first, not fire or air, and that it was one of the first things to be created, it will be quite correct to say that soul is preeminently nature. This is true, provided you can demonstrate that soul is older than matter, but not otherwise." *Laws*, Book X 892c.

24. *GR*, 269.

25. "In these lectures, which I will not attempt to summarize here, we find Heidegger adopting many of Aristotle's familiar criticisms of Plato, e.g., criticism of the ideas understood as numbers and of the relation of ideas to the things of our experience, i.e., the *chorismos* (separation) and *methexis* (participation) problems." Dostal, "Gadamer's Continuous Challenge," 291.

26. *IG*, 10. Aristotle writes of Plato and the Pythagoreans, "Only the name 'participation' was new; for the Pythagoreans say that things exist by 'imitation' of numbers, and Plato says they exist by participation, changing the name. But what the participation or the imitation of the Forms could be they left an open question." *Metaphysics* I, chapter 6, 987b.10. *Mimesis* refers to the existence of what is imitated or represented, *methexis* to the coexistence with something. *IG*, 11.

However, Gadamer suggests that Aristotle is entirely correct to attribute to Plato the Pythagorean identification of the number concept with ideas—not in order to establish a separation thesis, but on the contrary so as to exhibit both the self-sameness of the one and its participation in the many. According to Gadamer, the first indication that Plato advances beyond the Pythagoreans is that the language he uses to capture the relationship between idea and appearance is flexible ("presence," "interweaving," "coupling," "participation," "imitation," "mixture").[27] The flexibility of language suggests that the relation Plato is describing is nonconceptual, i.e., irreducible to a set terminology. Nevertheless, Gadamer continues, "Both the *Parmenides* and Aristotle's critique single out *methexis* from these expressions."[28] Gadamer reports that *methexis* "is not the harmless terminological variation it sounds like in Aristotle. On the contrary, it actually reflects a decisive turn which Plato takes."[29]

The decisive turn Plato takes from the Pythagoreans is derived from the very problems they posed. Gadamer recounts that the Pythagoreans had attempted to square the circle, to locate the point at which a curved line became straight,[30] and had been trying to "transform a circle into a quadrangle of the same area by circumscribing polygons, each with a greater number of angles than the previous one."[31] These tasks were, of course, futile. Gadamer explains why: "Pythagorean mathematics was certainly genuine mathematics, and its theorems and proofs obviously did not refer to the figures produced to illustrate them. But plainly it had no appropriate understanding of how its true objects—circle, triangle, number—differ from sense perceptions."[32] The Pythagoreans could not understand that the "true object" or concept was different from what is perceived. It is for this reason that they identified numbers and their exemplars in the starry heavens with perfect forms/concepts. For Gadamer, Plato's revolution consists in forcing a thought distinction that eluded the Pythagoreans.

27. *IG*, 10.
28. Ibid., 10.
29. Ibid., 12.
30. Ibid., 17.
31. *DD*, 106.
32. *IG*, 17.

According to Gadamer's Plato, the Pythagoreans failed to distinguish *aisthesis* (perception) from *noesis* (intellection). This is why they tried to square the circle. The distinction is conveyed by Plato's doctrine of numbers—the one is different from, yet the same as, the two or many. The mathematical paradigm, Gadamer contends, surfaces throughout the dialogues. In the last of the earliest dialogues, *Hippias Major*, each of the ideas are said to be what they are to the extent that they participate in the one idea of beauty.[33] In the *Theaetetus* the unity and difference in discourse also parallels the *arithmos* paradigm: "Now the classic examples of the systems which organize letters and harmonic intervals show how it is precisely the arithmos model which makes possible the solution of the problem of participation of ideas in one another."[34] Just as the sum is and is not its parts, so too is a syllable identical to, yet different from, the sequence of individual letters of which it is composed. In the *Phaedo* Socrates explains to Cebes that he is bewildered by the thought that, through addition, the nature of the one has changed and is not the same (97a). In the *Republic* Book 7 (524bc) the question is raised as to whether the finger between a larger finger and a smaller one is one or two.[35]

---

33. The problem is that sight and hearing are different but are also beautiful and thus have something (beauty) in common to which neither is reducible. Socrates explains to Hippias, of pleasure through sight and hearing, "Then they have some thing that itself makes them be fine, that common thing that belongs to both of them in common and to each privately. Because I don't suppose there's any other way they would both and each be fine." *Hippias Major*, 300b.

34. *DD*, 137. See *Theaetetus*, 201–206, where the syllable is a single unity with a character all its own that arises from letters (203e). Gadamer writes of this passage: "Does not the unity of discourse also have a certain determinate property not found in any of its component parts (letters, syllables, words) and is this not exactly the point? At the conclusion of the *Theaetetus* the logos or account which purports to explain something by listing its component parts ... is reduced to an aporia ... Either the syllable consists of the collection of its letters or it is an indivisible unit with its own special property. Here, I suggest, the true relationship of the One and the Many, which gives the logos its structure, is made evident in the analogy of the meaninglessness of the syllable and the dilemma with which it confronts us." Zuckert, *Postmodern Platos*, 98.

35. *DD*, 136. The same finger is one and two when it is distinguished as being self-same, or self-identical (one) yet also the same as the middle, index, and small fingers (many) which are conceivably also one. There are different ways of unpacking the paradox. Socrates refers to the soul perplexed by something being both hard and soft, and explains how counting removes the confusion: "In such cases, it seems, a soul first summons calculation and intellection and tries to examine whether each of the things reported is one or two" (524b–c). Something is both hard and soft when the "something" is differentiated from the sense perception. Gadamer thus reasons that

Each of these illustrations from the *Hippias Major*, *Theaetetus*, *Phaedo*, and *Republic*, writes Gadamer, is based upon "the number which serves as a model . . . for it is in fact the mystery of the number that one and one together are two without either of the units, which are each one, being two, and without the two being one."[36] The point of the paradigm is not that "seeing the participation of particulars in an idea" constitutes knowledge, but rather how it is possible that the one can be many and the many one.[37] The paradox confounds perception. Were thinking restricted solely to what is perceived, then the puzzle is a contradiction; the one cannot be itself and many at the same time. This would seem to be the route taken by Aristotle and tacitly by Heidegger in their conceptual formulation of Plato's doctrine of ideas. In other words, Heidegger's interpretation of Plato is wrong because he does not distinguish thinking from what is perceived. And this in turn is why he believes that the Good is an idea like any other.

3. THE GOOD

Heidegger follows Aristotle and reasons that the Good is an idea like any other idea, that Plato conflates *idea* (seeing) with *eidos* (what is seen), and that the Good has no bearing upon ethics; on the contrary, the Good defines what is useful and thus justifies a technical relationship to beings.[38] Gadamer challenges Heidegger by (1) taking to task his Aristotelian terminological bias; and (2) challenging his understanding of Plato's demiurge.

---

the relativity of sense perception points to the one (*DD*, 136); that the philosopher sees "through current opinions to the idea . . . and is capable of . . . forming and maintaining a stable political reality" (*DD*, 83); that for the same reason the philosopher can discern harmony and disharmony in the soul (*DD*, 88); that the philosopher can be distinguished from the activist (*DD*, 90–91).

36. Ibid., 134.

37. Ibid., 136.

38. According to Heidegger, Plato intensifies the light under which one aspect of an appearance is visible and equates that *eidos* (how something looks) with human seeing (*eidein*) in the Good. The Good is the identification of seeing with what is seen (*eido*). For Heidegger, it therefore does not have a character different from other ideas (or objects of knowledge); on the contrary, and in keeping with its numerological status, the Good is ontologically indistinguishable from other ideas of consciousness, which is the basis for the production thesis.

Terminology

Heidegger's tendency to read Plato in terms of Aristotle is mirrored in the Aristotelian terminology he imports into his discussion. Stanley Rosen attends to this problem directly, Gadamer somewhat obliquely (the exception being his essay "The Greeks"). While analyzing the "production thesis" in *The Basic Problems of Phenomenology* (1927), Stanley Rosen in his chapter "Platonism is Aristotelianism" comments on the terms Heidegger lists under the medieval term *essentia*, including *morphe, eidos, to ti en einai, genos, physis, horos, chorismos,* and *ousia*: "We see here Heidegger's implicit assimilation of Platonic to Aristotelian terminology."[39] Plato's "idea," Rosen later explains, is tacitly assimilated by Heidegger to the Aristotelian essence, *to ti en einai* ("the thing in accordance with that which it already was and is").[40] If the idea is an essence that precedes the coming-to-be of phenomena, then the truth of the phenomenon consists of making it conform to that prior determination of what it is. This transpires whenever people speak not about beings themselves but of this or that property of beings[41]

In another instance of the same tendency, while Socrates claims that the idea of the Good is beyond beings (*Republic* 509b), Heidegger equates it with any other idea of human consciousness in "Plato's Doctrine of Truth" (1931).[42] This step is possible because Heidegger is interpreting Plato's understanding of Being according to Aristotle's science of beings *qua* beings, i.e., *episteme*, which Heidegger in 1924, on the basis of *Nicomachean Ethics* VI, had reasoned is related to *techne*. *Episteme* is one of four kinds of perception that Heidegger equates with "a specific disposition (*Befindlichkeit*),[43] in which case, the truth (unconcealment) of beings depends upon human beings; specifically, a human perception (idea) that Plato, he argues, equates with "the Good."[44] Put succinctly by Heidegger, referring to Aristotle, "As possibilities of discovering entities,

---

39. Rosen, *Question of Being*, 5.

40. Ibid., 7.

41. Discussed in far more detail by Rosen in "Heidegger's Plato," 179.

42. For Heidegger, "The beginning of metaphysics in Plato's thinking is at the same time the beginning of 'Humanism.'" *PDT*, 269.

43. *BH*, 226.

44. Gadamer summarizes well this thought of Heidegger's Aristotle as Heidegger reconfigures it: ". . . 'factical' (*das faktische*) human *Dasein* is the origin of all meaning and thus must be the point of departure of all philosophical reflection . . ." *PDE*, 21.

techne and *episteme* do not let an entity be seen as, but not completely as, the entity that it is."[45] Epistemology privileges human seeing (idea), and thus does not think about beings in themselves; it "belongs positively to [productive behavior] and to its structure, and it guides the action."[46] With the Aristotelian notion of *episteme*—ideas and their relation to human making/*techne*—Heidegger had reason to conclude that, for Plato, the Good is the demiurge, the elevation of a craftsperson to the rank of the divine.[47]

Gadamer's questioning of Heidegger's Aristotelian Plato in matters of terminology is not as extensive as Rosen's, but it is precise. He disputes Heidegger's claim that Plato conflates seeing (*eidein*) with what is seen (*eidos*) by pointing out that the two terms "idea" and *eidos* have distinct meanings and that "Plato uses only the word *idea*, and never *eidos* for the *agathon*."[48] "Idea" means "view of something," but for Gadamer, when interpreted within the phrase in which it occurs, *idea tou agathou* from *Republic* VII, "idea" signifies "looking to the good" (*apoblepein pros*).[49] If the Good is that toward which seeing is directed by looking past something else, then the Good cannot be the same as any other idea. Rosen concurs with Gadamer, yet also indicates that Heidegger is right to consider "idea" and *eidos* synonymous because language is not fit to represent what is beyond itself; consequently, at times Socrates simply says "the Good."[50] That the Good is beyond beings suggests that it transcends phenomenon. Yet for Gadamer this must be thought dialectically alongside *praxis* or the concrete act of being virtuous. He thus argues that the virtues in *Protagoras* (329) and *Republic* IV "imply essentially

---

45. BH, 227.

46. BPP, 109.

47. Heidegger writes, "What makes every idea useful to an idea is, Platonically expressed, the Idea of all ideas and, consists therefore in making it possible for everything present to make its appearance in all its visibility (*Sichtsamkeit*)." PDT, 263. Heidegger states in *Basic Problems of Phenomenology* (1927) the production thesis: "The idea [*tou*] *agathou* is nothing but the *demiurgos*, the producer pure and simple." Quoted in Dostal, "Beyond Being," 87. Elsewhere Heidegger writes, "Technology is in its essence a destiny within the history of Being and of the truth of Being, a truth that lies in oblivion. For technology does not go back to the *techne* of the Greeks in name only but derives historically and essentially from *techne* as a mode of *aletheuein*, a mode, that is, of rendering beings manifest." "Letter on Humanism," 220.

48. IG, 27.

49. Ibid., 27–28.

50. PR, 401 n1.

the same thing, knowledge of the one, which is the Good."[51] Far from being of purely epistemological significance, the Good is visible in the act of being virtuous (*phronesis*), which is why it is beyond beings;[52] and Plato is able to recognize in the Sophists' actions a deceptive semblance of the Good, in Socrates its instantiation.[53]

The Demiurge

Gadamer writes, "From the very beginning Heidegger took over and transformed the Aristotelian criticism of the Idea of the Good and stressed especially the Aristotelian concept of analogy. . . . Only after World War II, with his decisive incorporation of Plato into the history of Being, was the ambiguity in regard to Plato removed."[54] While Heidegger may have varied in his assessment of Plato at Marburg, after World War II his views on Plato were consolidated. At that time, according to Gadamer, Heidegger made use of older manuscripts to challenge modern science with Aristotle's notion of *physis*.[55] Gadamer comments of Heidegger's essay on Anaximander: "The treatise on Aristotle's *physis* attempted with radical determination to recreate this Aristotelian concept and to set it off against the modern attack on 'nature' by contemporary science."[56] According to Heidegger, the early Greek notion of truth as *aletheia* was experienced in terms of the emergence-withdrawal of nature. Since human beings are implicated in truth as unconcealment, they stand within, or in some way belong to, *physis* (or the clearing). With this idyllic relationship between humans and nature Heidegger counterposed modern

---

51. *DD*, 130–131.

52. Although technical knowledge demonstrates something crucial about the Good, namely that it consists of accurately hitting the mark, reasoning about virtue along the lines of the crafts is precisely what Socrates refutes in the early dialogues, which is why they end inconclusively. Moral knowledge is not technical knowledge, nor is the Good, according to Gadamer, a matter of divine dispensation. To the evidence in the *Gorgias*, *Meno*, and *Republic* (429e) that virtue is a divine dispensation, Gadamer asserts that this must be interpreted within the context of Socrates's disagreement with the sophists, who equated virtue with the rhetorical skill of pandering to the people (*IG*, 51). In other words, the atheistic impulse of the sophists, according to Gadamer, provoked Plato to defend a nonreligious notion of the Good. *IG*, 54; *Phaedo*, 76d.

53. Gadamer, "Plato," 92.

54. *GR*, 347.

55. Gadamer refers to the 1939–1940 essay "On the Essence and Concept of *Physis* in Aristotle's *Physics* B1" in "Greeks," 141.

56. Ibid.

science and mathematical physics, which he traced to Plato's numerological metaphysics in the "Question Concerning Technology" (lectures, 1949) and "Age of the World Picture" (1938).[57] Given this conceptual lineage, the Good consists of making the things of the world, including human beings (the self), conform to a preestablished mathematical order.

Gadamer replies by investigating the roots of Heidegger's attribution of a numerological metaphysics to Plato. He points out that Aristotle, when he says in *Metaphysics* I.6.987b that for Plato things are imitations, also suggests something Heidegger does not recognize; namely, that *mimesis* is another word for *methexis*. Copying, or a kind of making that produces a pale imitation of an original (as discussed, for instance, in the *Republic*) is therefore not the last word in what making means for Plato. On the contrary, Gadamer considers Plato's criticism of the poets to be an ironic distortion of the truth of the matter: that there is in fact a dialectical relationship with art that includes both distinction and identification.[58] The copy theory itself, therefore, points to the participation (*methexis*) mentioned by Aristotle in *Metaphysics* I.6.

The question then is how does imitation (copying) include participation of the universal in the particular? Gadamer's reply draws on two sources: the Pythagoreans and Aristotle's notion of recognition in the *Poetics*. The mathematical numbers with which Aristotle associates Plato's ideas suggest to Gadamer a universal order that the Pythagoreans thought was at work in music. This entails an intrinsic relationship between the ideal and sensible realms that eluded the awareness even of the Pythagoreans. Gadamer introduces within this context the idea of recognition, that is, seeing in the transient the permanent with which one is already acquainted.[59] This is discussed by Aristotle in *Poetics* 1448b6–17 in relation to art.[60] Through the experience of artistic reproduction, therefore, Gadamer suggests that we participate in what he calls

---

57. Heidegger suggests that technological enframing originates in Plato's doctrine of truth, whereby beings are made to conform to a prior idea, and that his numerological metaphysics is the origin of modern mathematical physics.

58. Gadamer, *Relevance of the Beautiful*, 121.

59. Ibid., 47, 120.

60. In these passages Aristotle is describing how learning includes an "instinct for imitation" in which we delight to contemplate copies of originals.

a universal spiritual energy.⁶¹ Plato lit upon this as well, he says, with the idea that musical order is the basis for the order of human life in the *polis* (*Republic* 424d). In other words, Plato combines the Pythagorean abstract understanding of universal mathematical order with Aristotle's notion of recognition in the idea that music forms the self. This topic is taken up again in chapter 9.

---

61. Ibid., 103.

6

Hermeneutical Situations

1. PLATO

Heidegger's juxtaposition of Plato with Aristotle depends upon rendering Plato's philosophy a doctrine. If so, then Aristotle's phenomenology, in opposition to which Heidegger defines Plato's idealism, must be similarly regarded as a doctrine. The two halves of a binary opposition require each other, otherwise an antithetical relationship between them would be incomprehensible. Heidegger interprets Aristotle, no less than Plato, independently of his context—that is, independently of the living dialogue that Gadamer believes defines their common ground. In a challenge to Heidegger's positivism, Gadamer thus taps into the literary and historical contexts of Plato's and Aristotle's philosophy.[1] He writes of Plato:

> The methodological problem is clear. We must establish the philosophical significance of the scene, the setting of the dialogues, of the relationship of the speaker to what is spoken, of evolving meaning as it unfolds in live discussion. And we must apply what we can learn thereby to understand the philosophical questions which Plato puts to us.[2]

Since Schleiermacher and Schlegel had been taking into account the literary character and context of the dialogues during the previous century,[3] it is somewhat surprising that Gadamer should be invoking the

---

1. A shift to Socrates in order to clarify why Plato banished the poets in the *Republic* X is warranted by the *Seventh Letter*, and the overall trend in the late 1920s to foreground the political Plato. Sullivan, *Political Hermeneutics*, 5.

2. *DD*, 159.

3. For a discussion of their contribution see Kramer, *Plato*, 16–27.

same method in an indirect challenge to Heidegger. Since none other than Heidegger put forward "throwness," or the notion that we have no choice but to think out of a context we did not choose—what Gadamer called "effective history," the idea that we are in the grip of historical modes of reasoning about which we can never be fully aware—it is surprising that it was left to Gadamer to take historical conditions into account when interpreting Plato. The historical and literary reconstruction recommended by Heidegger's hermeneutical insights, but not practiced with respect to Plato, are performed by Gadamer during his interpretation of the dialogues—for example, the *Lysis*, *Phaedo*, and *Republic*.[4]

In "Plato and the Poets" (1934) Gadamer indirectly criticizes Heidegger's decontextualized conceptual analysis when he writes:

> It is also of no help in understanding the matter if one presupposes Plato as the metaphysician of the doctrine of ideas and then demonstrates that his critique of the poets follows logically from his basic ontological assumptions. On the contrary, Plato's attitude toward the poets is not a consequence of a system of thought which prevented him from more fairly evaluating poetic truth.[5]

In *Republic* X (595a–608b) Plato argues that since poets do not have knowledge of that which they make, yet pretend they do, they confuse people about the difference between reality and appearance and therefore merit banishment. In contrast to this ontological criticism of the poets, Gadamer indicates that the *Seventh Letter* is the clue to understanding Plato's cruelty. In the epistle Plato relates that when he met Socrates, he burned his tragedies. This was not evidence of Plato having discovered his true calling in philosophy (since Plato is a poet); rather, for Gadamer, it is symbolic of his opposition to Greek culture as a whole and, more specifically, to the domination of education by non-

---

4. In the *Lysis* it matters that Socrates is discussing friendship with two inexperienced boys and not adults; it matters that one of the boys is older and pursuing the younger. Similarly, contrary to a mathematical view of Plato that might reduce his teachings to a system or subject the dialogues to the rigors of purely logical analyses, Gadamer asserts that Plato is well aware in the *Phaedo* that the proofs for the immortality of the soul are not foolproof. Instead, they are tailored to turn the lapsed Pythagoreans, Simmias and Cebes, from an "enlightened mathematical" orientation toward religion. Since the emphasis is upon "a pedagogical turning of the students," the dialogue shifts attention from Simmias and Cebes to "the reactions of those recounting it." These kinds of insights are ignored by Aristotle, and are left unmentioned by Heidegger.

5. *DD*, 47.

philosopher-poets whose notion of education by imitation alienates the self from self-understanding. On account of this division within the self, those formed by poets were unable to resist the sophists' teachings and arguments against the conventional wisdom that the just life was best. As a result, Plato sought to replace poets with philosophers as educators, because a virtuous life cultivated through self-understanding could not be as easily swayed as a life shaped by imitating models external to the self. For Gadamer, Plato's banishment of the poets in the *Republic* has less to do with a theory of ontology than with the political conditions in fifth-century Athens.

2. ARISTOTLE

Gadamer observes, with incredulity, that Aristotle tends to interpret Plato literally and misrepresents him. Gadamer cannot believe that, after twenty years of associating with Plato, Aristotle could have misunderstood him. He explains Aristotle's misinterpretation of Plato as follows: "he must play down the 'transcendence of the good,' which, if he did not, would set it apart from all ideas. He must put the idea of the good in the same class as other ideas. Consequently, he must be particularly emphatic in insisting that like other ideas the idea of the good exists for itself separately (*choriston*)."[6]

In this passage Aristotle is said to have downplayed the transcendence of the Good while at the same time believing that, like any other idea, the Good exists separately. For Aristotle, things which are by nature (*physei onta*) are self-consisting; therefore, when he hears Plato assert that it is ideas that so exist, he reasons that the only grounds for the claim is spatial distance. As a result of applying a spatial category to what is for Plato nonspatial (beyond beings), Aristotle interprets Plato to mean that the ideas are physically separate from things. According to Gadamer, Aristotle is aware that this is not Plato's position, but nevertheless insists upon it for purposes of making his own position clearer. This is a tendency on the part of Aristotle, which Gadamer also points out in Aristotle's understanding of the *Timaeus*: "If Aristotle nevertheless takes the whole thing literally and then criticizes it, he does so because he is fighting, in reference to this and in many other playful passages in other dialogues, to carry through his own agenda, which is to defend

6. *IG*, 132–133.

the preeminence of nature and the merely secondary character of mathematics. I think that overall one has to picture the *Timaeus* as a game of Plato [*ein Spiel Platos*]."[7] In short, Gadamer argues that since Plato was responding to a political crisis, he emphasized the permanent ground of Being in its difference from sensible things, whereas Aristotle, since he was reacting to the separation thesis and its representation in mathematics, emphasized participation and the exemplification of the Being of the ideas in nature. Plato and Aristotle therefore differ not in kind, as Heidegger contends, but in degree, emphasis, and orientation.[8]

CONCLUSION TO PART TWO

Heidegger aimed to overcome the history of metaphysics with Aristotle, whom he believed provided a more radical treatment of the ontological problems raised by the pre-Socratics and Plato.[9] But this in turn was dependent upon an Aristotelian view of Plato represented in the nomenclature of Platonism. Dostal writes, "Heidegger's project of 1922 was to recover Aristotle phenomenologically and thereby breathe new life into an arid intellectual climate. Part and parcel of this project was a 'recapitulation' of Aristotle's critique of Plato."[10] However, by recapitulating Aristotle's criticism and developing a genealogy from Plato to humanism, Heidegger inadvertently exacerbates the intellectual climate he intended to challenge. Just as the neo-Kantians dismissed Aristotle "the naïve realist" on behalf of Plato "the idealist," Heidegger dismisses Plato the metaphysician-modernist on behalf of Aristotle the first-order phenomenologist-pre-Socratic.[11]

Gadamer may well have been thinking of Heidegger when he writes in 1974, the year during which Heidegger had thanked him for correcting his view of Plato:

---

7. *GR*, 400–401.

8. P. Christopher Smith explains that Aristotle knew that, for Plato, thinking of the ideas as wholly separate was a mistake and continues, "Hence we can only assume that he consciously slants Plato's thought in order to better articulate his own 'physicalist' position; in fact, he marshals Plato's very own arguments—again consciously—to attack the *choriston* idea (for example, the 'third man'). *IG*, 134 n6.

9. Dostal, "Gadamer's Continuous Challenge," 292.

10. Ibid., 290.

11. Gadamer, "Reply to Dostal," 308.

> With a persistence bordering on the absurd, the prevailing form of interpretation in which Plato's philosophy has been passed on to us has advocated the two-world theory, that is, the complete separation of the paradigmatic world of ideas from the ebb and flow of change in our experience of the sense-perceived world. Idea and reality are made to look like two worlds separated by a chasm, and the interrelationship of the two remains obscure.[12]

It is this interrelationship between "Idea" and "reality" that Gadamer develops in Plato's philosophy. The alternative advanced by Heidegger has a persistence, Gadamer suggests, that borders on the absurd. Of the tendency to contract Plato's teachings into a "doctrine" Gadamer writes:

> And even now there still exists the overwhelming countertendency to interpret the dialogical compositions critically as statements of a doctrine. One could learn from the precedent which Aristotle sets in this regard, but as I have noted above, Aristotle also seems to present a problem since in our approach to him we continue to be governed by our modern preconceptions of what scientific criticism ought to be.[13]

Aristotle represents Plato's philosophy as a doctrine so as to exaggerate the difference between his own approach and that of his teacher. But why Heidegger? Why would he give Aristotle's interpretation of Plato precedence, considering that in doing so he violates his own principles of a hermeneutical phenomenology? By unreflectively taking his orientation from Jaeger's privileging of Aristotle and Natorp's Kantian-Plato, and conrasting Plato the idealist with Aristotle the phenomenologist, Heidegger instantiates Gadamer's feeling, quoted above, that "in our approach to him [Aristotle] we continue to be governed by our modern preconceptions of what scientific criticism ought to be." Heidegger's tendency to interpret Plato's words independently of their dramatic context is but another indication of how his consciousness was historically affected. There can be neither an end to history nor a "new beginning" if the very prophet of the new era represents the tradition he renounces.

While much of this reconstruction of Gadamer's refutation of Heidegger is synthetic, in particular the crossing of paths with Jaeger, something of that refutation must have been effective. According to

---

12. *DD*, 156.
13. *DD*, 159.

Catalin Partenie, shortly after World War II Heidegger "confessed to one of his former students that the structure of Platonic thought 'is totally obscure to me,'" and wrote in a letter to Hannah Arendt in 1954, "I would like to begin my Platonic studies with the *Sophist* [lectures] (of 1924–25), to go through it again and to read Plato anew."[14] This is not the only evidence of Heidegger having changed his view that Plato is the father of the forgetfulness of Being.[15] Whether or not he was prepared to take the next step, to abandon his view that Plato's dialectic is indistinguishable from Hegel's and agree with Gadamer that it ought to be interpreted from the perspective of a living dialogue, is uncertain.[16] Nevertheless, a renunciation of the "metaphysical Plato" suffices to challenge Heidegger's claim to have created a new philosophical vocabulary, to have returned to the origins because they are transparent at the end of their development, and to have been done with metaphysics altogether.

---

14. Partenie and Rockmore, *Heidegger and Plato*, xiv. The student in question is Georg Pitch.

15. In "Reflections" Gadamer reports that the essays on Plato in Volumes 6 and 7 of his collected works "meant something to Heidegger in the last years of his life." Gadamer explains that he had argued against Heidegger's view that Plato prepares the way for ontotheology, and continues: "Even the metaphysics of Aristotle contains other dimensions than those Heidegger unlocked in his work. In this, I believe I was able to refer Heidegger to certain limits in his own interpretations. I am thinking especially of Heidegger's early fondness for referring to 'the famous analogy'—'die berühmte Analogie.'" Gadamer, "Reflections," 48–49. Dostal confirms, "Gadamer proudly, yet modestly, claims that his work on Plato had succeeded in persuading Heidegger late in his life, that Heidegger's account of Plato had fallen short." Dostal, "Gadamer's Relation to Heidegger," 251. Also, "Gadamer proudly suggested that his work on Plato was instrumental in persuading Heidegger at the end of his life of the inappropriateness of his reading and use of Plato." Dostal, "Gadamer," 30. Fried reports that in 1969 Heidegger retracted that Plato transforms the early Greek notion of truth. Fried, "Back to the Cave," 173 n3.

16. See Gonzalez, "Dialectic."

Part III
Gadamer's Plato

Introduction

GADAMER EXPLAINS THAT HEIDEGGER's interpretation of Aristotle was in the service of "an existential, situation-oriented, philosophic critique of the idealist tradition." By stepping back into the pretheoretical origins of idealism, Heidegger aimed to recover an existential-phenomenological sense of the meaning of Being. However, Gadamer asks, "does that suffice?"[1] By using Aristotle to critique German idealism, in which Plato was implicated, Heidegger overlooked what Plato and Aristotle have in common and hence the very thing that makes a criticism of either one by the other possible. Gadamer is referring to the inquiry into the Being of what is on the basis of how we speak about it.[2] This is the "second sailing" taken by Socrates in the *Phaedo* and reiterated by Aristotle in the *Physics* and *Nicomachean Ethics*, where he states that the starting point for philosophical investigation is what is better known to us.[3] By disregarding this common ground between Plato and Aristotle in the *logoi*, and insisting instead upon a nondialectical concept of Being in Plato's philosophy, i.e., a permanent idea, Heidegger reverts to a period of Plato's philosophical development that precedes the "turn

---

1. *DD*, 198.
2. See *PDE*, 70.
3. "This of course does not mean that the indirect tradition is of no concern to us. But in the sense which I have just explained, it is to be understood only on the basis of what is known to us." *DD*, 128. Aristotle writes, "We must start from what is known. But things are known in two senses: known to us and known absolutely. Presumably we must start from what is known to us." *Nicomachean Ethics* I:1, 1095b. Also, "The natural course is to proceed from what is clearer and more knowable to us, to what is more knowable and clear by nature, but clearer to us, and move on to things which are by nature clearer and more knowable." *Physics* I:1, 184.18.

to the *logoi*." As a result of this oversight, it is not Plato but Heidegger who forgets the meaning of Being.

In order to recover the meaning of Being that Heidegger forgets, Gadamer reverses Heidegger's version of Plato as Platonism by borrowing from Heidegger's insights of the early to mid 1920s. Gadamer agrees with Heidegger that what Plato really meant he did not fully state, but at the same time, does not unequivocally believe that Aristotle clarifies what Plato said either. Gadamer explains:

> The conclusion that Aristotle misunderstood Plato is rightly felt to be impossible. But it is equally certain that in this critique what is truly Platonic does not make itself felt in the positive character that it still has even today, for us. Aristotle projected Plato onto the plane of conceptual explication. The Plato who presents himself in this explication is the object of Aristotle's critique. What makes this critique problematic is that this projection cannot also catch the inner tension and energy of Plato's philosophizing as they speak to us, with such incomparable convincingness, in his dialogues.[4]

Aristotle's apodictic tests for validity, his observations, and his treatises clarify what Plato tacitly understood, but in so doing they obscure the "inner tension and energy" of the dialogue form. This follows from the nature of reflective thought. It is based upon the consensus reached through a lively exchange of views, and hence, by abstracting from the prescientific situation, tends to be impersonal and desensitized to motivations and contexts.

By identifying the limits of Aristotle's reflective science, however, Gadamer also opens up possibilities for reconnecting the latter to its origins in Plato's existential, situation-oriented philosophy. In contrast to Heidegger, who reads Plato in terms of Aristotle in order to achieve a critique of the idealist tradition, Gadamer steps back into Plato's prescientific Socratic philosophy in order to redeem Plato from Heidegger's assessment, and in so doing uncovers the origins of Aristotle's reflective-scientific thought. Gadamer thus reverses Heidegger's method in that he uses Plato to clarify what Aristotle meant. More specifically, according to Gadamer, Aristotle's notions of truth as unconcealment and non-Being as *steresis* are prefigured in the structure of Plato's dialogues, and Aristotle's ethic of *phronesis* in Plato's Socrates. Since Plato is philosophi-

---

4. PDE, 7. Zuckert alerted me to this passage in "Hermeneutics in Practice," 202.

cally, and historically prior to Aristotle in matters of truth, physics, and ethics, he is, in contrast to Heidegger's claim, more of an early Greek thinker than his scientific counterpart.

OUTLINE

The first two chapters of Part III investigate how, from Gadamer's perspective, Aristotle's understanding of truth and physics evolves from out of Plato's dialectic, exhibited at times in the dialogue form. Chapter 7, "Truth as Unconcealment," argues that Gadamer discerns in Plato's dialogues an early Greek notion of truth, which Aristotle later clarified. Chapter 8, "Physics," explains how Aristotle's insights into movement in nature developed from his understanding of the structure of Plato's dialogues. Since Gadamer's positive view of Plato and Aristotle is a reversal of the contrastive juxtaposition that Heidegger sets up between them, a reconstruction of Gadamer's Plato plays into Gadamer's correction of Heidegger as discussed in Part II, but from a different point of view: whereas Part II emphasized the ways in which Heidegger's Plato provoked a critical reply from Gadamer, Part III emphasizes how Heidegger also inspired Gadamer. Chapters 7 and 8 are prefaced by aspects of Heidegger's reading of Plato and Aristotle that parallel Gadamer's positive philosophy about them.

Chapter 9, "The Good," is about Gadamer's understanding of Plato's ethics. Essentially, Gadamer interprets Plato dialectically in that the Good is read back into Plato's discussion of virtue. This is Gadamer's way of rendering the participation of the one in the many intelligible to practice. Relating the Idea to virtue would seem not to have anything to do with Aristotle, whose *phronemos* does not require knowledge of the ideas, as pointed out by Rosen. But in the endeavor to weave them together, Gadamer modifies both Plato and Aristotle. Be that as it may, Chapter 9 is primarily about a tension, in Gadamer's thought on Plato's ethics, between Hegelian and Heideggerian impulses—that is, between a dialectical ethic and the ethics of authentic individuality.

7

Truth as Unconcealment

According to Heidegger, Plato does not have a genuine understanding of non-Being. Rather than think of a thing as something it is not, Plato merely, as Gadamer says, identifies non-Being with speaking of one thing as another; for example, the statement from the *Sophist*, "Theaetetus flies," is false because the concept of man implied in the name "Theaetetus" excludes the idea of flying. Alternatively, in the *Sophist* Plato argues that "what is not" refers to everything other than what is asserted. But in either case, whether by definition or exclusion, Plato's sense of non-Being is merely negation, because the matter in question is not being considered; what is under consideration is merely a series of propositions. The background to Plato's reasoning solely in terms of propositions is Heidegger's belief that the idea against which Plato gauges the meaning of beings is formed by intensifying a look at beings typical of daily living. According to Heidegger, Plato does not transcend everyday speech in which beings are disclosed; he elevates the "everyday" to the status of a science in which the non-Being of beings themselves cannot be thought (as in Parmenides). Heidegger suggests that Plato's concept of truth is summarized in *Metaphysics* X and that Aristotle overturns it by stepping back into its pretheoretical conditions in the early Greek experience of *aletheia* (unconcealment).[1]

    1. According to Heidegger, the tradition of philosophy arrives at three conclusions about truth: (1) truth belongs to judgment; (2) truth is a correspondence of thinking with reality; and (3) the correspondence theory of truth most agrees with common sense (*BH*, 220; also *BT*, 198 sections 1–3). While the tradition attributes these three conclusions about truth to Aristotle, Heidegger contends that nowhere does Aristotle discuss truth in passages about judgment. This then begs the question of why the three characteristics of truth are ascribed to Aristotle. Heidegger does not answer this question directly. In fact, he aims to undermine the tradition by finding in Aristotle a non-correspondence theory of truth; nevertheless, given Heidegger's argument that Plato's understanding of time (eternity), represented in the theory of ideas, is the reifi-

Gadamer agrees with Heidegger that Plato's thinking obscures the meaning of Being.[2] In contrast to Heidegger, however, he is attentive to Plato's hermeneutical situation and explains that, in response to the sophist's eristic arguments, Plato was justifiably focused upon unchanging ideas. Nevertheless, he also believes that Plato had a latent understanding of what Aristotle illuminated, which is also what Heidegger had intimated before he had become estranged from Plato in the late 1920s. After pointing out, in the 1927 summer session at Marburg, Plato's understanding that "the apparent and false is not nothing, not an *ouk on*, but a *me on*, a being, yes, but affected with a defect," Heidegger declares it trivial but also puzzling that in the *Sophist* the *logos* is *logos tinos* (or about something).[3] Heidegger is indicating that, for Plato, *pseudos* is not nothing, i.e., the sensible realm of non-Being in contrast to the intelligible realm of Being; rather, *pseudos* is a defect—a conclusion which, he suggests, has something to do with the fact that *logos* is about something.

Gadamer clarifies this relation, hinted at by Heidegger, between falsehood as lack and speech about something. He explains that Aristotle made a distinction between "this thing here" (*tode ti*) and what it is (*ti estin* or *eidos*) that brought into view the notion of falsehood as a lack. Whenever something is asserted about what "this thing here" is not, possible ideas of what it could be are also indicated. As a result, the idea of a thing is a possibility it lacks that invites the ongoing quest to understand it. This is essentially a notion of truth as unconcealment that belongs to the spoken word, to the dialogical character of the early Greek preliterate culture. It is, however, Plato who taps into the latter in his dialogues. Gadamer writes, "It is conceivable that one could find in Platonic philosophy one possible way to get behind the question as formulated in Aristotelian and the post-Aristotelian metaphysics, so that the dimen-

---

cation of the "now" in vulgar time, it is probable that when Heidegger cites Aristotle referring to common sense supporting both truth as correspondence (#2 above) and truth belonging to judgments (#1 above), he has Plato in mind. The scholastics may therefore have supposed that by referring to "common sense" Aristotle was expressing approval for truth as correspondence/judgment; according to Heidegger, however, by "common sense" Aristotle means "the vulgar." Contrary to the tradition's version of truth, Heidegger believes Aristotle is not justifying but rather overthrowing truth-as-correspondence inaugurated by Plato.

2. *DD*, 213.
3. *BPP*, 208.

sion of self-manifesting Being, the Being of *aletheia* that articulates itself in the *logos*, could be recognized in the dialectic of Ideas."[4] According to Gadamer, there is in Plato's philosophy a prior self-manifestation of Being as *aletheia* that is formalized by Aristotle. This "one possible way" toward the self-manifesting Being of *aletheia* is the dialogue form.

Heidegger also seems to have indicated that Plato is close to understanding the early Greek notion of truth. His reference to "*logos tinos*" in his 1927 lecture on Plato's *Sophist* is an Aristotelianism that opens up what Gadamer explains (above) in reference to Aristotle; namely, that falsehood is a defect (lack) and therefore of positive significance to what something is. Heidegger thus explains, with reference to the *Sophist* and Hermann Lotze, that the copula "is" in the statement "S is not P" is a positive judgment.[5] For Heidegger's Plato, Being includes non-Being in the sense of *steresis*. But if so, as Gadamer points out, then the alleged early Greek notion of truth as unconcealment is implicit to the dialogue form and, although articulated by Aristotle (and Heidegger), is presupposed by Plato.

Gadamer explains that Plato presupposed the distinction made by Aristotle. He writes, "Plato too in no way disputes that all speaking is ultimately speaking about something which is . . . but insofar as he analyzes the *logos* as *koinonia* of ideas, does not reflect upon this fact."[6] Insofar as Plato thought laterally about the formal relations between ideas, unity was a "sum of essences" or combination of ideas, and genuine deception or falsity was impossible because, as Heidegger-Aristotle points out, Plato was overlooking the real measure of truth in things themselves. Nevertheless, as Gadamer says above, Plato does not dispute that "all speech is ultimately speaking about something which is," i.e., Aristotle's *logos tinos*. Aristotle, therefore, formulates what Plato took for granted in any conversation.[7] If so, then there ought to be at least traces of the distinction between "this thing here" and its form in Plato's philosophy.

There are three ways taken by Plato to refer to a notion of non-Being as *steresis* in which the distinction between a "this thing here" and its form are implicated. First, he points out that the problem of the one and the many, to which he refers in the dialogues, includes what is not.

4. Quoted in Wachterhauser, *Beyond Being*, 178.
5. *BPP*, 199.
6. *DD*, 199.
7. Ibid. See also *IG*, 200.

The one is and is not many. Second, the quest for knowledge exhibited in the life of Socrates attests to the indefiniteness of knowledge—which is also captured by the *arithmos* paradigm, since the unit "one" is part of, and generates, a series of numbers. Third, both of these structural parallels between number and *logos* imply for Gadamer the incompleteness of all human knowing. This incompleteness, he says, Plato presupposed in crafting the dialogues, and therefore outlined in a lecture propaedeutic to instruction in his philosophy and summarized in the Excursus to his *Seventh Letter*.

In that Excursus, explains Gadamer, Plato develops distinctions between four symbolic means of knowing: words or names, illustrations or figures, explanations or conceptual determinations, and knowledge or insight.[8] For each of these means Plato demonstrates how they "not only convey the truth but also obscure it." Consequently: (1) there is no guarantee that the word corresponds to what it designates, because words are interchangeable and have no essential connection with what they designate; (2) the conceptual determination includes the contingency with respect to the genus one chooses to divide and what species it is divided into; (3) the illustration of a circle is not the same as the circle in the sand; and (4) humans are finite, hence an absolute or complete knowledge of what "is" is impossible.[9] In short, all the means of knowledge "assert themselves instead of the thing that they were intended to bring to light."[10]

In contrast to Heidegger, who circa 1929 argued that by identifying Being with a permanent idea Plato overlooked movement as movement, Gadamer argues that the latter is inchoate to the dialogue form and grounded, ultimately, in an oral teaching presented by Plato and observed by Gadamer many times in his lectures: namely, that absolute knowledge, or a complete system of ideas, is impossible because human beings are as finite as their means of knowing. The implications for Heidegger are twofold. First, on the basis of elucidating how Plato implicitly included non-Being (*steresis*) within his discussion of the means of knowing—namely, example, word, definition, and insight—Gadamer closes the gap between the indirect and direct traditions of

---

8. *DD*, 100–110.

9. These conclusions are paraphrased from Smith, "Gadamer's Heideggerian Interpretation of Plato," 216.

10. *IG*, 17 n17.

Aristotle and Plato, respectively. In so doing, he demonstrates that Plato is not the first metaphysician, as Heidegger contends, who obscures the early Greek notion of Being as appearing-withdrawal in an endeavor to ground truth in propositions, but instead that Plato reaffirms the early Greek notion of truth.[11] Smith reaches this conclusion using Gadamer's analysis of the Excursus to Plato's *Seventh Letter*. Smith writes:

> Clearly, this "dialogical" Plato is far removed from the Plato Heidegger portrays as a "metaphysical" thinker. On the contrary, he is one in whom the original sense of truth as disconcealment, presencing against a background of hiddenness, remains very much alive. There is no move here beyond the "cave" of language, rather a persistent being under way within it.[12]

> Hence far from being the first "metaphysical" thinker, Plato, in understanding the original nature of language, the experience of its spokenness, is the philosopher who has found perhaps the best means to preserve the earlier pre-"metaphysical" experience of truth – the play of equifundamental *aletheia* and *lethe*, answer and question, *euporia* and *aporia*, insight and confusion.[13]

For Gadamer's Plato the means of knowing never grasp that to which they refer. As Smith points out, a*letheia* includes *lethe*, *euporia* is *aporia*.

Second, it is but a short step from Gadamer's position regarding the relevance, in Plato, of human finitude to knowing, on the one hand, and to Heidegger's contention, on the other, that for Aristotle in *Nicomachean Ethics* VI what something is depends upon the "how" of human beings. The latter is a clarification of the early Greek experience of truth as concealment. Hence, by thinking of the truth of beings in terms of human beings and their finite ways of knowing, Gadamer's Plato no less than Heidegger's Aristotle touches upon the reasons why

---

11. Dostal writes of Gadamer, "In his reading of the pre-Socratics time and again, he shows how Plato and Aristotle take up pre-Socratic concepts in a positive way. Thus he shows a certain continuity between the pre-Socratics and the Socratics, unlike Heidegger who sees an epochal break between them." Dostal, "Gadamer," 260. See also Gadamer in "Plato," 87.

12. Smith, "Gadamer's Heideggerian Interpretation of Plato," 217.

13 Ibid., 219. Dostal summarizes Smith's argument and argues against him that while Gadamer does deliver a Heideggerian reading of Plato he is closer to both Plato and Aristotle than Heidegger. Dostal, "Gadamer's Continuous Challenge," 296–297.

beings appear to us as either for themselves, or something else. But even this achievement by Gadamer in the 1960s harks back to Heidegger, who in 1927 said that Plato understood the primary characteristic of an assertion to be *apophansis* ("letting something be seen from its own self").[14] For Heidegger, whether or not a being can be seen from its own self depends upon human beings' manner of existence, which Gadamer associates with the dialogue form and the drama of Plato's dialogues. That is to say, according to Gadamer, Plato understood that non-Being pertains to the existence of human beings; otherwise, it would have been impossible for him to have recognized the contrast between the Sophists and Socrates.[15]

---

14. *BPP*, 209.
15. Gadamer, "Plato," 92.

8

Physics

IN HIS LECTURES ON the *Sophist*, Heidegger says that Plato "is the *Umschlag* (sudden change or turn) between Parmenides and Aristotle." If Being is for Parmenides identical with contemplation, and for Aristotle in some sense identical with motion, then the *dynamis* to which Plato refers in the *Sophist* would seem to occupy a middle position between the Eleatic and the Peripatetic; Plato is a transitional figure in the development of the Greek notion of motion. However, Heidegger breaks from this genealogy and attributes *dynamis/Bewegung* in Plato's *Sophist* to Aristotle. He writes, in his 1922 essay "Phenomenological Interpretations with Respect to Aristotle," "The central phenomenon, whose explication is the theme of the *Physics*, becomes the being (or entity, *das Seiende*) in the mode of its being-moved (*Bewegseins*)."[1] According to Heidegger, *dynamis* in the *Sophist* is viewed negatively by Plato and positively by Aristotle. Gadamer reiterates this, pointing out that it was Heidegger who separated the question of rest from motion and attributed the former to Plato, the latter to Aristotle.[2] In contrast even to Hegel who had, according to Heidegger, a technical understanding of change, Aristotle very likely understood movement as movement because for Aristotle there is no time independent of motion.[3]

Gadamer agrees with Heidegger that Aristotle "wants to defend an older understanding of being against the Platonists,"[4] i.e., the disclosure of Being in the existent thing. But whether or not these Platonists include Plato or only his successors at the Academy is not clear. On the one hand, Aristotle complains that Plato cannot explain change because he

---

1. Dostal, "Gadamer's Continuous Challenge," 292–293.
2. Gadamer, "Plato," 83–84.
3. *BH*, 225.
4. *DD*, 200 n5.

has no notion of either formal or final causation. The idea (formal cause) of man does not explain how man comes to be unless the form participates in the material cause. On the other hand, however, Gadamer finds reason to contest this argument in Aristotle's *Physics* I. He paraphrases:

> There the observation is made that what Plato refers to as Not-Being actually can be said to have two meanings. Not-being is not simply and unequivocally the not-being of *heterotes* in the *eidos*, i.e., that which in any eidetic determination excludes all other determinations. There is a not-being in the *eidos* which has to do not with its relationship to other *eide* but with existence itself or, in Aristotle's forceful way of putting it, with being deprived of something, *steresis*.[5]

Gadamer is suggesting, as mentioned in the previous chapter, that Aristotle is shedding light on what Plato really meant. The *eidos* includes what is not "this thing here," to which it never adequately corresponds because the thing exceeds any eidetic determination, which is why there is always more to say about what something is; the idea of justice, for instance, includes everything that is not known about justice. This renders the initial idea privative, or not-yet being. However, as Gadamer says, this not-being in the *eidos* is related not to other *eide*, but to existence itself.

But why should Aristotle step out of the *logos* to the existent thing in order to grasp being deprived of something? Gadamer explains that Plato's mathematical model for Being cannot express the "being-not-yet" which becomes something. Viewed mathematically, the seed that grows into a tree assumes an eidetic determination that is different from what it was before. In order therefore to capture the dialectical notion of Being that he had discerned in the dialogue form, Aristotle adopted the language of physics where there is a transition from the ripe to the mature, where the *eidos* is always in matter and never separate by itself (as in mathematics).[6] In other words, the distinction Aristotle made in language convinced him that mathematics was not the best way to express the meaning of Being. This in turn is why he was critical of Plato's numerological metaphysics: it emphasized *choriston* (pure intelligible forms) of logical universality. While the one and the many captures the difference between Being and beings, it falls short of grasping the *steresis*

---

5. Ibid., 210.
6. Ibid.

or privation of *eidos* mirrored in the movement of dialogue, whereas the image of an acorn growing into an oak tree does not.

By way of contrasting Heidegger and Gadamer, then: Heidegger juxtaposes Plato's permanent and unchanging ideas with Aristotle's physics, and writes in *Being and Time* that dialectic is a "genuine philosophic embarrassment" superseded by Aristotle, who understood that beings show themselves in advance of speaking about them;[7] Gadamer, on the other hand, explains how Aristotle's position—that physics is a better way to grasp the structure of Being—evolves out of the early Greek notion of truth represented by Plato's dialogue form.

---

7. *BT*, 22–23.

9

The Good

HERMENEUTICS IS AN ACTIVITY of interpretation that cultivates *phronesis*, or the art of hitting the mark between two extremes that are contrary to one another. It follows from Heidegger's contrastive juxtaposition of Plato with Aristotle that a Gadamerian reply will aim to bridge the divide. Gadamer makes this bridge an interpretive principle for the *Republic*, and demonstrates it when he argues in *Plato's Dialectical Ethics* that the theoretical idea of the Good (wisdom) is manifest in practical life and that the virtues in the *Protagoras* and *Republic* IV are convertible into one another.[1] Gadamer's reading of Plato is not so much "Aristotelian" as it is informed by a prior decision about what dialectic means. Whether or not Gadamer's position on this score is also Plato's is discussed in Part IV, "Rosen's Rejoinder." At this point in an investigation of Gadamer's view of Plato's ethics, it is pertinent to observe that Gadamer's attribution of dialectical ethics to Plato, itself a residue of Hegel's influence, is in tension with his Heideggerian impulse. The result is a twofold understanding of what is true and good.

On the one hand, according to Gadamer, the ethics of dialogue is in the dialectical process.[2] By inquiring into the being of an existent thing with others a community of shared understanding is formed. When Socrates therefore turned, as he says in the *Phaedo* (99d), to investigating the intelligible order through the way in which people speak about things, by comparing points of view and modifying his own position and that of others, he was also founding a community dedicated to inquiry into the truth of things. The quest for the being of what "is" assumes a prereflective awareness of the Good that comes into focus incrementally

---

1. *IG*, 93.

2. The rules or components of dialogue are examined by Ambrosio in "Gadamer, Plato," 17–32.

during the activity of speaking together. Even those places where Plato might be interpreted to be advancing a personal and interior climb toward a transcendent Good are held by Gadamer to be social. Against such an "Augustinian" reading of Plato, he argues that the act of recollection that connects the *logos* of ideas to experiences in the *Phaedo* and *Meno* transpires in the company of others. There is no personal memory in Gadamer's Plato, only collective memory, because truth is a function of intersubjective agreement. Gadamer suggests this in the first sentence of his 1928 book: "The process of reaching a shared understanding of the matter in question through conversation (*Sachliche Verständigung im Gespräch*) is aimed at knowledge."[3]

Scholars have sided with Gadamer on the intersubjective nature of truth. Zuckert claims that, for Gadamer, dialogue aims to bring about agreement between people (the truth of things "is revealed in shared understanding of the whole").[4] Sullivan states that, for Gadamer, dialectic means "a mode of thinking that seeks and finds whatever anchorage it has in the agreement of others in conversation."[5] Francis Ambrosio repeats the same judgment: "What Plato learned from Socrates, and what Gadamer learned from Plato, is that truth occurs most originally and fatefully in human existence in conversation between persons . . . "[6] Truth is an event that arises through a mode of proceeding in conversation with others; and this mode of proceeding, Zuckert observes, is more important than the result.[7] Sullivan, summarizing the political implications, says: "Nearly everything Gadamer wrote in his early period may be construed as an argument against founded rationality; above all against the concept of a rationality based on a nature that shines over and against mind as 'reality.'"[8]

By emphasizing the dialogue form in relation to the concrete ethic embodied in the life of Socrates, Gadamer effectively undermined Heidegger's separation of Plato's ethics from his theory. The very activity of thinking together with others is ethical. However, Gadamer also

---

3. *PDE*, 17.
4. Zuckert, *Postmodern Platos*, 77–78.
5. *PDE*, 11.
6. Ambrosio, "Gadamer, Plato," 32.
7. Zuckert, *Postmodern Platos*, 77–78.
8. Sullivan, *Political Hermeneutics*, 11.

indicates a standard of morality and truth that is nondialectical and personal. In his commentary on the *Republic* he writes:

> An action is just which is in conformity with this inner order of the soul and which brings about and sustains that order. Thus the constitution of oneself as an internally well-ordered soul is the true measure of Dasein's self-understanding, i.e., of *sophia* (443e). Conversely, the destruction of the soul is *amathia* (444a), the diminution and darkening of this inner capacity to govern oneself.[9]

In this passage, Gadamer contrasts *sophia*, which for him means self-understanding, with its absence, *amathia*. The translator P. Christopher Smith says that *amathia* "characterizes a person turned away from himself in 'curiosity.'"[10] This "curiosity" (along with idle chatter and ambiguity) sounds like the absorption in the "they" that Heidegger at times attributes to an inauthentic mode of *Dasein*'s "Being-in."

That Gadamer may well be inclined to this direction is suggested again by Smith. He observes that Gadamer's depiction of the philosopher in contrast to the eroticist, the lover of sights, leads back to Heidegger's notion of curiosity (lust for the new) as it is set out in section 36 of *Being and Time*.[11] In "Plato and the Poets" (1934) Smith observes that Gadamer's description of the guardians as divided between the philosophical and tyrannical, the love of knowledge and the love of power, uses Heidegger's terms to indicate the concomitance of Being and non-Being, of being authentic and inauthentic (*gleichursprünglich*).[12] Smith is drawing attention to Gadamer's tendency to think of Being in Plato in terms of *Dasein*, which is clearly a Heideggerian reading of Plato. But it is in tension with the dialectical (Hegelian) reading insofar as, by locating Being in human beings, it removes standards of truth and goodness from a social and indeed linguistic context.

The Heideggerian impulse in Gadamer's interpretation of Plato inclines him to distinguish the authentic self from the inauthentic "they." For example, he singles out the dialectician from the community, saying that she "is characterized as one who strives to find what any and every existent reality is (*auto ge hekastous peri estin hekaston*) (533b);"[13] he

9. *DD*, 86.
10. Ibid., 86 n4.
11. Ibid., 91 n8.
12. Ibid., 57 n8.
13. *IG*, 84.

argues that the process of turning the soul around in the allegory provides immunity from the temptation to power and from flattery,[14] the ability to "resist public adulation and the hidden seductiveness of power which tempts them."[15] An education in the Good does not alienate the guardians from themselves, but rather makes it possible for them to remain constant (or true to themselves) amid the chaos, temptations, and external threats to their well-being posed by others. Training in the sciences therefore renders the philosopher steadfast amidst the threatening diversions and turmoil of the public space that Plato observed in the life of Socrates and compares to a battle in the *Republic*.[16] In contrast to the public *ethos* formed through dialogue, the philosophical knowledge of the Good, Gadamer says, is "in total opposition to a life led in *doxa*, that is, in mere conventions . . . With regard to the good . . . the consensus of others is of no importance to an individual."[17]

In contrast to Gadamer's intersubjective ethic, fewer scholars have isolated his ethic of autonomy. Kevin Decker discerns it in Plato, calling it a desire for self-sufficiency, but not in Gadamer *per se*.[18] Ambrosio observes the distinction between the collective and individualist ethic of autonomy in Gadamer and tries to negotiate them. He explains that the discipline of dialogue "is a discipline because it pertains to human existence and freedom; that is, it is a way of living that is in the service of autonomy . . . good is to understand truth for ourselves, but it is a truth shared with all persons . . . the truth of being in question."[19] According to Ambrosio, dialogue is in the service of autonomy in that it enables us to understand what is good for ourselves, but not by ourselves; however, this characterization is not consistent with Gadamer's Plato. On the contrary, the self-understanding nourished by the idea of the Good is said by Gadamer to render one immune to the temptations posed by flattery and power that originate outside the self, with others. Being with others

---

14. Ibid., 72, 96.

15. *DD*, 41.

16. Gadamer explains that the Good is an object "in just the same way (*hosautos*) [as other realities]" because knowledge of it consists of separating the idea of the good (*tou agathou*) from everything else, as if one were in a battle enduring tests of mettle. *IG*, 84. See Plato's *Republic*, 534c.

17. *IG*, 81.

18. Decker, "Limits of Radical Openness," 5–32.

19. Ambrosio, "Gadamer, Plato," 32.

is, from this side of the equation, not an opening to truth but a threat to it, a conclusion which in turn begs the question about the nature of the political realm for Gadamer.

Insofar as Gadamer contrasts the autonomous self, or metaphysical subject, with everyone (*das Man*), the public good is determined by a contract. In Gadamer's reading of Plato there is no other basis for relating to nonphilosophers, i.e., nonautonomous agents, than a guarantee of protection from being harmed by them. However, insofar as others are themselves philosophers, the problem is that there is not really any "other" to understand; everyone is a replica of the same one, a society of equals without substantial differences between anyone. This is a homogeneous state of like-minded persons wherein consensus is foregone conclusion. While a noncontractual notion of the good would find a place in such a society, since everyone is by nature philosophically political, the lawmakers would also be unjust to those who lack interest or time for rational deliberation.

CONCLUSION TO PART THREE

Both Gadamer and Heidegger use a hermeneutical and phenomenological method; however, Heidegger applies these methods only to Aristotle's works, not Plato's. Plato he reads instead through decontextualized Aristotelian concepts. Gadamer answers Heidegger by extending the hermeneutical and phenomenological methods to Heidegger himself. In so doing he penetrates the intellectual history of Heidegger's interpretation of Plato and demonstrates that it is congruent with the tradition of German idealism, and that, by privileging the indirect tradition (Aristotle in this case) over the direct (Plato's dialogues), it unfairly repeats Aristotle's one-sided view of Plato. However, this critical stand toward the Heidegger that provoked Gadamer also allows for constructive work. In keeping with the method of "destruction," Gadamer's criticism of Heidegger opens up a new way in which to think about the relation of Plato to Aristotle: the hermeneutical situations and dialectical ethic overlooked by Heidegger move Plato into the vicinity of Aristotle's thought. Far from being irrelevant to practical life, as Aristotle contends, the Good is revealed in the ethic of the *phronemos*; truth is not correspondence between ideas and things but includes concealment; instead of being opposed to nature, the ideas are potentially forms in phenomena that Aristotle makes explicit—because, by attending to that which speech is about (the particular), he is referred to things themselves (phenomena) that display the dialectical structure Plato discerned in speech.

The rapprochement Gadamer weaves between Plato and Aristotle has significant consequences for Heidegger's Plato. When hermeneutical situations and the dialectical structure of Being are taken into account in interpreting Plato, it becomes clear that he is neither a metaphysician nor an idealist opposed to Aristotle the realist; on the contrary, it is demonstrated that Plato thinks within the early Greek/Aristotelian context of *physis*. Far from being the originator of ontotheology, Plato's mathematical model prefigures Heidegger's thinking of the ontological difference as difference,[20] and Socrates's turn to the *logoi* prefigures the later Heidegger's own turn toward a groundless philosophy. Heidegger was not unaware of these results. In "Reflections on My Philosophical Journey," Gadamer reports that the essays on Plato in Volumes 6 and 7 of his collected works "meant something to Heidegger in the last years of his life." Gadamer explains that he had argued against Heidegger's view that Plato prepares the way for ontotheology, and continues:

> Even the metaphysics of Aristotle contains other dimensions than those Heidegger unlocked in his work. In this, I believe I was able to refer Heidegger to certain limits in his own interpretations. I am thinking especially of Heidegger's early fondness for referring to "the famous analogy"—"*die berühmte Analogie.*"[21]

---

20. Ontology of Being when identified with a universal and first cause is ontotheology. See Heidegger, *Identity and Difference*, 15. Heidegger writes, "Since the exposition of Being as idea, thinking about the Being of beings has become metaphysical, and metaphysics has become theological. Theology means here the exposition of the 'first cause' of beings as God and the misplacing of Being into this first cause, which contains Being in itself and discharges it from itself because it is the most being of beings." *PDT*, 268.

21. Gadamer, "Reflections," 48–49. Before leaving the University of Marburg for Freiburg in 1928, Heidegger had offered a valediction to his students, asking them to carry on the task of *Being and Time* in their respective areas of expertise: Karl Lowith in the social sciences and anthropology, Gerhard Kruger in theology, and Hans-Georg Gadamer in Greek philosophy and aesthetics. Grondin, *Hans-Georg Gadamer*, 130. Forty-two years later Heidegger remained enthusiastic about Gadamer's execution of that assignment. But the intervening years of discussion with his pupil had altered the original intent of Heidegger's request: whereas he might have expected in 1928 that Gadamer would broaden the scope for the analytic of *Dasein* within Greek philosophy, by the 1970s Heidegger realized that Gadamer's conclusions challenged and corrected his own.

If there is an analogy between Plato's idea of the Good and Aristotle's preference for a concrete human good, then how are they related to one another? Gadamer found the answer in the dialectical structure of the dialogue form. Yet the account of the latter is not so clear; while Gadamer privileges intersubjective truth, he also valorizes autonomy. The result is a contractual basis for political relations with nonphilosophers, or an exclusive community of philosophers that excludes those with no interest in rational discourse.

Part IV

Stanley Rosen's Rejoinder

Introduction

According to Gadamer, Plato's dialectic consists of interplay between contrary positions exhibited in Socrates's conversations. He finds this corroborated by what he calls Plato's "unwritten doctrine," the problem of the one and the many, and the "second sailing" in the *Phaedo*. In these instances of dialectical reasoning, Plato's ideas are shown to be not entities unto themselves that exist independently of speech, but linguistic hypotheses. However, there is a problem with Gadamer's actual account of what dialectic means for Plato, which in turn calls into question Plato's ideas and number theory as he understands them. On the one hand, Gadamer distinguishes himself from Heidegger by insisting upon the relevance of the literary dimension of Plato's work, including drama, character, and setting, to understanding Plato's philosophy. On the other hand, his actual interpretation of what dialectic means for Plato consistently bypasses the importance of the dramatic elements of the work. The explanation for this breakdown in what Gadamer lauds as the Doric harmony of speech and deed (in his essay "Logos and Ergon in Plato's Lysis") resides in his emphasizing the mathematical at the expense of the poetic aspect of Plato's dialectic.[1]

The two ways of philosophizing, the mathematical and poetic, identified by Rosen in "The Role of Eros in Plato's *Republic*," are in tension with one another but mutually sustaining.[2] The mathematical approach emphasizes the formal, structural, impersonal, and universal

---

1. For a contrary position on this question see Jean Grondin, "Gadamer and the Tübingen School."

2. Rosen, "Role of Eros," 452–475.

character of philosophical inquiry, and the poetic the particular content. Their symbiotic relationship is expressed by Aristotle in the *Poetics*. He states that poetry is more philosophical than history; this is because unlike history, which concerns itself with particulars, poetry concerns itself with particulars that include universals.[3] Yet Aristotle is silent about the madness that grips the poet, that is to say, the desire for creation (immortality) that Plato believes culminates in a vision of the Good for the philosopher-poet. For Rosen's Plato philosophy is not solely a matter of discoursing about ideas, but includes in addition a love of the Good that transcends all other ideas. This in turn accounts for the notion of dialectic as an ascent from lower to higher forms of intelligibility and makes sense of the transformation of the soul (*metanoia tes psyches*) that Gadamer intuits. To the extent that this love of the Good is suppressed in Gadamer's notion of dialectic, he remains more Aristotelian than Plato, more technical than poetic in his reading of the dialogues. This is why, despite his words to the contrary, in his actual interpretation of what dialectic and idea means for Plato he does not give due regard to characters, order of speeches, and dramatic context.

OUTLINE

Chapter 10, "Gadamer's Dialectic," is historiographical and philosophical in intention. I argue that the background to Gadamer's method of interpreting Plato's dialogues consists of Hegel, the Tübingen school, and Jacob Klein. This influence is evident in Gadamer's thesis about Plato's alleged *arithmos* paradigm and in his argument that Socrates's turn from a direct to an indirect inquiry into the being of what is in the *Phaedo* is the definitive statement on Plato's theory of Being (ideas). Chapter 11, "Incongruity of Speech and Deed," demonstrates an inconsistency between Gadamer's alleged regard for the literary aspects of the dialogue form, in which particular contingencies of existence are represented, and his explanation of what dialectic means for Plato. The latter is guided by a mathematical way that suppresses the poetic-erotic way and therefore the content of Plato's philosophy.

Chapter 12, "Plato's Dialectic Reconsidered," consists of three sections. The first deploys a method of interpretation that includes what Gadamer intends to account for but overlooks (drama). The result is a

---

3. *Poetics* IX, 1451b.

notion of dialectic exhibited in the *Symposium* and *Republic* that is characterized by a hierarchy of Being rather than an interplay between opposites. The second section addresses Gadamer's reading of the *Phaedo*. Based on the overall character of Gadamer's view of Plato's dialectic, there is reason to believe that his reading of Socrates's "second voyage" may not be balanced. In keeping with the reading of Plato that incorporates both patterns (mathematics or reason) and direction (poetry-*eros*), the ideas in the *Phaedo* are demonstrated to be not linguistic hypotheses, as Gadamer contends, but rather principles of intelligibility transcendent to speech. This in turn invites a reinvestigation of Plato's alleged *arithmos* paradigm, or the problem of the one and the many, in the third section. This paradigm effectively integrates the intelligible into the visible realm, which is Gadamer's version of Plato's dialectic, without presupposing a way of seeing that can distinguish the intelligible from the sensible sphere; however, Gadamer conflates what is perceived with an intelligible idea, and thereby closes down the alleged openness of his political philosophy.

10

Gadamer's Dialectic: Hegel, Tübingen, and Klein

ON THE ONE HAND, Hegel inspired Gadamer's understanding of Plato's dialectic in a similar way that Aristotle inspired his understanding of Plato's ethics. Just as Gadamer read the *Philebus* with a view to questions answered by Aristotle, thereby clarifying analytically what Plato expressed dramatically, so too does he position Hegel relative to Plato. Gadamer explains in "Hegel and the Dialectic of Ancient Philosophers" (1961) that Hegel "is the first to actually grasp the depth of Plato's dialectic" and that Plato's dialogue is the substrate of Hegel's logic.[1] Hegel integrated into his logic of Jena a systematic philosophy based on the *Philebus* and *Parmenides*, and the principles of Plato's unwritten doctrine as known, for example, through Aristotle and Sextus Empiricus.[2] Not unlike Aristotle, who explained Plato's ethics of *phronesis*, Hegel explicates the inner logic of the dialogue form. Gadamer would therefore seem justified, as he says of his early career, in "setting about the task of relating the dialectic of the ancient philosophers to Hegelian dialectic in order to elucidate both in terms of the other."[3] The affinity between Hegel and the ancients consists in thinking in contradictions, which Gadamer also says has its source in the Eleatics, and later in Plato. In this way of thinking, the consequences of opposing hypotheses are drawn out without knowledge of the essence or "whatness" of the things being discussed.

Gadamer's focus on the formal structure of Plato's thought received new impetus from Schadewald as early as the 1940s, and later in the 1950s from his followers Gaiser and Kramer (the Tübingen school). In an endeavor to reconstruct Plato's secret teachings, they took up

1. *HD*, 7.
2. Kramer, *Plato*, 157.
3. *HD*, 3–5.

Aristotle's reference to the One and indeterminate dyad, and identified this "one" with Plato's idea of the Good (as had Plotinus). While Gadamer was critical of their claim that Plato had an esoteric teaching, and that it consisted of a Plotinian hierarchy from point to line to plane and then to solid, he was also inspired by the possibility of an arithmetical structure in Plato's (Hegelian) dialectic. In a revised version of his Heidelberg lecture in the 1960s, Gadamer connects Aristotle's one and the dyad to Plato's doctrine of the one and the many ("Plato's Unwritten Doctrine"). Later, in *Idea of the Good*, he argues for the development of Plato's number theory from a criticism of the Pythagoreans, whose notions of the limited and unlimited had previously informed his reading of Plato's practical philosophy in the *Philebus* (1928). That Plato's philosophy was structured by a formal dialectic to which Hegel was keyed seems to have been certain.[4]

On the other hand, Gadamer recognized the limits of mapping an arithmetical dialectic onto Plato's philosophy. Gadamer explains in 1961 that, after having been "schooled in the sound and solid handicraft of phenomenology" and studied dialectics with Nicolai Hartmann and Martin Heidegger, he was vexed with Hegel's claim "that in his dialectic the idea of philosophic demonstration has been restored." In contrast to dialectic, defined by pure categories of identity and nonidentity, reconfiguring itself into an apodictic science in which all differences are resolved in the Absolute, Gadamer aimed to "bring the productive unclarity of dialectical thought back to life."[5] The productive ambiguity he refers to is the indeterminate meaning of Being visible in the literary form of Plato's dialogues—that is, in the original movement of a conversation—which Gadamer contrasts with degenerate forms of speech such as rhetoric. In contrast to rhetoric, which sways an audience by manipulating its emotions, is long-winded or monologic, and aims at winning (showing oneself to be a knower who cannot be refuted), a Socratic conversation is characterized by short questions and answers, adjusts itself to rational inquiry, and above all prioritizes the question;[6] there is no conversation if the answer is a foregone conclusion. For Gadamer, the dialec-

---

4. I am in debt to Grondin, "Gadamer and the Tübingen School."

5. *HD*, 3.

6. "Degenerate Forms of Speech" are discussed by Gadamer in *PDE*, 44–51, section 4. In the *Gorgias* it is compared to a knack, pretending to have knowledge when one really does not.

tical structure of Plato's dialogues departs from Hegel's closed system by being undogmatic because it has the logical structure of openness. This is evinced by the inconclusiveness of the Socratic dialogues and is discussed extensively by Gadamer in "The Hermeneutical Priority of the Question: The model of Platonic Dialectic" in *Truth and Method*.[7]

After having used the methods of phenomenology in *Plato's Dialectical Ethics* (1928) to show that the character of dialectic in later dialogues such as the *Statesman*, *Sophist*, and *Philebus* are rooted in live philosophical discussion,[8] Gadamer took a different direction in his study of Plato. Roughly fifteen years after his first book, Gadamer reconsidered and thought that he had pushed Plato's doctrines too much into the background. He recalls that his emphasis on the dialogue form affirmed the "inherent inconclusiveness and open-endedness of dialogue," but at the same time "turned against establishing any doctrine of Plato's." In 1943, explaining his focus on the form of Plato's philosophy in his 1928 book, he writes, "This tendency went to an extreme, and on that account my own Plato book at the end of the 1920s must also be faulted. Using the tools of phenomenology, it attempted to tie Plato's dialectic to Socratic dialogue, but in so doing the basic theme of Plato's doctrine was pushed all too much into the background."[9] Gadamer's phenomenological approach to Plato submerged the question of Plato's doctrine while highlighting the dialogue form. He reiterates the same problem in 1968:

> Our situation in respect to the tradition demands that we give philosophy and not philology methodological priority when it comes to uncovering the subject matter at issue behind the different literary forms in which the tradition is given to us and when it comes to orienting ourselves in terms of that subject matter"[10]

According to Gadamer, philosophy penetrates behind the literary form to a hidden doctrine. Reconstructing what was thought to be left "unsaid" was characteristic of some of the very thinkers whose image of Plato motivated Gadamer's work: Kant claimed to have understood

---

7. *TM*, 325–341.
8. *DD*, 93.
9. *DD*, 125.
10. *DD*, 197.

Plato better than Plato understood himself,[11] Natorp suggested Plato was a proto-Kantian, and Heidegger observed that Plato was a Nietzschean.[12] In Gadamer's case, the catalysts for investigating an "unwritten doctrine" (not necessarily an esoteric teaching) in Plato's philosophy were Plato himself, who at the end of the *Phaedrus* says that orality is superior to writing because it is written on the soul; Aristotle, who in *Physics* (209b 11–16) refers to Plato's unwritten doctrine; the Tübingen school (Kramer and Gaiser); and, above all, according to Gadamer, Jacob Klein's theory of Greek numbers.

In the preface of the 1967 edition of *Plato's Dialectical Ethics*, Gadamer says that when he wrote his book in 1928 he "had not learned the significance of the Greek concept of arithmos from Jacob Klein or seen the importance of the unwritten tradition concerning Plato's teachings."[13] Gadamer is referring to his colleague at Marburg, Jacob Klein, and his book, *The Concept of Number in Greek Mathematics and Philosophy* (1934). Klein alerted Gadamer to the relevance of number in Plato's philosophy: that the one is composed of all numbers, but distinct from them; that sevenness, for example, can be separated intellectually from that which it characterizes and each instance of seven can be recognized independently of sevenness, solving the problem of participation.[14] The locus for a convergence between the number theory and

---

11. In the *Critique of Pure Reason* Immanuel Kant writes of the term "idea" in Plato: "I shall not engage here in any literary enquiry into the meaning which this illustrious philosopher attached to the expression. I need only remark that it is by no means unusual, upon comparing the thoughts which an author has expressed in regard to his subject, whether in ordinary conversation or in writing, to find that we understand him better than he understood himself. As he has not sufficiently determined his concept, he has sometimes spoken, or even thought, in opposition to his own intention." Kant, *Critique of Pure Reason*, A 314, quoted in Politis, *Paul Natorp*, 457.

12. Heidegger explains of the unsaid, "The 'doctrine' of a thinker is that which is left unsaid in what he says, to which man is exposed in order to expend himself upon it." *PDT*, 251.

13. Zuckert, *Postmodern Platos*, 96.

14. Summarized from Zuckert, *Postmodern Platos*, 14. Although Gadamer concludes his 1942 essay "Plato's Educational State" with an allusion to the number doctrine, it was not until after a break from Plato studies (1945 to 1960), in the 1968 essay "Plato's Unwritten Dialectic" and the 1974 lectures at Heidelberg (compiled in *Idea of the Good*, 1978), that Gadamer works out the significance, for Plato's teachings, of the dialectical structure of Being in the *arithmos* paradigm. For a criticism of Gadamer's appropriation of Klein, specifically the argument that Klein never refers to an arithmos structure of *logos*, see Hopkins, "Klein and Gadamer," 151–157.

the structure of dialectic is precisely what Heidegger and the tradition, through a one-sided Aristotelian perspective, found wanting in Plato: a theory of participation.

Klein's insight into the Greek number theory was a model for the participation of ideas in one another, a concept that Gadamer thought was Plato's unwritten doctrine. Contrary to those who criticized Plato for not having a theory of participation, Gadamer reasoned that the theory was "hidden" within the problem of the one and the many alluded to throughout the dialogues, from the earliest to the latest.[15] This, he says, is evinced by the Excursus to the *Seventh Letter*, which, having been written for the novice, states the principles Plato expressed many times in private lectures and considered propaedutic to philosophy. The distinction between the means of knowing and the object of knowledge outlined in the Excursus, he says, was "not at all a Platonic problem but rather a Platonic presupposition. Plato had always viewed the participation of the individual in the idea as self-evident and as that which makes the acceptance of ideas at all reasonable."[16] Having taught the theory of participation in private lectures, Plato did not think it necessary to reiterate that teaching in the dialogues; moreover, having been motivated by the sophists' eristic, he emphasized separation. Consequently, "participation" is only alluded to by Plato even though it is implicit in the problem of the one and the many.

Alongside the Tübingen school's arguments about Plato's esoteric teaching, Klein's number theory thus alerted Gadamer to Plato's unwritten doctrine, the problem of the one and the many, or what Gadamer calls the *arithmos* paradigm. It is a theory of participation in the sense that the numbers one and two are a model for bringing together opposed hypotheses in a third that is implicated in both but distinct from them. Gadamer can be heard giving voice to just this structure in his characterization of Plato's dialectic. He writes, "Surely one of the most difficult problems which Plato's philosophy presents is that of establishing how these two procedures which he develops from Socrates's art of conversing, i.e., the exercise of thinking in opposites, on the one hand,

---

15. The mathematical puzzle is represented in the *Hippias Major* (300) during a discussion of beauty and in the *Protagoras* and *Republic* during a discussion of virtue; it is alluded to in the *Sophist* and *Statesman* and is integral to Socrates' reasoning in the *Philebus*, to mention a few.

16. Dostal, "Gadamer's Continuous Challenge," 305.

and the differentiation of concepts on the other, are related to each other."[17] Thinking in opposites entails finding unity, but the unity is contingent upon making distinctions within that very unity; for example, in a conversation neither person knows precisely the whole meaning of the subject matter under consideration. The "whole" is effectively a question—but it enters into, and unfolds from, the process of making distinctions during an exchange of views.[18] Jacob Klein's insights into the Greek number theory connect with Hegel's dialectic in that in both cases the mind is forced to think a contradiction that presupposes yet also yields something else. The one is paradoxically two, but they both consist of one(s) which when combined generate three. Hegel and Klein together (as understood by Gadamer) were a catalyst for Gadamer's thesis that the ontological structure of Plato's dialogue form (or a phenomenological description of it) is dialectical. This structure is corroborated for Gadamer by Socrates's "second sailing."[19]

Gadamer argues that in the *Phaedo* Socrates turns away from thinking about ideas in themselves and toward Aristotle's starting point for philosophical inquiry: the way in which the world is given in an everyday sort of way. The steps that Socrates takes toward this "second voyage" are dialectical in that he considers two positions on the study of things, that of the materialists and metaphysicians, that are contrary to one another before finding a way that combines both. While there is no evidence of Gadamer actually incorporating the dialectic of contraries into his reading of the *Phaedo*, it is striking that Socrates justifies his

---

17. *DD*, 94. The puzzle states that a contradiction, that the one is many and the many one, is not a contradiction. In other words, it is by transcending perceptual knowledge and thinking independently of the latter, relating what is given in perception (many) to what is thought (one) that the contradiction is removed.

18. Gadamer comments on the logic that is immanent to the Socratic dialogue: "What emerges in its truth is the *logos*, which is neither mine nor yours and hence, so far transcends the subjective opinion of the partners to the dialogue that even the person leading the conversation is always ignorant." *TM*, 331. Although both participants are ignorant of the inner logic that animates and unites the conversation, understanding the being of "x" nevertheless unfolds.

19. In "Plato's Unwritten Dialectic" (*DD*, 130–140) Gadamer argues that the *arithmos* paradigm recurs throughout the dialogues, from the earliest to the latest, and is referred to by Plato as the problem of the one and the many, by Aristotle as the one and the dyad. Gadamer thus reasons that Plato and Aristotle find common ground in a dialectical ontology couched, for Plato, in the problem of three fingers being fingers, words being composed of letters, and beautiful things also partaking in the beautiful itself.

turn toward the *logoi* with reference to deficiencies in natural scientific and metaphysical theories. I thus construct Socrates's rationale for the "second voyage" according to Gadamer's dialectical perspective.

In reply to Cebes's question about the immortality of the soul, Socrates recounts that he had initially sought to understand the coming to be and passing away of things with the help of the natural sciences (96b), but became exasperated. If physical causes alone, or what Aristotle called efficient and material causes, are relied upon to explain change, then Socrates could not understand how numbers are generated from one another (97a). It seems absurd to pose a question about the causes of numbers to the physical sciences; in so doing, Socrates intends to highlight their limitations. The natural sciences are fit for understanding what is perceivable; but perceived forms, such as the large and the small, he suggests while discussing numbers, do not admit of opposites. Since thinking in opposites is precisely what is required in order to understand the cause that is responsible for the generation of two from one, the quest for the first cause of all things falls to another level of inquiry: the nonmaterial or metaphysical notion of *nous*/reason, espoused by Anaxagoras.

Socrates had learned from Anaxagoras that "Mind" "arranged everything and caused everything" (97c). In contrast to the physical sciences, "mind" is neither an efficient nor a mathematical cause. It is a final cause, and meant to Socrates that which is best, or that for the sake of which everything exists (97c). As Gadamer says, the consequence of reason is the reasonableness of what is.[20] However, although Anaxagoras's insight touched Socrates, he was disappointed with Anaxagoras because his explanation for the coming to be of beings was stated in terms of material causes such as "air and water" (98c). Not unlike the Pythagoreans, who had, according to Gadamer, conflated perceived numbers with the concept of number and hence could not untangle the contradiction of the two being one, Anaxagoras conflated what is perceived, and therefore changing, with the intelligible and unchanging realm of things. Anaxagoras thus claims, on the one hand, that everything Socrates does is to be attributed to mind (or what is best) and, on the other, explains that Socrates's bones and muscles are responsible for sitting there in prison (98c). Anaxogoras may have been on the right track when he conceived of *nous* as the reason for all things because it entails that exis-

20. *PDE*, 69.

tence aims for harmony; however, his explanation for change remained scientific and independent of what was best. Socrates is thus critical of him, saying that his argument is slipshod.

Just as the natural scientists could not think a contradiction, neither could the metaphysicians. The scientist thought of causes solely in terms of physical causality, thus eclipsing that for the sake of which everything exists. Anaxagoras, with his notion of "reason," seemed to have recognized that for the sake of which everything exists, but conflated it with physical causation. Because he failed to distinguish between the intelligible and sensible causes, he, no less than the scientists, could not solve the number problem and explain why the one was also two. Sensible perception, to repeat, cannot combine opposites.

Socrates, therefore, sought to circumvent this shortcoming by adopting a different method or way of understanding. He noticed that the natural scientists and metaphysicians could not make the requisite distinction between the intelligible and visible spheres because they attempted to study objects of knowledge directly. This, he reports, blinded and bedazzled their eyes, and prompted him to opt for an indirect method of inquiry. With it he might make such a distinction and thereby discover the cause of generation and growth of everything that his contemporaries missed. This indirect study was of things as they are given to us in speech. Speech has a referent and therefore fluctuates; but at the same time, as Gadamer says, "the words by which we designate things already have the character of a universality that remains the same."[21] Speech consists of both particulars and universals: "this thing here," and its idea (hypothesis). That which neither the natural scientists nor the metaphysicians could achieve, a distinction between the specific and general meaning due to a direct approach, becomes clear to Socrates when he reflects upon the way in which things are spoken about during a conversation. The dialectical structure of Being thus becomes visible by analyzing a dialogue.

---

21. *PDE*, 70.

11

Incongruity of Speech and Deed

BY EMPHASIZING THE DIALECTICAL structure of Being in Plato's philosophy and the literary aspects of the dialogues, Gadamer seeks to undermine the *Altertumswissenschaft* tradition of subsuming Plato to an objective science. Given the structure of dialogue, no definitive doctrine can be established; it is simply contrary to the give and take of a conversation, animated by a question, to put forward a definitive idea about what something is. Every answer is another question. The literary form of Plato's work dovetails with Gadamer's reading of Plato's open-ended dialectic in that any pretense toward an objective doctrine is an abstraction from the poetry in which the meaning of a particular being is embedded.

As a result of this regard for the coming to be of the thing-in-itself, Gadamer contends that an understanding of what Plato means—for example, in the *Lysis*—must consider to whom it is that Socrates speaks as well as the circumstances of their discussion.[1] After observing that "the overwhelming tendency to interpret the dialogical compositions critically as statements of a doctrine" is due to a modern preconception of what science ought to be, Gadamer explains:

> The methodological problem is clear. We must establish the philosophical significance of the scene, the setting of the dialogues, of the relationship of the speaker to what is spoken, of evolving meaning as it unfolds in live discussion. And we must apply what we can learn thereby to understanding the philosophical questions which Plato puts to us.[2]

---

1. This is Smith's observation ("Plato as Impulse and Obstacle," 154) about Gadamer's essay "Logos and Ergon in Plato's Lysis" (*DD*, 1–20).

2. *DD*, 159. Also, Gadamer writes, "The particular literary form which Plato invented for his Socratic discourses is not merely a clever hiding place for his 'doctrines;' it is a profoundly meaningful expression of them within the possibilities which the art

The proper method for interpreting Plato, Gadamer says, is to apply the significant scenes, settings, and character of the speakers to the philosophical arguments. He says of the *Republic* that its argument is not easily discerned from a style and form of writing that is fraught with both contrived coincidences and arbitrariness; nevertheless, these are not dispensed with for the sake of the "statement of a doctrine." Rather, the literary dimension of Plato's work is integral to discovering the "sequential logic" and "inner unity" of the argument's development.[3] The dramatic dimensions of Plato's dialogues are integral, suggests Gadamer, to understanding the argument. The convention of interpreting Plato according to a prior decision about scientific validity is thus challenged by Gadamer's sensitivity to the literary, and therefore particular, in Plato's thought in conjunction with an indeterminate ontology.[4]

Despite this expressed regard for particular beings and their circumstances, Zuckert complains that "Gadamer makes sweeping claims and arguments that weave together a variety of texts. He often violates his own strictures about the need to read the dialogues as discrete works or wholes in which the character of the particular participants must be related to the specific setting and action."[5] According to Zuckert, during his actual interpretation of Plato's dialogues Gadamer violates the strictures of his own method. Rather than include the contingent particular in his interpretation of Plato, he excludes it. The reason Gadamer fails to fulfill his intention in this regard is his consistent privileging of what Rosen calls a mathematical way to philosophy—that is, a focus upon universal and anonymous structures—which, for Gadamer, is a dialectical logic of uniting contraries with one another. As a result of this emphasis upon the formal side of philosophy, Gadamer bypasses (1) the significance of *eros* to understanding what dialectic means for Plato; and (2) the literary aspects of the dialogue. The latter are opened up by a love of philosophy, because love is creative and therefore attuned to the character of the speakers and the drama of the dialogues. By stressing logic, or variations upon Hegel's logic, Gadamer's account of the meaning of

---

of writing allows." Ibid., 95.

3. Ibid., 77.

4. Wachterhauser reports "that for Gadamer the various settings of Plato's work show his sensitivity to the contingent particularities of human thought." Wachterhauser, *Beyond Being*, 32.

5. Zuckert, "Hermeneutics in Practice," 219.

dialectic for Plato ignores desire and the phenomenological-existential conditions under which it is conveyed by Plato.[6]

Early in his career, while he was guided by Heidegger, Gadamer interpreted ancient dialectic in terms of Hegel's logic.[7] Although he claimed to have recognized that Hegel's logic abstracted from the oral tradition in which meaning is reinterpreted intersubjectively, and while he believed that Plato despised the "macros logos" and was not a "Euclidus writ large,"[8] Gadamer's interpretation of the meaning of dialectic for Plato nevertheless exhibits a preference for the Euclidean rather than the poetic impulse toward philosophy. Consider the following: Gadamer refers to the *Sophist* (253d–e) and *Statesman* (285) in support of the mathematical structure of Being in Plato's philosophy.[9] However, the rather complex passages he adduces, wherein the sophists are criticized for not making divisions according to "real classes," are

---

6. Gadamer investigates the meaning of dialectic in the *Phaedo*, *Republic*, *Sophist*, and *Statesman* in *Plato's Dialectical Ethics* (65–100). I consult this source selectively and rely primarily upon his rendition of Plato's dialectic from his essays "Plato's Unwritten Dialectic" (*DD*, 124–155) and "Dialectic and Sophism in Plato's 7th Letter." (*DD*, 93–123).

7. Wachterhauser, *Beyond Being*, 5.

8. This is from Grondin, "Gadamer and the Tübingen School."

9. *DD*, 95. Plato writes, "For it is indeed the case, in a certain way, that all the products of the various sorts of expertise share in measurement. But because of their not being accustomed to carrying on their investigations by dividing according to real classes, the people in question throw these things together at once, despite the degree of difference between them, thinking them alike—and then again they also do the opposite of this by dividing other things not according to parts, when the rule is that when one perceives first the community between the members of a group of many things, one should not desist until one sees in it all those differences that are located in classes, and conversely, with the various unlikenesses, when they are seen in multitudes, one should be incapable of pulling a face and stopping before one has penned all the related things within one likeness and actually surrounded them in some real class. So let this be enough for us to say about these things, and about modes of defect and excess; and let's just keep hold of the fact that two distinct classes of measurement have been discovered in relation to them, and remember what we say they are." *Statesman*, 285. "Aren't we going to say that it takes expertise in dialectic to divide things by kinds and not to think that the same form is a different one or that a different form is the same? . . . so if a person can do that, he'll be capable of adequately discriminating a single form spread out all through a lot of other things, each of which stands separate from the others. In addition, he can discriminate forms that are different from each other but are included within a single form that's outside them, or a single form that's connected as a unit throughout many wholes, or many forms that are completely separate from others. That's what it is to know how to discriminate by kinds how things can associate and how they can't." *Sophist*, 253d–e).

advanced not by Plato's Socrates but by a "Visitor," an Eleatic stranger and student of Parmenides. Gadamer presupposes that the Visitor's depiction of dialectic is that of Plato. But it cannot be assumed that they are one and the same person. Furthermore, Gadamer does not consider that the definitions proffered by the Visitor might be suitable for the habits of thinking proper to his interlocutor, the mathematician Theaetetus.[10] As Plato suggests in the passages to which Gadamer refers, mathematicians divide parts according to a class, and distinguish forms that are included in a single whole or are external to that whole. In other words, mathematicians use a method of collection and division in order to understand the whole, its parts, and their relations to one another; however, the advantage of this method is also its shortcoming. Mathematics is a universal science intelligible to the mind independently of the character of the mathematician. In reply to Socrates urging Theaetetus to seek the essence of knowledge, the young mathematician does not speculate upon an end or purpose of all things, as had Socrates in the *Phaedo*; he recalls what he had recently learned from Theodorus: a procedure of inquiry that is value-neutral and impersonal. Gadamer takes this to be Plato's statement on the meaning of dialectic.

Contrary to the thesis herein defended, that Gadamer's understanding of Plato's dialectic abstracts from the experiential dimension of knowledge because logic is indifferent to the erotic impulse toward creativity typical of the poets, are Gadamer's assertions about the expe-

---

10. Also relevant to Gadamer's thesis on Plato's dialectic is the following passage from Plato: "So it's settled. We'll divide the craft of copy-making as quickly as we can and we'll go down into it. Then if the sophist gives up right away we'll obey the royal command and we'll capture him and hand our catch over to the king. But if the sophist slips down somewhere into the parts of the craft of imitation, we'll follow along with him and we'll divide each of the parts that contain him until we catch him. Anyway, neither he nor any other kind will ever be able to boast that he's escaped from the method of people who are able to chase a thing through both the particular and the general. . . . Going by the method of division that we've used so far, I think I see two types of imitation here too. But I don't think I can clearly tell which type or form we're looking for is in." *Sophist*, 235. The two types of imitation (or copy-making) to which the Visitor is referring are likeness-making and appearance-making. The former is a likeness of the beauty of a thing (as in sculpting) and thus resembles the real entity; the latter does not even resemble the real entity because it consists of creating from a viewpoint that isn't even beautiful. In either case, the sophist or imitator is caught through the process of compelling him to make distinctions in his craft before being handed over to the king, presumably the magistrate. The Visitor seems to believe that the misuse of speech is unlawful.

rience of insight. Quoting Simplicius on Plato against Antisthenes, he says, "He who has no eye for the idea could not be made to see it even by a Lynceus,"[11] and continues:

> Now the moral example which we have used makes clear at once what is meant when the text says that he who is himself supposed to get a vision of the thing itself or he who would engender that vision in another must have an "affinity" for the thing besides having the intellectual gifts of comprehension and memory.[12]

Gadamer is indicating a personal experience of knowledge that he suggests is contingent upon having an affinity for the thing itself. He writes, "The best that can be hoped for is a meager 'indication' which could illumine the thing only for someone who has the prerequisite nature to understand it."[13] By creating room within the quest for knowledge for a personal insight, Gadamer would seem to have provided grounds for grasping the idea of the Good itself in the erotic language of poetry. However, in his explication of Plato's dialectic in the *Statesman*, *Sophist*, and *Phaedrus*—that is, in his actual interpretation of Plato's works—Gadamer is notably silent about the end of dialectic as well as the erotic character of knowledge of the Good. For example, with respect to the passages from the *Statesman* and *Sophist* mentioned earlier, he overlooks the following: after explaining how sophists fail to divide their thoughts according to real classes (see the quote above), the Visitor in the *Statesman* speaks to the aim of making divisions; it is "for the sake of our becoming better dialecticians generally" (*Statesman*, 285d). And following the passage from the *Sophist* (235d–e, quoted above) to which Gadamer refers the reader,[14] Plato writes, "you'll assign this dialectical activity only to someone who has a pure and just love of wisdom" (*Sophist*, 253e). We cannot be certain what the Visitor means by becoming "better," but it presumably includes "a pure and just love of wisdom" of a kind that, as stated in the *Sophist*, mathematicians may not understand because they are not personally implicated in the distinctions they make.

11. *DD*, 96.
12. Ibid., 116–117.
13. Ibid., 118.
14. Ibid., 95.

With respect to the *Phaedrus*, in *Plato's Dialectical Ethics* Gadamer says that the context for Plato's definition of dialectic is a criticism of rhetoric. Whereas rhetoric strives for persuasion and uses deception, dialectic strives for common understanding.[15] But at the same time, this distinction is made in a dialogue about love. Gadamer suppresses the topic *per se*, referring to *eros* as a mere example to convey the requirements of a definition before enumerating the structural requirements of dialectic. These include: agreement about the subject matter; collection; and division.[16] In "Plato's Unwritten Dialectic" he alludes to the passage 256c–266a-c of the *Phaedrus*, where Socrates compares cutting up speeches to splicing flesh from the bones of a sacrificial carcass,[17] but he stops short of explaining why Socrates identifies himself with a dialectician. According to Plato's Socrates, the purpose of dialectic is to think and speak well; or, as Gadamer says, dialectic proves to be "a prerequisite for the artful mastery of speech."[18] Yet that purpose must be understood within the context of Socrates's recantation speech, wherein he overturns Lysis's praise of sex without love (230d–234c) and "atones" for his own better "immoral" speech with an account of love that is directed toward the bliss of immortality (*Phaedrus*, 243e–257b). The fact that Socrates shares these thoughts with the eroticist Phaedrus outside the walls of Athens, in a natural setting, speaks to a transpolitical end of dialectic in the vicinity of the gods, divinities, and muses, to which Socrates's rationality yields (235c-d, 238d, 241e–242a, 262c-d). But it is precisely this transpolitical end symbolized by the setting, and the references to that end being in the vicinity of the gods (where rationality succumbs to poetic madness), that Gadamer does not mention in his definition of Platonic dialectic. By not taking into account the personal, which is to say the erotic side of dialectics, Gadamer violates the tenets of his own method explicitly designed to include particular phenomena in an understanding of the whole.

To speak on Gadamer's behalf, it is possible that the indeterminate meaning of Being that he emphasizes is typical of the earlier and not the middle or later dialogues. Decker concurs with this, observing that the underlay for Gadamer's dialectic is the process of inquiry characteristic

15. *PDE*, 84.
16. Ibid., 85.
17. *DD*, 146.
18. *PDE*, 88.

of the early dialogues.[19] In the absence of a *telos* or positive teaching from the dialogues, the ascent through a hierarchy of Being is presumably similarly absent. In the early dialogues we would not expect to find a dramatic structure that unfolds toward higher degrees of intelligibility, only the back-and-forth movement of a process punctuated by "aha" moments. And yet a closer examination suggests that this is not unambiguously the case. Kenneth Dorter explains that the term "dialectic" is not used in the early dialogues; instead, we find the term "elenchus."[20] Nevertheless, Dorter sees that, like the middle dialogues, "the *elenctic* dialogues leave us with an opposition whose paradoxical character invites us to find a way to reconcile the opposites by embracing them within a higher conception."[21] Dorter consults the *Meno* and *Protagoras* (*elenctic* dialogues) to demonstrate the progression which he describes in the early dialogue, *Republic* I, as follows: "In Book I of the *Republic* the distinctions Socrates makes in the course of his refutation point toward positive doctrines that will be formulated in later books."[22] Dorter goes on to explain that the distinctions made through the method of division render explicit the prior understanding of the subject matter in question. "However, it proceeds systematically rather than ad hoc and aims to provide not only a definition based on genus and differentia" (which Gadamer isolates and says is the "core of dialectic"), but in addition "a genealogy of the concept sought that shows its location on a conceptual tree."[23] In the early dialogues, what Plato refers to as "the source itself" in which to "secure confirmation" (*Republic*, 533d) is never fully articulated but is nonetheless evident, according to Dorter, in the dialogues' structure.

CONCLUSION

An investigation of Gadamer's account of Plato's dialectic demonstrates that he ignores the dramatic elements of Plato's work such as setting and character of the conversationalists. Part of the reason for this is the

---

19. Decker, "Limits of Radical Openness," 5, 22.

20. "Dialectic" is used for the first time in the following dialogues: *Philebus*, 16e–17a; *Meno*, 75d; *Cratylus*, 304c and 348d. Dorter, *Transformation of Plato's Republic*, 9–11.

21. Ibid., 11.

22. Ibid., 12.

23. Ibid.

influence of Hegel and the sources Gadamer consults, including the *Sophist*, *Statesman*, and *Parmenides*. Stanley Rosen points out that these later dialogues exaggerate the mathematical character of philosophy, "and any attempt to interpret them must take this fact into account."[24] Mathematics, as mentioned, is characterized by anonymity and "in this sense is public rather than private."[25] Consequently, even though Gadamer refers to an insight proper to the individual rather than the public at large, and thus seems to create a tension between a personal and an intersubjective experience of truth, nevertheless by divesting *logos* of *eros* he supplants the apolitical ontology transcendent to human beings with a linguistically mediated intersubjective dimension of reality. By cutting dialectic off from its transpolitical end, and characterizing it solely in terms of a mathematical or logical procedure of collection and division, Gadamer renders knowledge of the Good nonerotic and subject to the contingencies of consensus. This is mirrored in his suppression of the erotic dimension of Plato's dialectic—a dimension that is opened up by thinking about the order of the souls in Plato's works and that is typically discernable to the poet, who is more attuned to human nature than to universal and objective structures.

---

24. Rosen, "Role of Eros," 453.
25. Ibid., 467.

12

Plato's Dialectic Reconsidered

1. SYMPOSIUM AND REPUBLIC

GADAMER'S MATHEMATICAL APPROACH DENIES him the methodological precepts needed to access the literary dimensions of the dialogues in which particular contingencies of existence are represented. In this regard the work of Leo Strauss is pertinent. Above all, he emphasizes the importance of the dramatic structure of the dialogues to their philosophical meaning; but at the same time, according to Rosen, he downplays the significance of discursive reasoning that is "mathematical" insofar as it is rational, or oriented toward an impersonal truth of beings. By including, along with an eye for the mathematical form of Plato's thought, an ear for the dramatic qualities of the dialogues and their contribution to that form, an alternative view of Plato's dialectic bubbles to the surface that is in keeping with the erotic, hybristic character of the philosophic life—specifically, a hierarchy of being based on an idea of the Good beyond beings. This alternative notion of dialectic, that includes the contingent particulars for which Gadamer expresses regard, is sketched below with reference to the dramatic elements of the *Symposium* and *Republic* because they represent the two sides of Plato's philosophy: the erotic and the mathematical, respectively.[1]

The setting of the *Symposium* symbolizes the erotic dimension of philosophy. The inquiry into the meaning of love takes place in a private home, Agathon's, where the guests are more likely to speak freely in a quest for understanding that defies the city's norms. This climate of inquiry is compounded by the guests who are, with the exception of the resilient

---

1. I am in debt to Rosen, "Role of Eros" for my argument about the two ways toward philosophy.

Socrates, slightly inebriated. Their rational faculties are relaxed, which befits the topic at hand and also suggests that love is potentially dangerous to the sobriety and moderation of the public space. Rather than concern himself with the desire for personal security and the means of obtaining it, Socrates focuses on a love that transcends the city. This love of philosophy accounts for the structural cohesion of the dialogue.

The order of the speeches in the dialogue indicates a direction of inquiry that is transpolitical and therefore conceivably transgresses public norms. In the words of Allan Bloom, the speeches exhibit an ascent "from the most common experiences toward the peaks, beginning with the real bodily sexual attractions of individuals for one another."[2] The dialectical climb from base to higher forms of love begins with Phaedrus. He praises love for the usefulness of the lover to the beloved (178b); Pausanius distinguishes vulgar from heavenly love and eulogizes the latter for its duration (180c); Eryximachus locates love within a divided cosmos, opposite strife (185c);[3] Aristophanes urges love of the whole (192a); Agathon claims love is beautiful (195a); and Socrates asserts that love is philosophy (201d). At the end of the dialogue, Alcibiades completes the ascent by praising Socrates and declaring his love for him despite the fact that Socrates did not requite Alcibiades's show of affection (213a). One among the most handsome, powerful, and popular persons in Athens cedes to the superior power of philosophy.

The superiority of philosophy thus evolves from the base and self-serving Phaedrus toward higher levels of perfection, until even the most erotic man of Athens yields to his estranged love of philosophy. Bloom recapitulates of Plato's *Symposium*, "There is a dialectic established among these rhetorical speeches because they contradict one another, and one must try to resolve the contradiction in order to get any kind of a coherent account of the phenomenon."[4] Dorter echoes this assessment: "Each of the speeches of the *Symposium*, although presented in an apparently haphazard order, conveys a view that either stands in contradiction to its

---

2. Bloom, *Love and Friendship*, 433.

3. The "strife" in the cosmos between opposites, raised by Eryximachus, is resolved if the myth concerning the birth of Harmonia is taken into account. Harmonia, the wife of Cadmus, founding King of Thebes, was born from the union of Ares (war) and Aphrodite (love). Harmony arises from the unity of opposites.

4. Bloom, *Love and Friendship*, 434.

predecessor or else reconciles a previous opposition."[5] The ascent in the speeches toward higher degrees of knowledge corresponds to the "ladder of love," whereby love of bodies is transcended toward bodies in general, laws, branches of knowledge, and finally, immortality and timeless ideas (*Symposium* 205d–209e). In contrast to Gadamer, whose account of dialectic relies on a nonerotic model for understanding Plato's meaning and therefore abstracts from context, a turn toward the poetic aspect of the dialogues marks a return to pretheoretical experiences that exhibit gradations of meaning, culminating in a love of Beauty expressed by Diotima.

The *Republic* would seem to be ideally suited to a version of dialectic put forward by Gadamer. Plato's Socrates is notably brutal in his treatment of anything that might be a catalyst for the guardians' erotic desire; they are deprived of private property, the freedom to choose a wife, and private meals. They seem always to be subject to the scrutiny of rulers. Yet the dramatic setting of the dialogues and the character of dialectic in the *Republic* suggests that the topic under consideration, justice, is no less revolutionary than those who inquire into it. The conversation takes place at the home of Cephalus who is oblivious to the dangerous character of his guests' thoughts; in particular, those of the budding tyrant Thrasymachus and the philosopher Socrates. They represent the hubristic character of *eros* in its twin modes: love of the body and of the soul. In the *Republic*, love of the body is thwarted; consequently, in contrast to the *Symposium*, where the tyrant Alcibiades has the last word in judgment of philosophy, in the *Republic* the love of power is transformed through education in the creation of a perfect state. This education is in the sciences, but nevertheless culminates in a vision of the Good that Rosen points out is replete with sexual imagery in Books VII and VIII.[6]

---

5. Dorter, *Transformation of Plato's Republic*, 21. Dorter writes, "In the first speech, Phaedrus praises justice in terms of self-sacrifice, and is followed by Pausanius, for whom its value lies not in self-sacrifice but self-interest. Eryximachus follows these one-sided oppositions with a speech according to which the value of *eros* lies in its power to reconcile opposites. In the next speech too, that of Aristophanes, *eros* is a reconciling power; but where Eryximachus saw it as a corporeal force, Aristophanes portrays it as a spiritual one, piety. Agathon's speech, which follows, includes key aspects of all the previous speeches but opposes Aristophanes' divine-centered conception of virtue as piety with a human-centered conception of virtue as wisdom. Socrates explicitly rejects this in the next speech, and takes a position midway between Aristophanes' piety and Agathon's wisdom, by choosing a model of virtue that is in between them, namely love of wisdom."

6. Rosen, "Role of Eros," 473. Rosen observes that the sun generates visible things

When a turn is made, then, to the literary aspects of the dialogues alongside a regard for the universal character of knowledge as emphasized by Gadamer, an idea of the Good that transcends the city comes into view that accounts for the ascending character of Plato's dialectic. Socrates states that "... dialectic is the only inquiry that travels this road, doing away with hypotheses and proceeding to the first principle itself, so as to be secure" (533d); "anyone who can achieve a unified vision is dialectical, and anyone who can't isn't" (537c); and, finally: "Therefore, dialectics is the only method that advances this way—by demolishing assumptions—up to the source itself to secure confirmation; it gently drags the eye of the soul out of the odious ooze in which it lies buried and leads it upward, using the studies we've gone through as helpers for turning the soul around."[7] According to Plato's Socrates, dialectic is related to a synoptic vision of the whole, to first principles, and, finally, to a turning of the soul toward the idea of the Good (Book VII). The ascent toward the latter is described by Allan Bloom in reference to the *Republic* (533d, cited above):

> One is thus forced to seek for another and more adequate opinion which can comprehend the phenomenon covered by the contradictory opinions. The thoughtful observer recognizes that the opinions of the men in the cave are self-contradictory and thus meaningless as they stand. But this very contradiction points beyond them to more intelligible opinions and to objects which do not admit of such ambiguity. The many contradictory opinions are solicited by the one, comprehensive, opinion. Dialectic, beginning from commonly held opinions, will lead to an ultimate agreement.[8]

According to Bloom, dialectic does not oscillate between the visible and intelligible spheres, between *aporia* and *euporia*. It transcends the visible and reaches toward the intelligible through sciences that broaden and deepen the mind as it draws closer to its home in a wholly transcendent ground of Being.[9] Dialectic for Plato is a gradual climb through

---

and is an offspring or child of the Good.

7. *Republic*, 533d.
8. Bloom, "Interpretive Essay," 406–407.
9. John Sallis writes, "Like the upward-moving *dianoia*, [dialectic] begins with hypotheses and, according to Socrates' account, attempts to move upward so as to get 'behind' the hypotheses. In this respect, then, *episteme* is described as simply an upward-moving *dianoia* carried through to completion. From the viewpoint of *di-*

higher forms of intelligibility.¹⁰ But, as mentioned, the ascent beyond the cave is not exclusively of a rational or mathematical character. The *Republic* as a whole comes to be through a poetic or creative act; the philosophical life is compared to that of the eroticist, and is introduced with reference to love of boys, glory, and wine; and knowledge of the Good in the *Symposium* and *Republic* is revealed to be prophetic insight or divine madness.¹¹

2. PLATO'S IDEAS IN THE PHAEDO

When the poetic-erotic dimension of Plato's philosophy is taken into account alongside the mathematical-rational dimension, the character of Plato's dialectic shifts from a rational inquiry with others to an ascent from the way in which things are commonly spoken about to the vision of the Good experienced by Socrates. This climb is not visible independently of the setting, speeches, and order of speakers. There is thus a

---

anoia it is, of course, difficult to say very much about what this completion involves. Nevertheless, in Book VII the completion is described in various ways; yet in every case it is the analogy with *dianoia* that is primarily operative." Quoted in Decker, "Limits of Radical Openness," 16.

10. The ascent through higher orders of understanding is represented in the Divided Line. Socrates concludes the teaching of the Divided Line (509d–511e) with a summative statement on the rank order corresponding to forms of knowing and their objects: "Now for these four segments take four states that arise in the soul and give intellection to the highest segment, understanding to the second, trust to the third, and imaging to the last. Arrange them in a proportion and regard each as participating in as much clarity as its object does truth." *Republic*, 513e. Four parts of the Divided Line correspond to four affections in the soul (*noesis, dianoia, pistis, eikasia*) arranged in a proportion where "their degrees of clarity correspond to degrees in which their objects participate in truth." The lowest level of clarity belongs to fantasy, the highest to the intellect. Dialectic is the process of moving through the different states of the soul not simply toward a multiplicity of ideas, but toward an insight into Being itself above and beyond particular ideas, where hypotheses are discharged, where reasoning processes employ only ideas in dialectic (511b). If, however, what "is" is mistaken for an image, then the capacity to think has been eclipsed by the imagination; if what "is" is mistaken for something visible, then the intellect has been shrouded by the senses; if being is identified with a mathematical formula, then a higher level of insight has been achieved. But such an insight still depends upon images "of some higher cognitively original" (510e). Consequently, mathematical demonstrations are transcended toward the thing itself which the mathematicians presuppose. The dialectical ascent towards a permanent and unchanging idea in the Divided Line is coordinate with an existential transformation conveyed in the Allegory of the Cave.

11. Rosen, "Role of Eros," 473.

relation between the ideas as intelligible forms and experience that is not available to Gadamer's Plato. But if so, then the "second sailing," and the status of Plato's ideas and knowing as Gadamer understands them, must be reexamined.

Ideas

According to Gadamer, Socrates's solution in the *Phaedo* to the impasse of the nondialectical mode of inquiry illustrated by the natural scientists and metaphysicians is to inquire into the meaning of being through language, where it is possible to think a contradiction and so to converse about both a particular and a universal meaning, the many and the one, at the same time. The implication of this second sailing is that the ideas no longer transcend phenomena, but rather, in the words of P. Christopher Smith, "We see here that we humans, even in positing the forms of things, never leave the level of our human discourse."[12] The truth of the *logoi* does not refer to anything more real or outside of speech. The ideas within a linguistic context of meaning are linguistic hypotheses.[13] In so reasoning about the ideas, Gadamer effectively creates common ground between Plato and Aristotle—specifically, Aristotle's categories (which Gadamer takes over from Heidegger).[14]

At first this does not seem plausible. In the Categories a thing is identified by means of a defining property. In this case, the idea of man that is being negotiated in a conversation would be the properties of the man being spoken about, e.g., whether he is tall or large, a rational or speaking animal. However, as Gadamer explains in his discussion of the means of knowing, the essence or idea is irreducible to the means of knowing it. This suggests that the idea is a nondiscursive essence, hence Gadamer is surely not an Aristotelian. Yet the idea cannot be extralinguistic, because knowledge, including not-knowing, is mediated by language. Consequently, Gadamer says that the idea seen while speaking about it is absent. After stating that "unlike the thing itself, science in the soul is not timeless," and "insights do not belong to reality but to becoming (genesis)," Gadamer asserts:

12. Smith, *Hermeneutics and Human Finitude*, 143.
13. *PDE*, 70.
14. This is pointed out by Decker, "Limits of Radical Openness," 8. He says that, for Heidegger's Plato, truth is communicated by "a holistic network of interrelated meaning-structures" and not by "divine speech."

> Closest to the thing itself is obviously that moment of insight in which suddenly everything which contributes to the intelligibility of the internal relationship of the thing to itself is present to me all at once: the steps of the proof, the auxiliary construct, which was so hard to find, and its function in the proof, and so forth. More than anything else this evidentness, which makes one want to say, "I've got it!," contains the intrinsic relationship of the mathematical structure as such.[15]

In this passage Gadamer seems to be accessing a metaphysical principle that, in the context of the turn to the Good, would be a noniconic identification between what is said and what is meant (the idea). There is evidence of both Gadamer and Heidegger affirming such a possibility. In *Being and Time* Heidegger argues that "for primitive people the sign coincides with what it indicates."[16] In *Truth and Method* Gadamer argues that Greek philosophy began when the intimate unity of word and object, to the extent that the name was a substitute for the person, began to break down.[17] However, the identification of word and idea cannot be spoken, and it is certainly not a metaphysical principle. Instead, the identification is a result of thinking reflectively about a moment of insight. The proper locus for truth is therefore an experience about which nothing positive can be said. Gadamer writes:

> Plato wants to show that in speech, with its claim that speech's word names are right, no truth about how things actually are is attainable, and that one must know things that are, purely, starting from these themselves ... As a dialogue of the soul with itself, pure thinking of the ideas is voiceless [of speech], is merely the stream of sound through the mouth that originates in such thinking: anyone can see that this perceptible sound can claim no meaningful truth for itself.[18]

The positive meaning of the idea experienced "in truth" is represented by silence, but is still a part of the spoken language. Gadamer therefore finds space within linguistically constituted meaning for an idea that is beyond reason while nevertheless remaining within the horizon of language.

15. *DD*, 103.
16. *BT*, 76.
17. *TM*, 366.
18. Ibid., 368.

But is this position on the nature of ideas and the event of knowing them congruent with Plato's *Phaedo*? When Socrates turns to the *logoi* to study the ideas indirectly, he states, "I do not at all agree that he who investigates beings in *logois* is looking in icons any more than is he who investigates beings in *ergois*."[19] Studying beings in language is compared to studying them in actions. As Rosen says, courageous actions express the idea of courage, which is a condition of the soul (and not a deed). Similarly, language is an image or icon of ideas, but not an idea itself. In the passage quoted above, Socrates is, therefore, advising not to employ icons in the investigation of beings, but rather noniconic *logos* or divine speech. Noniconic *logoi* is *logos*. *Logos* is discernable, as Rosen says, to the mind's eye or Idea that is common to both speech and beings.

Socrates thus concludes, of the approach to study that he adopted after abandoning physics: "And positing in each case a *logos* which I judge to be the strongest, I establish [take my stand on the *logos*] as true whatever seems to me to agree with it, whether with respect to the cause or to any other things whatsoever; what does not [agree with the *logos*], I establish to be untrue."[20] According to this passage, *logos* is not a linguistic artifact, rule, or concept, nor an Aristotelian category. The truth of beings is not accessible through speech *qua* imagery but rather, through the intellect that sees the *logos* of things and can measure them against it.[21] This suggests that Gadamer's endeavor to render language primary, on the basis of the turn to language in *Phaedo* (99d), presupposes that he has apprehended the idea or essence itself; he asserts that, in language, one comprehends the entity in what it always is. In order for a meditative statement or essential definition to be uttered, Gadamer would have to have apprehended the look or idea of the being in question, would have to have seen "the essence" or identity of the thing apart from and in advance of its properties; for example, prior to identifying humans as rational animals he would have to have had a precategorical intuition of the human being.[22]

To recapitulate in slightly different terms, Gadamer argues that the ideas are linguistic hypotheses that cannot be reduced to the spoken word

---

19. Rosen's translation of *Phaedo*, 99e6–100a2. Rosen, *Question of Being*, 67.

20. Rosen's translation of *Phaedo*, 100a2–7). Ibid., 72.

21. Rosen writes, "Socrates looks through speech as the icons of things (in his example of the sun) to the sense or truth of the things as independent of thought revealed by the activity of looking." *Nihilism*, 152.

22. Rosen, *Question of Being*, 48, 51.

or any other means of knowing. But then on what basis does he know that he is speaking truly about anything? Gadamer's reply is that there is an "aha!" moment in which an identity obtains between what is said and what is meant.[23] This moment is a non-iconic linguistic moment, a moment of silence. However, as Rosen says of the Divided Line in the *Republic*, equally applicable to the *Phaedo*, "From the outset, *noesis* is associated with *logos*. It is not used anywhere in this section of the *Republic* to refer to silent intuition, if by 'silent' is meant the absence of discursive thinking."[24] Instead of Gadamer's event of "silent intuition," Rosen finds *logos* known by *noeisis*. From Gadamer's perspective this entails a transgression of human facticity, that is, the belief that we can step outside of our time and place to an eternal position transcendent to beings. In this case, the resultant language of *nous*/mind cannot but be an objective science. However, this argument bypasses the role of love and its creative act, poetry, in knowing what the being of a thing (idea) is. The *logos* seen by *nous* is translated (copied) by what Rosen calls a psychic demiurge into a poetic idiom.[25] The philosopher is thus separated from a direct noniconic knowledge of the ideas, not by death or mortality, but rather by love. It is after all love, according to the *Symposium*, about which Gadamer is notably silent, that is suspended between the mortal and immortal and accounts for philosophers yearning for the divine.

The ramification of this rereading of Socrates's turn in the *Phaedo* is that, contra Gadamer, the ideas are not icons or linguistic images. The motivation for equating them with the latter, I contend, is the impossibility or fear of an objective science (noniconic language) that is in turn circumscribed by an insistence on the limit of human knowing, i.e., death. However, this is a misunderstanding of Plato's ideas and way of knowing them. It is possible for the ideas to be principles of intelligibility transcendent to human making, i.e., language, insofar as it is not through death but through love, and therefore through a poetic medium of speech, that they are grasped. The doctrine of ideas is therefore represented by Plato in myths, allegories, parables, and similes, and is at bottom a likely story; the quest for an identity between the spoken

---

23. See *DD*, 116–118, 140.

24. *PR*, 265.

25. Rosen, *Question of Being*, 67–68. We can see this in *Republic* X where the ideas are made by a craftsperson but the making is comparable to growing or *poiesis*. This suggests that the "science" of eternal *a priori* ideas indicated in the *Phaedo* is a likely story.

word and the thing-in-itself is what motivates Gadamer's insistence upon human finitude or mortality as that which both separates us from and brings us experientially close to "the truth." Underlying Gadamer's understanding of Plato's dialectic, therefore, is another hidden doctrine. Stated otherwise, an identity between word and thing-in-itself is impossible because there is no scientific or mathematical understanding of the ideas by themselves without divesting *logos* of *eros*.[26]

The One and the Many

Gadamer reasons that the problem of the one and the many is Plato's "unwritten doctrine" that unlocks the dialectical structure of being in the dialogue form. There is, as Rosen says, a relationship between Plato's theory of ideas and his conception of mathematics and number.[27] Rosen points out that Being for Plato is a relationship between one and many— or, as he says, referring to Aristotle (*Metaphysics*, 987b19–988a15), between the monad and the dyad.[28] However, he is not prepared to follow Gadamer in equating the "one" with an idea. Were the number "one" the same as an idea, then there would be no position from which to recognize the one as one and in relation to the many. Another way of looking at this is through the problem of unity and identity of being. On the one hand, the identity of being "is that by virtue of which we know it to be the being that it is and hence, what it is." Conceptually, this means there are many different things, each countable and independent of one another (the many). On the other hand, the unity of the identity is "that by virtue of which the identity coheres and is available as what it is to our intelligence."[29] Unity is that which makes it possible to count in the first place and is always the same (one). We may then have many chairs, but they are nevertheless classified as "chair." However, neither identity (many) nor unity (one) is intelligible in and of itself, as Gadamer supposes. It is only possible to see that the many are one on the basis of a third that is common yet transcendent to both. It is thus from this third

---

26. Rosen also contests Gadamer's reading of the *Philebus*, arguing that it is about the physical universe and not eternal ideas *per se*, but is nevertheless of utility in understanding the triadic structure of the ideas. The physical thus casts light on the eternal. Rosen, "Ideas," 417–418.

27. Ibid., 409.

28. Ibid., 410.

29. Rosen, *Question of Being*, 71.

position, also referred to by Rosen as *logos*, that it is possible to recognize many chairs as chairs, or many as one. By thinking about the one and the many without this third term, Gadamer places himself in the position of being unable to differentiate the one from the many, a chair from chairs. Rosen captures this dilemma when he states that seven cows counted would be equivalent to asserting that the theoretical number seven is a cow.[30] By a circuitous path Gadamer returns to the very problem that perplexed the natural scientists and Anaxagoras in the *Phaedo*. By renouncing the transcendent status of the idea, he is unable to see what the particular and universal have in common that would enable him to recognize their difference, hence he conflates the intelligible with the sensible realm.

Gadamer is not without a retort to the prioritization of unity over difference and, by implication, the affirmation of an Idea transcendent to human making that grounds a dialectical hierarchy in Plato's philosophy. He reasons that the pyramidal structure in Plato's work captures the experience of advancing insight, but that this has nothing to do with Plato's ontology. He explains that "exemplary mathematics" (defended by Gaiser and Kramer) exhibits a "unified continuum extending from the number to the point, the line, the plane, and the solid (from arithmetic to stereometry)," and adds, "What this doctrine actually describes, I contend, is the felicitous experience of advancing insight, the *euporia* which the *Philebus* says (15c) happens to the person who proceeds along the proper path to the solution of the problem of the One and the Many—the way of discourse which reveals the thing being discussed."[31] The logic of point, line, plane, and solid represents the experience of advancing insight that corresponds to steps toward the idea of the Good; however, Gadamer is not prepared to grant that this experience points to a hierarchical ontology of Being in Plato's philoso-

---

30. *PR*, 292. Or as Rosen puts it, "But we cannot say that 'being' and 'many' can be used interchangeably, because each item in a manifold is what it is by virtue of its unity. I can say that a cow has many attributes, but in order to say that it is a many, I must first see it as the unity of many elements. Being is of course both one and many, but unity is prior to multiplicity because each element of that multiplicity is itself a unity, and so too is the manifold itself. A manifold could not exist, let alone be intelligible, if it were not this particular manifold, of such and such a kind, consisting of definite elements of such and such a kind, and thus it is a unity in two different senses, both of which are the foundation or basis for its manyness." Ibid., 287.

31. *DD*, 119. See also 150, 202, and *IG*, 134.

phy. Instead, he divorces the experience of advancing insight, or rather, Plato's phenomenological description of it, from such an ontology and maps the latter onto an arithmetical logic of one and two. The ontology he attributes to Plato is thus inconsistent with an experiential account of it. This interpretation is tantamount to separating Plato's ontology from his phenomenology as Gadamer understands it.

CONCLUSION TO PART FOUR

Despite having turned away from Hegel's dialectic because it resolved itself into an apodictic science, and having attempted instead to keep the meaning of the matter in question open by thinking about it in terms of a living conversation, Gadamer's account of dialectic remains doctrinaire. He develops a dialectical ontology that befits the dialogue form, but is nevertheless an abstraction from the existential-phenomenological character of Plato's dramas. By implementing Hegel's dialectic, Klein's number theory, and Aristotle's Categories in his reading of Plato, Gadamer arrives at an account of Plato's dialectic that is not in fact Platonic. Rather than subvert the tendency to reduce Plato to an objective system, Gadamer replaces Heidegger's theory that, for Plato, Being is permanently present with a theory that it is impermanent. As such, and despite claims to the contrary, Gadamer's Plato interpretation is regulated by a prior decision about the meaning of Being, in advance of the phenomena itself or of the direct tradition of interpreting Plato.[32]

---

32. Smith points to the same argument in Plato's *Theaetetus*. He argues that it is on the basis of the written word that we are inclined to envision an eidetic realm independent of and apart from the phenomena that might have been spoken about during a genuine conversation. After listing things we name *episteme* in reply to Socrates' question, "What is knowledge?", Socrates urges Theaetetus to think about the thing itself, to which the young mathematician replies by advancing a mathematical example of what he thinks Socrates means. Models direct thinking to permanent forms of things that detract from what Socrates is after in *dialegesthai*, whereby things "take on their being in the process of our finding the word (*onoma*) to name them." In short, *dianoia*, as mathematical reason, detracts from thinking about things by talking through them (*dialegeshtai*). There is a tension between these in Plato's philosophy that, according to Gadamer in *Truth and Method*, Plato resolves in the *Cratylus* in favor of the mathematical model of perfect forms. But Gadamer himself, I contend, reaches the same eidetic realm of forms, not through reflection upon the printed word—which, as Smith says, is Eric Havelock's thesis—but rather by a mathematical method of interpreting Plato's work that originates in Hegel and Klein. Smith, "Audible Word," 329.

Gadamer thus explains that his first book, *Plato's Dialectical Ethics* (1931), intended to develop a genetic-historical relationship between Aristotle and Plato using phenomenology.[33] Yet the starting point for a phenomenological description of the *Philebus*, he says, "... was Aristotle's two treaties on 'pleasure' in the *Nicomachean Ethics* (VII:10–13 and X:15)." The justification for starting to read Plato according to Aristotle, explains Gadamer, was that Aristotle's work is a response to questions raised by Plato in the *Philebus*. This is confirmed during an interview with Jean Grondin: Gadamer says that his first book was molded by Heidegger, and continues, "Plato is only a preparation for Aristotle."[34] However, if the starting point for interpreting Plato is Aristotle, then the question of what Plato thinks has been answered before Plato has even had a chance to speak. According to Gadamer, *Plato's Dialectical Ethics* "was an Aristotle book that got stuck."[35] Gadamer's self-confessed approach to interpreting Plato cannot be considered phenomenology if he interprets Plato according to an *a priori* knowledge of the answers to Plato's questions.[36] His professed prioritizing of the direct tradition or reading of Plato starting with the dialogues themselves is dubious. This fact in turn begs the question as to what the theory of human nature might be that underlies his mathematical method.

33. *GR*, 15.

34. Ibid., 425.

35. Grondin reasons that since Gadamer considered Aristotle to be answering Plato, Gadamer foregrounds the question in Plato's philosophy. Grondin, *Hans-Georg Gadamer*, 135. But if the questions are conceived after the answers, then they are not questions.

36. Sullivan observes that Gadamer adopted Aristotle's format for doing political philosophy: viewing the *polis* as both a reflection of the ethical individual and as a model by which to educate the person. Sullivan, *Political Hermeneutics*, 6.

Part V

The Politics of Exclusion

Introduction

By returning to the pretheoretical experience out of which the question of Being is asked, Gadamer decenters Heidegger's Plato and discovers in the dialogue form that the meaning of a thing's being is open to new interpretation, because in conversation the answer is not a foregone conclusion. The inquiries undertaken by Socrates typically end inconclusively, and Gadamer's dialogue with the tradition of philosophy is equally open to reinterpretation and revision. Inquiry, as Kevin Decker says on Gadamer's behalf, consists of attempting to bridge the situations of the interpreter and interpretant.[1] Dialogue thus has a dialectical structure that is open to and inclusive of different points of view. For neither Plato's Socrates nor Gadamer is there a definable standard of truth or goodness; instead, their meaning is negotiated within an intersubjective context exhibited by Socrates in Athens and formalized by Gadamer in his philosophical hermeneutics. It is thus not surprising to find Gadamer expressing his appreciation to Plato and the ancients. He writes that, "Insofar as they are my constant companions, I have been formed more by the Platonic dialogues than by the great thinkers of German Idealism;"[2] and that it was "ancient philosophy from which the whole of philosophy and its history disclosed itself to me."[3] Plato was instrumental in the development of Gadamer's hermeneutical philosophy. As Grondin relates, "The dialogical understanding of language that Gadamer intends to develop owes much, if not everything, to Plato

---

1. Decker, "Limits of Radical Openness," 9.
2. *PA*, 184.
3. Quoted in Wachterhauser, *Beyond Being*, 4.

and to his putting into perspective the order of pronouncements."[4] And at a Heidelberg conference in 1993, Gadamer said in response to a paper of Wachterhauser's that called hermeneutics anti-Platonic, "I am a Platonist."[5]

But it is not clear that Gadamer is a Platonist. Part IV demonstrated that, despite his intent to include the literary dimension of the dialogues in his reading of Plato and antipathy toward science and systems, Gadamer's actual performance is notably dismissive of those concerns. As a result of emphasizing the mathematical approach, he does not take into account the poetic-erotic vision of the Good in Plato's dialectic. This suggests that, even while speaking about openness and inclusion, Gadamer actually bases his hermeneutic on a theory of human nature about which he is not explicit but at which he nevertheless hints. He hints at it, for instance, in his depiction of Plato's school, which he describes as a community of participants engaged in ongoing didactic discussions "for whole days at a time" in "a living community" established among them.[6] But at the same time, what of the many, such as Callicles in the *Gorgias*, who have no desire to become philosophers? What of the majority of Athenians who snickered and thought that Socrates was foolish, or those who would prefer to be a musician like Meletus in the *Apology*, or a general like Nicias? What of those who simply believe that the highest truths are not available to either reason or rational discourse? If the light of the Good belongs to human beings, then everyone is equal but also the same—a position that is blind to substantive differences among persons. By exhorting philosophers to transform society into an image of themselves, Gadamer is urging a permanent revolution against the nonphilosophers Rosen believes Plato is decrying. Since this is carried out in the name of equality and inclusion, it is somewhat sinister in comparison to regimes that are openly totalitarian.

Gadamer would naturally shrink from this assessment of his hermeneutical philosophy. As Grondin points out, Gadamer's dialogical conception of language "owes much, if not everything, to Plato" because a living conversation precludes a fixed, objective order of statements.[7] Dallmayr fondly recalls that Gadamer was the "personification of the

4. Grondin, *Philosophy of Gadamer*, 131.
5. Wachterhauser, *Beyond Being*, xi.
6. *DD*, 126.
7. Grondin, "Universality of Hermeneutics," 326.

Socratic spirit: a spirit relentlessly committed to lively conversation in which all fixed positions are dissolved or transformed . . . "[8] Gadamer's Plato studies challenge the period of Heidegger's thought that roughly coincided with the rise of Fascism; to associate Gadamer's hermeneutic philosophy with yet another ideology of exclusion is incredible. It may, then, be possible to challenge the thesis that Gadamer's politics excludes the other as other by inviting into the conversation someone whose position on the nature of Being is contrary to Gadamer's—thus meeting the criterion of dialectic—and whose philosophical convictions have been loosely associated with a "closed society."

Stanley Rosen is one such candidate. He poses questions about the whatness of beings oriented toward a hierarchical classificatory scheme of ideas that culminates in the highest idea of all—an idea wholly transcendent to, rather than immanent to, beings. This would seem to be the theoretical justification for a conservative regime typically thought to be intolerant of differences and pluralism. In the *System of Logic* J. S. Mill writes of truths known by intuition, independently of observation and experience, that they are "the great intellectual support of false doctrines and bad institutions."[9] By "bad institutions" he means the conservative establishment, represented by such scholars as Coleridge, to which he and the Radicals were opposed. Since Rosen's Plato is continuous with the tradition Mill calls "intuitionism" insofar as he privileges truths arrived at through insight rather than demonstration alone, he is an ideal gauge by which to measure Gadamer's degree of commitment to an open society.

However, contrary to appearances, Rosen's interpretation of Plato is notably inclusive of the other as other. This is above all evident in his reading of Book I, where the most diverse characters in the *Republic* appear. Rather than draw a line between philosophers and nonphilosophers, authentic and inauthentic existence, Rosen (and other philosophers such as Allan Bloom, Kenneth Dorter, and Waller Newell) unearths possibilities in the character and thought of those dismissed by Gadamer as tyrants, and so allows them a place in the just state. Somehow the Good of Rosen's Plato, transcendent to beings, translates into a more inclusive politics than does the immanent Good of Gadamer's Plato, i.e., the Good brought into the cave. This then is the mystery: how a hierarchically

---

8. Dallmayr, "Hermeneutics and Justice," 92.
9. Quoted in John Passmore, *A Hundred Years of Philosophy*, 15.

ordered notion of Being that culminates in a transpolitical Idea of the Good can underlie a dialogical ethic that recognizes the other as other.

OUTLINE

Chapter 13 is a summary of Gadamer's interpretation of Plato's *Republic*. It is incomplete, but so is Gadamer's reading of Plato as he emphasizes themes that he believes are relevant to understanding the purpose of the dialogue; namely, to educate philosopher-citizens. Chapter 14 is a summary of Rosen's reading of the same dialogue, or rather of themes in it that intersect with those that interest Gadamer. Both of these chapters are preliminary background to a critical engagement of Gadamer's central claims. Chapter 15, "Human Nature," investigates what Gadamer takes to be the true nature of the human being: a rational nature, fulfilled in a state for philosophers, where differences between the private and public sphere and between classes and types of souls are dissolved. This interpretation of Plato is assessed using key passages from the *Republic* that support Gadamer's position, such as the watchdog imagery, and claims he makes about them, e.g., that desire is also rational. The final chapter, "Politics of Inclusion," consists of a detailed study of Gadamer's reading of Book 1. In contrast to Gadamer, whose ideal state consistently excludes nonphilosophers such as Thrasymachus, Rosen demonstrates in his interpretation of Plato a regard for nonphilosophers such as Glaucon and Cephalus. This suggests that a notion of the transcendent Good pure and simple is more consistent with a pluriform society than Gadamer's perspective that the Good-One is many.

13

Gadamer's Interpretation of the *Republic*

INTRODUCTION

IN KEEPING WITH GADAMER'S reticence regarding a synthetic representation of a philosophical system in its entirety, his interpretation of Plato's *Republic* principally appears in the following three essays: "Plato and the Poets" (1934), "Plato's Educational State" (1942) and "The *Polis* and Knowledge of the Good" (1978).[1] Despite Gadamer's openness to revising his point of view, there is no discontinuity in his thinking about the *Republic* over the forty-four years separating these works;[2] it is thus possible to construct with some measure of accuracy his overall view of the *Republic*. It is divided into themes, identified in the section headings below as hermeneutical situation (Book I); poets and education (Books II and III); city-soul-justice (Book IV); dialectic (Book V); the Good (Books VI and VII); and the myth of Er (Book X).

1. HERMENEUTICAL SITUATION: BOOK I

Gadamer introduces his interpretation of Plato's *Republic* with an account of Plato's motives and context that indirectly rivals that of the Straussians. Whereas the latter are inclined to consider the best life for Plato to be a private and apolitical reflection upon the nature of reality,[3]

---

1. "The Polis and Knowledge of the Good" is in *IG* and the other two essays are in *DD*.

2. The most poignant discrepancy is in Gadamer's interpretation of Plato in "Language and Logos," where he argues, using the *Cratylus*, that in reaction to the separation of word and object Plato grounds meaning in ideas that are opposed to language. *TM*, 366–378.

3. Gadamer asks, "Does Plato seek nothing more than to show that the conflict

Gadamer positions that reflection within a broader socio-political context from which he argues it never departs. Gadamer observes that, after World War I, Wilamowitz, Hildebrandt, Kurt Singer, and Paul Friedlander argued in favor of interpreting Plato according to his political circumstances as captured in the biographical *Seventh Letter*, which had recently been authenticated. The result of this approach is summarized by Gadamer: "We know from Plato's biography and above all from the unique testimony which he himself gives us in the *Seventh Letter* that Plato by no means used abstract theory to deduce this requirement that philosophers rule. On the contrary, it arose as the natural consequence of the political experiences of his youth."[4] Gadamer does not deny that the *Republic* contains "doctrines regarding the actual structure of the state or its institutions," but according to him they ought not to be the starting point for an interpretation of the dialogue. As indicated by the early dialogues, what is basic for Plato is not a theory of ideas, but rather the existence of Socrates from which Plato's philosophy springs. Gadamer thus defends interpreting Plato's philosophy according to the original political context to which Plato was responding. He reports somewhat emphatically of the *Seventh Letter*, "My view is that this autobiographical statement reveals something about the purpose of all of Plato's writings. Note that it does *not* say that Plato gradually came to the realization that his political aspirations were in vain after he was already an influential writer."[5]

In reply to what political dilemma did Plato write the *Republic*? Gadamer quotes at length from the *Seventh Letter* (325), wherein Plato explains that he decided to achieve societal reform through philosophy rather than politics. Although destined for political life, he was motivated by the corruption of Athens and the persecution of Socrates to develop a political philosophy demonstrating that the injustice of the city will not cease until philosophers become rulers. The philosophic life, therefore, ought not to be interpreted as an ideal independent of politics; on the contrary, it is the fulfillment of political or civic virtue. Consequently, Gadamer relates in "Plato and the Poets" that if Plato burned his tragedies, it was not because he had discovered that his talent lay in philoso-

---

between *theoria* and politics is irresolvable?" The note to this question reads, "Such is the opinion of Leo Strauss and Allan Bloom." *IG*, 70 n3.

4. *DD*, 73.
5. Ibid., 75.

phy; rather, after he met Socrates, Plato realized that the arts were not sufficiently robust to achieve the political reform he desired, whereas Socrates's philosophy was.[6] After meeting Socrates, therefore, Plato attempted societal reform through education, the *Republic* being one of at least twenty-five dialogues whose aim was "an education in citizenship. Ultimately, however, the latter is education in philosophy."[7] Far from being a threat to the stability of the political sphere, or extricable from it, the philosophical life is integral to the sustenance of politics. This claim has significant implications for Gadamer's interpretation of the *Republic* as a whole.

The initial focus of Gadamer's research during the war years was the education of the guardians and Plato's criticism of poets.[8] In the 1970s his Platonic studies turned to an account of the idea of the Good that was consistent with what he had already established; namely, that the principle of unity in the dialogues is practical reason or *phronesis*, exhibited in the figure of Socrates.[9] Just as he believes Plato worked his way toward philosophy from out of a nonphilosophical milieu, Gadamer finds that Plato has crafted Book II as a reply to a nonphilosophical circumstance. Gadamer writes of Book I:

> Hence the very failure of the discussion to define justice shows us how accurate Plato was in his characterization of the existing state as decadent. What began as mere ignorance of the just order in society and ignorance of justice as the power in the soul which sustains that social order, has now developed into a total perversion of justice.[10]

---

6. Ibid., 41.

7. Ibid., 73.

8. While the Nazis were in power, Gadamer immersed himself in classical studies, an interest represented by "Plato and the Poets" (1934) and "Plato's Educational State" (1942), both in *DD*.

9. So Gadamer's main concern includes Book II and IV, since the definition of the virtues and the structure of the healthy state are outlined in relation to the guardians' education; Books III and X, wherein Plato criticizes the poets; and Books VI and VII, since an education in the sciences, and the idea of the Good to which this leads, are discussed therein. Books VI and VII are the topic of "The Polis and Knowledge of the Good" in *IG*. Gadamer tends not to make much of the "myth of the metals" or "noble lies."

10. *DD*, 81.

In this passage Gadamer blurs the distinction between Plato's experience of a decadent Athens and the definitions of justice in Book I of the *Republic*. Book I, in particular the views of Polemarchus and Thrasymachus, reflects Plato's understanding of the moral dilemma confronting Athens. Unlike Cephalus, the "bearer of cult and custom" (or tradition, which Gadamer says is the "natural mirror image of philosophic life"),[11] his son and the teacher of rhetoric, having succumbed to the insidious effects of sophistry, implicate justice either implicitly or directly in the desire for power. Despite the pernicious influence of the Sophists upon the youth, it is not they who are Plato's primary concern, Gadamer believes.

2. POETS AND EDUCATION: BOOKS II, III, AND X

Gadamer observes that the poets are criticized first in Books II and III, and later in Book X. In the earlier books he argues that Plato objects to the poets on two grounds. First, he observes that Plato reproves Homer for portraying the gods as quarrelsome human beings; and second, that he is critical of Homer's image of Hades because it arouses a fear of death.[12] In Book X Gadamer reports that Plato criticizes the poets for taking the measure of their work from those who know the least (the many).[13] The criticism that their work is thrice removed from reality (595a–602b), he argues, is intended to emphasize "the claim of philosophy as dialectic to knowledge of true essences."[14] It is not art, but philosophy as a pure science of idealized forms that is being ridiculed. If so, then for Gadamer's Plato art-poetry in some way harbors truth. In a circuitous way, the ontological argument against poetry in the *Republic* returns to the importance of poetry to philosophy.

According to Gadamer, Plato's primary concern with the poets is that they equate education with *mimesis* rather than self-knowledge. Mimesis consists of copying models of excellence external to the self, thus alienating the self from self-knowledge. As a result of being formed by means of models external to themselves, the youth developed subjective self-understanding estranged from praxis (i.e., an aesthetic con-

---

11. Ibid., 78.
12. Ibid., 43.
13. Ibid., 61.
14. Gadamer, *Relevance of the Beautiful*, 121.

sciousness), which in turn compromised their ability to stand firm in the face of the Sophists' twisted instruction to pursue power and pleasure rather than nobility and justice. Gadamer suggests that this shortcoming is illustrated by Homer, and points out that in Book X, Plato contrasts Homer to such figures as Solon and Chardonas, Thales, Anarcharsis, and Pythagoras. The latter were renowned for their achievements, a fact which for Gadamer means that they had self-knowledge, since it is impossible to order one's life well on any other basis. Without the same self-knowledge, by contrast, Homer left behind neither a school of thought nor followers, and instead merely stirred the passions.[15] Plato's ontological criticism of the poets is thus motivated by the moral ramifications of their neglect of self-knowledge, witnessed by him in the breakdown of Athenian culture.

With a view to what was required in his own culture, therefore, Plato begins the *Republic* by demonstrating the effects of the Sophists' teachings on Polemarchus and Thrasymachus. Upon cross-examination these two exhibit distorted views of justice that, according to Gadamer, demonstrate the need for education based on something other than the "imitation" advanced by the poets. Although Socrates has been present to the discussion from the outset, representing the potential for philosophy in the midst of sophistry,[16] Gadamer suggests that the formation of genuine citizenship does not become an issue until Book II, when Glaucon and Adeimantus join the conversation. Their presence signals a shift in the questioning from matters of *techne* and power to care of the soul.[17] However, Socrates argues that justice may be easier to see "writ large" in a state than in a soul; consequently, he proceeds to construct a description of a just state and from there to make inferences about the condition of an ordered soul (368c).

15. Ibid., 41. Gadamer concludes on p. 60, "For this reason Homer fails the test which Solon, for instance, passes: the test of having been effective in shaping human life." (See *Republic*, 599d–600d.)

16. Gadamer writes in "Plato's Educational State," "Thus the paradoxical philosopher-king, though long kept in the background and explicitly introduced only after considerable delay, is essentially implied in the way the question is put from the beginning." *DD*, 83.

17. Glaucon and Adeimantus want Socrates to demonstrate what justice and injustice are in themselves. Toward this end Glaucon presents the "popular view" of justice, that it is not natural but conventional, an agreement of the weak to protect themselves from the strong (357a); and Adeimantus, that people praise justice not for itself but for the rewards it brings. By refuting them Socrates demonstrates what justice is.

With respect to this construct of a just city (an education in understanding what justice is) Gadamer explains that, for Plato, the city of pigs, in which each does a singular job because bound by necessity, is an "inimitable mixture of nostalgia and satire," irony and caricature.[18] This assessment is derived from Plato's assertion that the city is healthy and true.[19] Gadamer considers this statement ironic because truth is historical, whereas the city of pigs, as he says, never has and never will exist because it omits the fact that "man is a profligate being who desires to prosper beyond his present circumstances."[20] Plato's attribution of "truth" to the "healthy vegetative state" is a caricature of the truth about justice that is confirmed by the rise of the second city, the city of excess. According to Gadamer, the state of discontent is, in fact, for Plato "true" because it is historical and parallels his own life: the rise of justice (Socrates) amidst injustice. Were it not for a prior condition of injustice in the luxurious city, the just city could not have come into being historically. The guardians, he points out, are distinct from the workers because (1) their work does not aim at production and (2) their skill is the knowledge that distinguishes friend from foe.[21]

After having described the coming-to-be of justice in terms of the luxurious state (372d–427c), Plato turns to the education of the guardians (376c–415d). In this regard, Gadamer argues that Plato, as mentioned, is shifting the basis for education from the imitation of a measure external to the soul (*mimesis*) to a standard that is internal to the soul (self-knowledge). According to Gadamer's Plato, the soul is divided by two contrary impulses, the bestial and the peaceful, which would divide the self against itself were it not for self-knowledge.[22] Self-knowledge for Gadamer's Plato is *sophrosyne*/wisdom, which weaves a harmony between the two contrary impulses. Rather than being an enemy to itself, through self-knowledge the soul becomes a friend to itself. On the basis of the self-understanding won through what is ultimately an education in "the Good" (discussed below), the person is capable of ordering his external affairs according to what is right for the soul. Gadamer explains this in a reference to Book V,

---

18. *DD*, 54.
19. Referring to the city of sows, Socrates says, "I think the city we just described was true and healthy" (Plato's *Republic*, 373).
20. *DD*, 51.
21. Ibid., 56.
22. Ibid., 54.

where he interprets a "concluding expatiation on the philosophical education of the guardians and ruler" as follows:

> The Greeks have a lovely expression for this intrinsic correlation between the good constitution of the soul and *Dasein*'s knowledge of itself. They call it *sophrosyne*, which Aristotle glosses as *sosoussan ten phronesin* (*Nicomachean Ethics* 1140b). In preserving *phronesis*, in existing as knowing, *Dasein* attains to a lasting governance of itself.[23]

The highest form of knowledge is not silent communion with the pure and unadulterated Ideas; instead, the best life for Gadamer is "a lasting governance" of the self.

But this requires maintaining a correlation between the good (of the soul) and practice. Such a correlation yields *phronesis* (Aristotle) or Plato's equivalent, *sophrosyne*, which is to say, the unity of theory (*sophia*) and practical wisdom (*phronesis*) in what Gadamer calls existing as knowing. The fact that Gadamer refers to the self as *Dasein* is significant to understanding the identification of existence with knowing. He is referring to Heidegger and the thought that Being belongs to human beings, which in the passage above surfaces in terms of "the good constitution of the soul." Following Heidegger's existential ontology, "the Good" for Gadamer belongs to the soul and empowers or enables the philosopher to resist temptation and flattery and abide in self-knowledge in order to arrange life accordingly.[24] Insofar as philosophers exist according to what they know, then they are self-governing; or, as Aristotle says in the *Politics*, they both rule and are ruled by themselves.[25]

---

23. Ibid., 88–89. Also, he writes on p. 86, "Thus the constitution of oneself as an internally well-ordered soul is the true measure of *Dasein*'s self-understanding, i.e., of *Sophia* (443e)."

24. Gadamer writes, "Plato seeks precisely that power of the human soul which constitutes and sustains the state, its political 'fertility', as it were (*gonima*, 367d), from which arise the state and what is right and just." Ibid., 82.

25. Aristotle explains that the good citizen must have the knowledge to both rule and be ruled. The knowledge to rule comes from being ruled, so the citizen is free but also governed. *Politics*, 1277b. By suggesting that the citizen has knowledge of "Being" ("the Good"), Gadamer "platonizes" Aristotle's notion of the citizen who does not require a knowledge of ideas. This may be because Gadamer reads Heidegger's notion of authenticity into *phronesis* and *sophrosyne*.

3. CITY-SOUL-JUSTICE: BOOK IV

Gadamer observes of the *Republic* "that the disclosure of what justice is starts by displaying it in the order of a just state and then proceeds to a translation of what is seen there, into justice in the soul (427d)."[26] Justice in the state, Gadamer goes on to explain, consists of each class minding its own business (*ideopragein*), which is included in the notion of each class (workers, guardians, and rulers) doing that for which it is fit. The order of the soul is the same. Gadamer writes, "The order of the state would of necessity correspond to that of the soul (435bc)," and continues, "in a quite remarkable analysis Plato shows that there are indeed three parts to the soul, which correspond to the three classes in the political order."[27] Love of learning corresponds to the rulers, zeal to the guardians, and desire to the workers. There is a one-to-one correspondence between the state and the soul for Gadamer. As for the virtues (wisdom, temperance, justice, and courage), he assigns courage to the warriors, wisdom to the leaders, and *sophrosyne* (temperance) and justice to all classes.[28] By *sophrosyne* Gadamer means "unanimity about the 'thinking for everyone' carried on by the governing classes (430d–432)."[29] He then stipulates that the justice of the state (i.e., the classes) and the flourishing of the virtues presuppose "everyone's doing what befits him, or *ideopragein* (433b)."[30] Just as *ideopragein* gives unity to the state and soul, so too does it give unity to the virtues. Gadamer calls the latter "political justice," which he says is derived from the order of the soul.[31] Political justice is derived from the order of the soul presumably because it is what remains after the other virtues have been defined, i.e., when every virtue and part of the soul minds its own business.

The correlation between the parts of the soul and "political justice" might at first seem perplexing. How can outer virtue or action

---

26. *DD*, 83.

27. Ibid., 85.

28. Gadamer writes, "The doctrine of the parts of the soul cannot be disassociated from the definition of the virtues insofar as the latter is based upon the former." Ibid., 87–88. He does not, however, explain how the virtues are individually based on the parts of the soul.

29. Ibid., 84.

30. "*Ideopragein* is required of the class of workers as well as the governing classes and it alone gives the state its unity." Ibid.

31. Ibid.

correspond to an inner condition of the soul? In reply, the editor P. Christopher Smith explains that Gadamer agrees with Hegel's claim in "The Law of the Heart" that Kant and Rousseau could not reconcile what is thought subjectively with what occurs in the external world. Smith adds on Gadamer's behalf, "no such discrepancy afflicts Greek moral philosophy."[32] The order of the soul is thus reflected in the virtues; or, as Gadamer says, the latter are derived from the former. That is to say, the virtues are derived from the order of the soul and are mirrored in the order of the state. Gadamer, therefore, refers to the "inner order of the state" that brings about "the reconciliation and unification of the three classes," and says that justice of the soul similarly consists of an "inner action by which it attains unity with itself (443cd)."[33] In short, for Gadamer there is a correspondence between the order of the state (classes) and the soul (virtues).

If there is a correspondence between the order of the state and that of the soul, then the question arises as to the basis upon which that argument might stand, considering that Plato makes distinctions between classes and thus presumably between kinds of souls. Gadamer argues that the guardians are the class of all human beings, hence everyone in the just state partakes of their nature. Gadamer supports this position with reference to *sophrosyne* in Book IV. The latter means "The intrinsic correlation between the good constitution of the soul and Dasein's knowledge of itself."[34] Gadamer also argues that *sophrosyne* is what Plato means by *phronesis*.[35] *Sophrosyne* (temperance or moderation) therefore consists of a correspondence between self-knowledge and, as mentioned earlier, practical goodness or right living. Since Plato says that *sophrosyne* is wisdom, as noted by Gadamer (443e), and belongs to every class, he reasons that everyone in the just state is a philosopher.

It is notable that in Book IV, where the order of the state, soul, and virtues are discovered, there is no mention of the idea of the Good. Nevertheless, Gadamer says that the Good, although discussed in Book VII, seems to follow from Book IV because at the outset of Book VI, where the Divided Line and Simile of the Sun are discussed, "Plato

---

32. Ibid., 86 n5.
33. Ibid., 89.
34. Ibid., 88–89.
35. Ibid., 89.

reminds us of the achievements of Book 4."[36] In addition, and more importantly, Gadamer reads Plato dialectically, and thus integrates the ideal or utopian demands of the *Republic* in Books VI and VII into the previous chapters so as to yield a unity of theory and practice in a concrete good.[37] He therefore claims, after discussing the components of the soul that correspond to classes in the city in Book IV (434d–444e), that the conclusion of the dialogue has been reached;[38] that in Book IV the Good, although not mentioned there, is simply recognized as being indispensible to the virtues.

4. DIALECTIC: BOOK V

Despite connecting Book IV directly to Books VI and VII, Gadamer comments on two themes in Book V: the best regime (449a–474a) and the definition of a philosopher (474b–480a). He also comments on the decay of the best regime in Books VIII and IX. In the background is his conviction that Plato intends us to read dialectically; or, as indicated, to relate the theoretical dimensions of the dialogue (such as the Allegory of the Cave and education in the sciences) "to their opposite, in order to find, somewhere in between, what is really meant—that is, in order to recognize what the circumstances are, and how they could be made better."[39] In short, Gadamer treats the theoretical dimensions at one pole in order to balance them against the dystopian reality of historical existence at the other ("the so-called democracy of Athens at that time and not only there"), and thereby strike a middle ground between them that he understands to be Plato's authentic teaching. With respect to the best

---

36. *IG*, 67. *Republic*, 504a.

37. Gadamer has mixed thoughts about this possibility and argues for it despite the following note about the Good: "Plato's reservation of the actual question about the Good for Book 6 would seem to be fundamental to the composition of the *Republic* as a whole. Whether a four-book *Republic* ever existed or not, the effortless and fortuitous introduction of the question of the sharing of women and children, which leads to the extended discussion, may surely be assumed to be as deliberate as the avoidance of the word *agathon* in Book 4." *IG*, 80 n7. Gadamer's argument is that the Good is presupposed in Book IV, so Plato is silent about it.

38. "Once the *aretai* have all been shown to have the character of knowledge, the analogy between the harmony of the classes in the *polis* and the harmony of the soul—its "health"—would seem to suffice as an answer to the question about the definition of justice. With the conclusion drawn in Book 4 the goal has been reached." Ibid., 66.

39. Ibid., 71.

regime in Book V, where wives and children are held in common and the family is thus eliminated (457c–461e), Gadamer explains that it must be understood according to a prior context of "the ruinous role of family politics, nepotism," and the rule of philosophers according to dynastic power politics at that time.[40] As for Books VIII and IX, where degenerate regimes and souls are analyzed (545c–592b), he argues for the merging of reason with historical reality, and says that Plato teaches that "no system of human social order, however wisely planned or thought out, can endure."[41] Historical reality is defined by contingencies and limits that defy control by any rationalized system. Nevertheless, that is not to say that reason and utopias are useless or irrelevant. Gadamer writes, "human reason is not restricted to the realm of utopia and strict ideal order. On the contrary, it is fully capable of expanding into the historical world of vague regularities. The disorder of human things is never complete chaos."[42] The extremes of rationality are no less damaging than the extreme of nonrational existence, i.e., disorder. The key to understanding Plato's dialogue is to see how reason expands into historical life, and not the renunciation of either politics or theory.

According to Gadamer, discussion of the possibility of creating the just state culminates in the high point of the dialogue, the office of philosopher-king. This leads him to reflect upon Plato's comments on the nature of philosophy in Book V (474b–503e). Gadamer reasons that Plato contrasts the life of philosophers with that of the eroticist, the lover of sight, and the dreamer. The philosopher participates in these three dispositions, but in a fundamentally different way from others. Whereas the eroticist "is not predisposed to any specific love in preference to others" (474), the philosopher's *eros* will "aim at fundamentally one thing in all loves"; whereas the lovers of sight love all things that are beautiful, the philosopher's sight yearns to see "the one Absolute Beauty in all things." In contrast to the dreamer whose mind is captivated by images, the philosopher's mind is awake and in a position to see "true Being itself." However, even this depiction of the best life is biased toward an extreme; namely, the love of learning. Gadamer thus argues that Plato

40. Ibid.
41. Ibid., 73.
42. Ibid. In "Plato's Educational State" Gadamer suggests that the perfect regime declines when citizens both lack knowledge of the whole and relate to one another through *techne* and their tyrannical nature takes over. *DD*, 85–87.

unites the philosopher's love, sight, and knowledge of the one true Being with politics in the office of the philosopher-king (503b).

5. THE IDEA OF THE GOOD: BOOKS VI AND VII

Gadamer disagrees with those who maintain that Plato seeks "no more than to show that the conflict between *theoria* and politics is irresolvable."[43] On the contrary, Gadamer believes that Plato argues for their unification, even in matters pertaining to an education in the sciences (Book VI) and the idea of the Good (Book VII). An education in the sciences, from the particular and concrete to the universal and abstract (521c–535a), is, on the one hand, intended to habituate the philosopher in thinking independently of the senses. An education in the sciences that raises the soul out of the mire and turns it toward universal truths is preparatory for knowledge of an ultimate good that transcends convention.[44] The aim of a theoretical education is, therefore, not about the application of general rules to particular cases; that sort of theory is proper to the crafts. Instead, the training in the sciences has for its aim matters of an ethical or moral import that are distinct from conventions. As Gadamer says, an education in the sciences enables philosophers to know that for the sake of which all things are carried out, i.e., their ultimate justification.

However, even the vision of the Good is not wholly "other-worldly," even though it is independent of the senses. Gadamer explains that the message of the Allegory of the Cave is not only that philosophers are blinded before the light of the Good, but also that by returning to the cave they must adjust themselves to the darkness, which has positive value for Gadamer in that "it enlightens us regarding the putative worthlessness of the theoretical human being in practice."[45] Those who return will have to contend with shadows and images of justice in human affairs (517d). But having envisioned a universal and unchanging idea, they have also learned to "resist public adulation and the hidden seductiveness of power which tempts."[46] That is to say, an education in the idea of the Good enables the philosopher to resist the erotic side of his nature

---

43. *IG*, 66.
44. Plato's *Republic*, 526e, 533d, 534d.
45. *IG*, 75.
46. *DD*, 41.

that might yield to the temptation of power and popularity.[47] Rather than becoming an Alcibiades, philosophers become, through an education in the sciences and the Good, a Socrates: the best of citizen-philosophers.

The Good for Plato is therefore separate from what is technically good yet participates in the sensible sphere in the sense that the Good is the ground of practical wisdom (*sophrosyne*), which Gadamer takes to be Plato's word for what Aristotle meant by *phronesis*.[48] To illustrate the Idea of the Good in its concrete manifestation, he cites Socrates, who inspired Plato by his ability to remain steadfast, to hold to what is right in discourse and deed amidst a crumbling society.[49] Insight into the immovable and permanently present Idea is translated by Gadamer directly into the practical virtue of remaining true to oneself—that is, authentic, existing as knowing. To demonstrate Plato's commitment to the "incarnation" of the Good as practical virtue, Gadamer cites dialogues in which the ideas are typically demonstrated to be "separate"—namely, the *Philebus*, *Phaedo*, and *Republic*—and observes that they address the good in human life. Dialogues on the immortality of the soul, wisdom, and the idea of all ideas are framed by the question of what should be done here and now. This suggests that there is an inner connection between "Plato's universal ontology . . . and making distinctions that links up with the good in human life."[50] By developing a structural coherence in the *Republic* on the basis of synthesizing the metaphysical and physical realms in Books VI and IV, Gadamer is justified in reasoning that knowledge of the Good is presupposed by every other virtue, part of the soul, and class in a just city. He thus concludes that justice is realized when the citizens become philosophers.[51]

---

47. *IG*, 95–97.

48. *DD*, 88–89. Gadamer writes, "*Sophrosune* belongs to all the classes, to the rulers as well as the ruled." Ibid., 84.

49. *IG*, 83; 96–97.

50. Ibid., 93. Gadamer also remarks (82) that the Good appears as early as Book I during a discussion of power and self-control.

51. So we find Gadamer reasoning, "For Plato each person belongs to the whole." *IG*, 69. "The state is an ordering of government and populace founded upon the fact that the whole is present in each individual and his action" (*DD*, 84), where "the whole" refers to knowledge of the Good/Being. And finally, in reference to Hegel, "It was the purpose of this education to strengthen the philosophical element in the guardians in order that the general and universal (Hegel: *das Allgemeine*), *koine sympheron*, might prevail." *DD*, 87.

6. THE MYTH OF ER: BOOK X

According to Gadamer, the myth of Er in Book X is the culmination of the moral education of the philosophers. Books I to IX were intended to mend the rift between the inner self and the practical life (aesthetic consciousness) created by the imitation of false models of virtue, e.g., Achilles. According to Gadamer, this was accomplished by praising justice. Praising justice does not detract from the order of the soul but resonates with it; in so doing it brings that which is external to the self, i.e., the creation of a just state in word, into harmony with the inner self or self-knowledge. The *Republic* is a work of art, but for Gadamer it is not imitation of an external reality (and for the same reason is not *mythos*). It is a projection of what the soul already is that corrects or educates the self divided against itself (or ignorant of its own justice). By the end of the dialogue Socrates celebrates the achievement of this philosophical education by creating a myth that is, like the dialogue as a whole, a figurative expression of self-knowledge (which is of concern to everyone). However, while elements of the myth of Er such as the transmigration of the soul and governance of eros "derive their existence from the inner certainty of the soul," Gadamer points out that the myth is suffused with irony, jocular play, and jest. This suggests that, within the image of perfection created by Plato, the truth speaks playfully, or is experienced playfully—a conclusion that necessarily follows from a prolonged Socratic and systematic interrogation of appearances for the sake of a genuine reality, since it is precisely an appearance or illusion of sorts that in the end truth becomes visible by chance.[52]

---

52. *DD*, 66–72.

14

Rosen's Interpretation of the *Republic*

INTRODUCTION

Rosen's interpretation of the *Republic* is in debt to the methods and teachings of Leo Strauss. This is particularly true of Rosen's development of an approach to the dialogue that he believes is coordinate with the mathematical and poetic dimensions of Plato's philosophy. This chapter begins by elucidating the rudiments of Rosen's Platonic studies from his conversation with Strauss, after which Rosen's view of the *Republic* is examined according to the three themes of poetry and education (Books II, III, IV, V, and X); philosophy and poetry (Books VII and X); and ascending forms of intelligibility (Books VI and VII).[1] Rosen's commentary covers Books XIII to IX, but since Gadamer is not concerned with those chapters, including them in a summary of Rosen's interpretation would add nothing to an understanding of the contrast between the two thinkers.

1. ROSEN AND STRAUSS

Stanley Rosen's view of Plato was developed over decades of reflecting upon his teacher's interpretation. After completing his dissertation on Spinoza in 1955, Rosen's research initially affirmed Strauss's reading of the *Republic*.[2] In *Plato's Republic: A Study*, Rosen expresses his debt to Strauss above all with respect to understanding the dramatic structure of the dialogue, yet at the same time points out why he eventually came to

---

1. Rosen's commentary includes Books VIII to IX, but since Gadamer is not concerned with those chapters, including them in a summary of Rosen's interpretation would not add anything to the contrast between them.

2. *PR*, 5.

disagree with his teacher and develop a different reading of the purpose of the *Republic*, Plato's doctrine of ideas, and esotericism. A sketch of the similarities and differences between Rosen and Strauss helps bring into focus a summary view of Rosen's understanding of the dialogue.

According to Rosen, Strauss did not take seriously Plato's doctrine of ideas, suggesting that he did not take seriously the possibility of noetic perception of pure forms.[3] However, if this is the case, then Strauss, as Rosen points out, has no metaphysical or ontological foundation for his own claim to have discerned fundamental and comprehensive solutions and problems through Plato's philosophy. But then what could be the foundation for such claims? Rosen suggests that it is poetry or rhetoric.[4] If the idea of the Good is then known solely to poetry, poetic madness, or divine dispensation, then philosophical truths are surpassed by revealed truths (which Strauss places in opposition to one another in *Natural Right and History*).[5] In keeping with this hypothesis, Strauss suggests that the (esoteric) truth revealed by Plato in the *Republic* is that the perfect regime is impossible because it is against nature. And it is against nature because, as Strauss says, it insists upon the equality of the sexes and absolute communism, which is destructive of a love of one's own and the body. In the ideal state parents and children do not know one another as such, nor do siblings.[6] According to Strauss, no amount of rhetorical force could bring about this total dissolution of the family.

Rosen's reply to Strauss is to question the assumption that Plato's teaching about the impossibility of the best regime is esoteric (or revealed to a few). Rosen agrees with Strauss on the impossibility of the just state, but disagrees that it is a hidden teaching. On the contrary, he points out that Plato is notably blunt about the impossibility of the just state; for example, it is stated explicitly that everyone over the age of ten is expelled (which would include the founders),[7] and that familial

---

3. The fact that Plato's theory of ideas is, as Strauss says, incomplete is not an argument against the possibility of philosophy; it is an invitation to develop better arguments for the necessity of the ideas. Rosen, "Role of Eros," 425.

4. Rosen, "Strauss and the Quarrel," 162–163.

5. Ibid., 159.

6. Living arrangements and communism (no private property or money) are discussed in 415d–427c of the *Republic*.

7. *PR*, 391.

reforms contradict and offend the Athenians.[8] Above all, Rosen points out, the creation of such a state is not feasible for Plato because human beings are at best lovers of wisdom; consequently, there is neither a detailed discussion of laws nor any provision for interpreters of them, i.e., those astute in practical wisdom. Rosen concludes, "One of the great weaknesses of the Socratic city is that it never establishes the practical value of the intuition of pure Ideas."[9] Rosen's point is that the pure intuition of ideas has no practical value, which is why Plato is clear about the impossibility of creating a perfectly just state.

The positions held by Rosen and Strauss on Plato's esotericism is relevant to what they consider to be the purpose of the dialogue. On the one hand, Strauss believes that although the best regime is impossible, it is nevertheless a standard against which to "see the essential limits" of a city.[10] But, as Rosen says, Strauss also denies that this standard is intelligible to reason, in which case the *Republic* cannot have been written to educate philosophers; it must, rather, have been written for gentlemen—that is, rural aristocratic citizens who love what is best but cannot explain why, or who accept noble lies without understanding why they are medicinal. From Rosen's perspective, by displacing the philosopher with the poet Strauss severely compromises Plato's intentions.

Contrary to Strauss, Rosen believes that Plato is blunt about the impossibility of the just regime because he is warning the many to guard against the hubris of philosophical *eros*. If philosophers truly become kings, they will be brutal toward nonphilosophers, as love of the Good and True is uncompromising. This indicates that no matter how great the philosophers' desire to rule, and so to fulfill their erotic longings (i.e., to create a world that is a mirror image of themselves), it is best for them to retire into a private life where truth and justice can be contemplated in peace. The perfect state for philosophers is a palace of the mind, which is why they want to discuss the *Republic*.

---

8. Ibid., 390.

9. Ibid., 392. Rosen argues that if the best regime is impossible, then Socrates would not take seriously the account of the best city and approve of its extreme measures to achieve justice (390–393). Rosen also looks to Aristotle and reasons that if the unfeasibility of the polity were the central message of the work, as Strauss contends, then it "could have been defended directly" by Plato. Rosen looks to Aristotle in this regard who openly denounces Plato's ideal regime as impossible and recommends instead, in the words of Rosen, "a moderate aristocratically inclined democracy" (5).

10. Ibid., 138.

From Rosen's perspective Strauss overlooks the duplicity of Socrates speaking to two audiences: philosophers, whom he attracts, and non-philosophers, whom he repels. Furthermore, he believes that Strauss overlooks the danger of hubris within philosophical *eros* (which cannot be fulfilled without being unjust).[11] Nevertheless, as suggested earlier, Rosen initially agreed with Strauss's approach to Plato; specifically, he agreed with Strauss's literary approach to the dialogue, evident in both interpretation and style of composition. Strauss writes:

> One cannot separate the understanding of Plato's teaching from the understanding of the form in which it is presented. One must pay as much attention to the How as to the What. At any rate to begin with one must even pay greater attention to the "form" than to the "substance," since the meaning of the "substance" depends on the "form." One must postpone one's concern with the most serious questions (the philosophic questions) in order to become engrossed in the study of the merely literary question.[12]

Strauss foregrounds the literary aspects of the dialogue—the way a speech is phrased, its location relative to other speeches, the character of the speaker, and the setting. These issues, he says, precede and indeed direct an interpretation of the "substance" of Plato's teaching.

With respect to his own literary style, in *The City and Man* Strauss plays the role of a Socratic conversationalist contesting with a challenger. He first denounces the possibility of setting forth anything like a doctrine or theory of Plato's ideas. This is not possible because although Plato is mentioned twice in the dialogues (present at the trial of Socrates, absent during his death), "In none of his dialogues does Plato ever say anything."[13] In other words, there is no more sense in saying "that Plato held such and such a view" on the basis of the dialogues than to reduce Shakespeare to the words of Macbeth. Continuing to mimic a conversation, Strauss hears the objection that surely Socrates is Plato's spokesperson. He counters that this "is still sillier" and explains that Socrates is being ironical, that he varies his speech according to the character of those with whom he speaks, at times interrogating their assumptions, at other times speaking at length in

---

11. As Rosen says, "every attempt to enact the truth in human affairs without compromise leads to a reversal of that truth." Ibid., 9.
12. Strauss, *City and Man*, 52.
13. Ibid., 50.

order to yield or confirm agreement on "salutary opinions."[14] Socrates is, moreover, taught by others, e.g., Parmenides and Diotima. The best place to discern Plato's views, Strauss argues, is in the selection of speakers, themes, and titles of the dialogues.[15]

Rosen shares with his teacher a concern for the dramatic form and rhetorical elements of the text. He says that he agrees with those "for whom the successful interpretation of a Platonic dialogue depends, among other things, upon careful attention to such topics as these: the dramatic setting, the character and intelligence of the main interlocutors, the difference between the rhetoric of living conversation and scientific or analytic discourse, . . . "[16] This influence of Strauss upon Rosen's approach to reading Plato carries over, as it does for Strauss, into his style of composition. Like Strauss, who simulates a conversation in his interpretation of the *Republic*, Rosen writes, "I have made a special effort to write in a style that is compatible with that of Socrates himself."[17] Rosen contends with adversaries named and unnamed throughout his study of Plato. Strauss is one such interlocutor.

Yet Rosen is critical of Strauss's lack of technical detail and analytic rigor. He argues that Strauss's discussion of the titles of Plato's works is inconclusive and that his distinction between the narrated and performed dialogues is inaccurate.[18] Rosen identifies Strauss's strength, an emphasis upon the dramatic aspects of the dialogues, acknowledges that it had a significant influence on his own interpretation of Plato, and so dedicates his book to his teacher's memory;[19] yet this very strength, for Rosen, plays into a weakness of philosophical argument. In other words, whereas Strauss prioritizes the literary aspects when interpreting the substance of Plato's teachings, Rosen distinguishes the literary and philosophical dimensions and weaves them together. He writes, "It is now acknowledged by competent Plato scholars that we cannot arrive at a satisfactory appreciation of his philosophical teaching if we ignore

---

14. Ibid., 53.
15. Strauss writes, "It is above all through this selection of conversations, apart from the titles, that we hear Plato himself as distinguished from his character" Ibid., 57.
16. *PR*, 2.
17. Ibid., vii.
18. Ibid., 11.
19. Ibid., vii.

the connection between discursive argument, on the one hand, and the dramatic form and rhetorical elements of the text on the other."[20]

2. POETRY AND EDUCATION: BOOKS II, III, IV, V, AND X

Rosen's interpretation of the *Republic* is directly related to Strauss's influence. Just as Strauss emphasizes the literary aspects of the dialogues, and Rosen supplements them with discursive argument, so too does Rosen find these dimensions exhibited in Plato's philosophy. He argues that, for Plato, philosophy is not the sum of poetry (divine madness or intoxication focused on the particular) and mathematics (intellectual cognition focused on the universal). He points out that Plato is critical of both the madness of the poet and the sobriety of the logician, and continues, "Instead, I am suggesting that for Plato, philosophy includes as its most fundamental dimension two methods, literally 'ways' or 'paths' which are analogous to poetry and mathematics."[21] Both poetry and mathematics are what he calls a "refraction" of *eros*, i.e., of the striving for wholeness or perfection; however, it is philosophy, and in particular a love of the Good in Plato's *Republic*, that Rosen says unites the two. Love of the Good satisfies both the mathematical and poetic impulses.

The poetic method that Rosen finds included in Plato's philosophy is exemplified in the *Symposium*, which he considers a companion piece to the *Republic*.[22] Plato's *Symposium* is a record of songs in praise of *eros*, expressed by Alcibiades, Agathon, and Socrates, that Rosen says relate *eros* to hubris and tyranny.[23] It seems strange to place Socrates in the same category as the democratic politician Alcibiades and the tragedian Agathon, yet their erotic strivings expressed in poetry collectively represent a transgression of society's norms and codes of acceptable conduct.[24] The difference is that whereas Alcibiades's passions and poetry

20. Ibid., 1–2.
21. Rosen, "Role of Eros," 425.
22. Rosen writes, ". . . I shall argue that there is a specific relationship between the *Symposium* and the *Republic*, which turns upon the role assigned in each to Eros, whereby each dialogue illustrates primarily or exaggeratedly one of the two main aspects of philosophy." "Role of Eros," 454.
23. Rosen observes that Socrates is said by Alcibiades at 215b7 and 219c5, and by Agathon at 175e7, to be hubristic. "Role of Eros," 457 n7.
24. Drawing upon Strauss's approach, Rosen finds it significant that the setting is the home of Agathon during the Dionysian festival, and that the guests had been drinking and are likely (with the exception of Socrates) slightly intoxicated. Being inebri-

are in servitude to the body and Agathon's to self-aggrandizement in the eyes of the many, Socrates's passions are directed toward the good of the soul. The three personalities, Alcibiades, Agathon, and Socrates, thus display a refraction of *eros* in different directions while nevertheless illustrating that *eros* is tied to hubris, which is to say that it tends to raise itself above the laws of the city. Alcibiades was therefore not only a leader of the democratic faction, but an adulterer and criminal, and Socrates, although fulfilling his duty and fighting (defensively) at Delium and Potidaea,[25] was also consumed by a love of the whole. The latter Socrates conveys in the *Symposium* while recalling his conversation with Diotima. She had explained to the young Socrates that *eros* is by nature a longing for immortality and that since the Ideas alone are eternal, they are also the proper objects of love.[26] Love of immortal ideas represents the desire to become divine, and is the reverse image of Alcibiades's love of political power and fame. According to Rosen, the *Symposium* teaches that *eros*, be it acquisitive or philosophical, desires immortality (either worldly or philosophical); and that this is a hubristic desire threatening the stability of the city—which is why Socrates was persecuted, tried, and condemned to death.

In the *Republic* the transgressive nature of *eros* is above all characteristic of guardians destined to become philosophers, because they would not love the whole were they not more erotically driven than most. Since tyrants are also unusually erotically driven, this means, for Rosen, that those characters who are potentially the best are also potentially the worst.[27] The worst of the best, he points out, arise if they are

---

ated, within the confines of a private home isolated from a public arena and amongst friends, they are less likely to subject their thoughts to the strictures of social constraint. In short, the environment in the *Symposium* indicates that something is at hand that threatens the order of the city. This is affirmed when Phaedrus suggests that they sing songs in praise of *eros*. The singing of songs places the understanding of *eros* within a poetic context that Plato is suggesting does not belong to the public sphere.

25. Alcibiades reports of Socrates, "There was another occasion on which his behaviour was very remarkable—in the flight of the army after the battle of Delium, where he served among the heavy-armed—I had a better opportunity of seeing him than at Potidaea, for I was myself on horseback and, therefore, comparatively out of danger." *Symposium*, 220e.

26. Diotima asserts, "Then the simple truth is that men love the good. To which must be added that they love possession of the good. And not only possession, but the everlasting possession of the good." *Symposium*, 205d.

27. PR, 207.

deprived of a good education. Alcibiades is a case in point: although Socrates was enamored of the youth's potential, Alcibiades matured into a hedonist. In an odd twist of fate, at the end of the *Symposium*, the decadent Alcibiades reveals his love for Socrates, who rebuffs him.[28] With respect to the fragility of *eros* in the *Republic*, Rosen highlights Glaucon. Glaucon's character is divided between a love of competition and honor (spirit), and a love of learning (philosophy).[29] He is a potential philosopher who is keenly interested in understanding why justice is worthy for its own sake (expressed at the outset of Book II).[30] He senses that justice is noble, but lacks a philosophical understanding of it. However, while Rosen points out that Glaucon urges Socrates on when the argument begins to fade, this proclivity is an expression not of Glaucon's desire to know but of his ambition. This fact is indicated by his reaction to the idea of the Good. After Socrates has given an account of the Good, Plato records the following: "'Apollo!' Glaucon cried comically. 'What divine transcendence!'" (509c). As Rosen points out, Glaucon is not in fact a philosopher; at best he is an auxiliary or assistant to philosophers in the *Republic*. This makes him vulnerable, like the young Alcibiades, to the temptations of power, and indeed, Rosen reports of Glaucon that in Athens he supported the tyranny of the thirty.[31]

The principal challenge for Rosen's Plato is to regulate the erotic nature of the guardians, since without an education they are a grave danger to the city. In his commentary on the *Republic* Rosen specifies that *eros* is a desire for self-preservation, an acquisitive desire that can manifest itself in the gluttony and selfishness depicted by Plato in the "Luxurious City" (372d–427d) and by Hobbes in a war of all against all. In order to suppress that possibility, Plato is ruthless toward the poets. But why poets? According to Rosen, in Books II, III, and X Plato uses extreme measures, what Rosen calls a mathematical way of impersonal and universal standards, to suppress the guardians' *eros*. The problem for Rosen's Plato is that not that the poets do not have knowledge; on the

28. At the end of the *Symposium* Alcibiades relates that he tried to seduce Socrates, who treated him like a brother.

29. Rosen, "Role of Eros," 470.

30. Glaucon asks Socrates into which category justice falls; into things loved for their own sake or things loved for their consequences (357b).

31. Rosen points out that Glaucon's spirited nature eventually yielded to desire, that is to say, to the quest for power. Glaucon supported the tyranny of the thirty. Rosen, "Role of Eros," 463.

contrary, Plato is aware that they understand the nature of the soul as well as he does and so paint the brightest, as well as the worst, pictures of human life.[32] Nevertheless, poets choose to foster division and civil war in the soul, to turn desire and spirit against the truths revealed to reason. They are thus a threat to the singularity of a coherent and ordered life typical of philosophers. The poets, in other words, know what is true but lack the character (i.e., education) to live by it, so they produce works of art that celebrate diversity. Rosen points out that the variety of Platonic dialogues attests to diversity in the lives of philosophers as well; but in contrast to the poets, philosophers do not pursue diversity for the sake of diversity, or novelty for the sake of novelty.[33] Consequently, Plato censors the poets in Books II and III (376e–398c) and drives them out of the city in Book X for deforming character (595a–608b).

Removing from the just city anything that might be a catalyst for the guardian's erotic-acquisitive desire entails, as mentioned, controlling the poet's love of inner fragmentation and lack of direction. Rosen adds in the same regard that the guardians are deprived of private property, a choice of wives, and family, and are subjected to a severe education in the sciences that will habituate their minds to thinking independently of the senses.[34] Yet this is only half of the new curriculum. While suppressing poetry by mathematics, Plato simultaneously condones poetry of a different ilk according to Rosen: specifically, medicinal lies (414c), because they correct the sick nature of human beings displayed in the city of excess (373d),[35] which, by comparison with the city of necessity (368e), is tantamount to a herd of pigs without a leash. Medicinal lies are thus intended to change human beings from mere lovers of their private well-being, and the means to sustain it, to lovers of a just city. Love of a just city more than one's own life is what Rosen calls nobility, hence the medicinal lies are also called noble lies. Rosen points out that they are approved by the gods and that even if they are not true, they ought to be told to the young guardians in order to modify their acquisitive, erotic nature.

Human nature is, therefore, malleable according to Rosen. This has repercussions for other aspects of his interpretation of Plato; for example, it entails that there be no correspondence between the just city and the

32. PR, 353, 369.
33. Ibid., 356.
34. Rosen, "Role of Eros," 462.
35. PR, 136.

soul until the soul has been cured. Yet Rosen does not believe that every soul is equally sick. He points out that, while every soul of every class in the just city is a composite of reason, spirit, and desire, some are more intelligent than others. This harks back to his belief that the poets' myths are heard differently by different kinds of people: some will understand that death is not to be feared because they are banking on a life after death, while others will understand that death is not to be feared but is in fact preferable if beautiful. That is to say, the different classes of a just city (workers, guardians, rulers) are prefigured in those children who find the unconditional pursuit of self-preservation desirable and those who find it aesthetically revolting. The latter are by virtue of their earliest education aesthetically predisposed to become philosophers because they find pleasure in what is impersonal and universal rather than in what is particular and private.

Nobility is typical of guardians but is also an impediment to philosophy. With reference to Book IV, where the best life is presented (474b), Rosen points out that the guardians destined to become philosophers have two dispositions: one is martial and is steadfast and firm, while the other is quick to learn and of good memory. The martial nature without the philosophical is slow to learn, and the philosophical without the martial is erratic and changeable. For Rosen, Plato aims not to unite them, but to balance them against one another. It is not possible to harmonize politics (spirit) and philosophy (reason), because the ideas are something to be contemplated, while ruling requires practical action. The purpose of the *Republic*, says Rosen, is therefore (a) to recruit a few to philosophy and (b) to warn the many against philosophers who might aspire to rule, because without inhuman strictures and constraints philosophers in office become tyrants.

3. PHILOSOPHY AND POETRY: BOOKS VII AND X

In contrast to the *Symposium*, the *Republic* suppresses *eros* for the sake of a just society, yet also combines both a mathematical and a poetic way toward philosophy and thus at the same time allows for *eros* and even for poetry. According to Rosen, although *eros* is suppressed it is also camouflaged. Desire is hidden, says Rosen, in that the *Republic* would never have come into being were it not for an erotic-reproductive longing, nor would it decline were it not for the origin of *eros*. The just state declines when rulers elude the laws and have children out of wedlock.[36] In short, *eros* is responsible for the birth and death of the just society because it, in contrast to the intellect, is subject to the laws of genesis or change. Yet there are two places in the dialogue where Rosen argue that *eros* becomes visible and is not camouflaged. Both are in the middle of the work, hence at the height of the ascent to the ideas and the furthest removed both from the beginning (Book I) and from the demise of a just society into a tyranny of either many (democracy) or just one (dictatorship) (Book IX).

Rosen argues that *eros* surfaces in the middle of the dialogue during a discussion of the philosophical life and vision of the Good. At these points in the work, the mathematical and poetic ways toward philosophy converge in the sense that there transpires, on the one hand, a vision of universal and unchanging ideas, and on the other, a private experience of them that is erotic. In short, reason and *eros* merge during the contemplation of the ideas. According to Rosen, this is reflected in the sexual and reproductive imagery to which Plato resorts in these middle sections of the *Republic*.[37]

Just as mathematics and poetry coalesce in the middle of the dialogue, so too they do at the end, although in a way that for Rosen brings out the limits of philosophy. He explains that the Myth of Er reverses the achievements of previous books. Whereas in Books VI and VII the ideas are eternal, in Book X they are "grown" by a god;[38] whereas previously no mention was made of the soul's immortality or piety, in Book X both are central to the notion of reincarnation.[39] In Book X, philosophy is replaced by carpentry.[40] These "reversals," as Rosen calls them, are nevertheless instructive. He says that the Myth warns the reader not to take seriously the philosophical claims to truth presented in the main books of the dialogue.[41] While the god who creates ideas may be a philosopher-poet,

---

36. Rosen, "Role of Eros," 462.

37. Rosen writes, "When we see the intricacy of the total design, it comes as no surprise that the description of philosophy in the middle books is permeated with erotic language." "Role of Eros," 472. He cites *Republic* 499b7–c2, 493a, and 490a8–b7.

38. *PR*, 389.

39. Ibid., 387.

40. Ibid.

41. Ibid.

that is, one who knows the truth and creates it, the very nature of that being calls into question the veracity of the author Plato's words about the eternity of the ideas and the Good in Book VII. In other words, for Rosen the reader is called to question Plato's philosophy—to scrutinize it independently, as Rosen himself demonstrates, and treat it as a likely story rather than as fact. Rosen concludes, "The more we think about it, the less the *Republic* seems to be an attack upon poetry and the more it vindicates philosophy's need for poetry." Were it not for poetry the *Republic* would never have come into being; at the same time, however, because the utopia is created, it is also fundamentally flawed.

4. ASCENDING FORMS OF INTELLIGIBILITY

Rosen's interpretation of the dramatic structure of the dialogue corresponds to the ranking of objects of knowledge and forms of knowing in the Divided Line.[42] It is thus possible to discern in his interpretation of Plato a climb from the sensible to the intelligible realms. Consider the following excerpt from his commentary:

> The theme of descent plays an important role in the dramatic structure of the *Republic*. To note only the obvious, Socrates and Glaucon descend from Athens to the Piraeus at the very beginning of the dialogue; Book Seven begins with a descent from the sunlight into the cave of shadows that represents the subpolitical nature of the human soul: the dialogue closes with an account of the descent of Er into Hades.[43]

According to Rosen, there is a descent from the intellectual to the sensible realms in the dramatic structure of the *Republic*, i.e., from Athens to Piraeus, from the sun back into the cave, and, at the end, into "Hades" (Myth of Er). Yet there is an ascent as well, beginning with the ascent out of the Piraeus in Book I and continuing with the climb out of the cave into the light of day in Book VII. These two movements are coordinate with the structure of the Divided Line. In the words of Rosen's student Kenneth Dorter, "The modes of thinking through which the dialogue passes during its rise and return exemplify the different levels

---

42. Book 6 (509d–511e) where forms of knowing and corresponding objects of knowledge include imagination-fantasy, opinion-visible things, mathematical-numbers, and intellection-ideas. Analyzed by Rosen, *PR*, 263.

43. *PR*, 19.

of thought processes classified under the Divided Line."[44] Rosen affirms Dorter's claim and writes, ". . . it makes sense to say that the dialogue as a whole is the story of the attempt by Socrates to rise from the Piraeus to the Idea of the Good, and then to descend via the account of the deterioration of the cities and the final discussion of poetry, immortality, and the myth of Er."[45] The climb up and down the divided line corresponds with a movement toward and away from life.[46]

The hierarchy that Rosen believes is integral to Plato's philosophy shapes his interpretation of the dialogue. He reads it as exhibiting an incremental movement from lower to higher forms of intelligibility; for example, while the characters in Book I display some redeeming qualities, they are also preoccupied with goods that pertain to the body, e.g., reputation, saving face, appeasing public norms. The entrance of Adeimantus and Glaucon in Book II begins to transform the initial direction. Given this order in the dialogue, Rosen is not inclined to interpret chapters in terms of one another except insofar as the earlier ones point to a higher level of understanding in later chapters. But at the same time, it would be wrong to attribute a "system" to his interpretation of the *Republic*. The hierarchical structure is not a template or blueprint for the composition of the dialogue, but rather is submerged within the dramatic settings and at other times within the order of speeches and speakers; for example, it is significant for Rosen that the conversation about the just state transpires in the privacy of Cephalus's home rather than in the marketplace. Cephalus represents convention, yet also shelters revolutionary ideas or novelty that would be unsettling and misunderstood in the marketplace or agora.[47] It is also significant for elucidating the hierarchy of being that it is the less practically oriented Glaucon, and not Adeimantus, who joins Socrates in an ascent toward a vision of the Good in Book VII.

In short, Rosen's interpretation of the *Republic* presupposes a theory of Being. However, it is not a mathematical doctrine but rather a play be-

---

44. Dorter, *Transformation of Plato's Republic*, 7.

45. *PR*, 19.

46. Uniting the beginning and the end are the themes death, religion, and piety introduced by Cephalus in Book I (sacrificing to the gods) and concluded by the Myth of Er in Book X. Between these themes philosophical *eros* moves toward what is best and everlasting life in the contemplation of the ideas in the middle chapters. Philosophy is structurally flanked by religion, wisdom by piety, love of learning by reverence for the gods.

47. *PR*, 22.

tween the discursive arguments and the literary or poetic aspects of the dialogue form, both of which he believes capture the creative and mathematical refractions of philosophical *eros*. His "theory" is therefore more than an affirmation of *a priori* ideas, because these ideas are unintelligible without an inevitably poetic, metaphorical form of speech which itself depends for its comprehension on the very ideas it indicates. There is no philosophy without poetry. Nevertheless, the interplay of poetry with universal and unchanging forms, this contraction and expansion of thought, is not simply a cycle, but rather builds incrementally upon itself so as to form higher degrees of understanding. This experience of development through the pursuit of wisdom is intelligible because of an idea of the Good that is the cause for the generation of ideas leading up to it. While the hierarchy of being and forms of cognition are explicated by Plato in the middle of the dialogue, the ranking is implicit in the order of speakers, speeches, and dramatic contexts leading up to that point. Plato's manner of writing communicates as much about the Good as what he says; the *telos*, so to speak, silently inheres in stages throughout the dialogue and in the climb toward the vision of the idea itself in Book VII.

15

Human Nature

INTRODUCTION

GADAMER'S VIEW OF PLATO'S theory of human nature is influenced by Heidegger. As mentioned in Part II, he reverts to Heidegger's term *Dasein*, and believes that Being, in this case the Good, belongs to human beings as self-understanding. But if so, then the difference between Being and human beings must be identified. Gadamer's view is that Plato does so in the Excursus to the *Seventh Letter*. According to Gadamer, Plato believes that human beings, including their reason or insight, are finite, separated from the Good by infinity; understanding-of-Being is an unending task because humans are mortal.

Another way toward the same conclusion about human nature is from the side of dialogue. Conversation can conceivably terminate in a consensus on which a scientific theory might be built. In order to maintain the open-endedness of the dialogue form there must, therefore, be something deeper than language or speech with which to ensure that Being remains a question and the ideas hypotheses. According to Gadamer, we ask questions because of the distinction between the object of knowledge and the means of knowing it. This is very close to siding with Heidegger on the significance of thinking the ontological difference, which circles back to the *Dasein* of human subjectivity since this notion of difference is tantamount to "death." For Gadamer it is not the living context of a conversation that ultimately grounds the open structure of Plato's dialogues, but rather the residue of Heidegger's thinking about transcendence.

It is thus not by mere coincidence that Gadamer emphasizes the division within the guardian nature between the harsh and savage on the one hand and the gentle and philosophical on the other, as imaged in the watchdog. This is a reflection of the bivalent nature of *Dasein* (authenticity and inauthenticity). However, unlike Heidegger, who undertakes an existential analysis of *Dasein*'s structures, Gadamer leans toward the position that humans are by nature rational-political.[1] Consequently, he assumes that it is the purpose of education to synthesize the different parts of the soul; that in Book IV *eubolia* is *sophia*, that moderation includes wisdom, and that wisdom is distributed, like justice, amongst every class; that the Good is fulfilled in *phronesis*; and that philosophers are happy in a just state.[2] But does Gadamer's position on the nature of Being in Plato's philosophy bear scrutiny when measured against the *Republic*? Does Plato's Socrates agree with Gadamer that Being is dialectical in structure because it belongs to finite human beings (*Dasein*), and hence that there are but two ethical possibilities: authenticity or inauthenticity, philosophy or tyranny?

In the interest of testing Gadamer's theory that humans are by nature rational (otherwise a just state would be for him impossible), a series of interrelated propositions upon which his argument depends are subjected to examination in this chapter: (1) that the watchdog imagery proves that the guardians are by nature philosophical; (2) that the city of sows proves nothing about the nature of the guardians and their erotic nature partakes fully in reason; (3) that everyone is wise because temperance includes wisdom and is identical to justice; and (4) that the nature of the guardians is the nature of every class because there is a correlation between the order of the soul and that of the state.

---

1. Gadamer believes that, for Plato, human beings are by nature philosophical and their nature is fulfilled in political life; but he muddies the water when he claims that humans do not have the potential, by nature, for a philosophical existence. He writes, "For the potential of the human being to be a human being among other human beings, in short, to be a political being, depends upon this unification of the philosophical and martial natures in him. But this potential for political existence is not given to man by nature, for even if both these elements in him are natural and necessary, man becomes a political being only insofar as he resists the temptations of power which arise from flattery." DD, 56. On balance there is no further evidence in Gadamer's interpretation of the *Republic* to support the view that humans are not philosophical by nature. Virtually his entire reading of the dialogue depends upon the latter.

2. Gadamer says that Plato's "ontological critique" of the poets in Book X is aimed at the ethos they encourage, in which "virtue and happiness are placed in opposition to each other." "Such a juxtaposition," says Gadamer, "can result only from a false conception of virtue and happiness which makes them seem incompatible." Ibid., 62.

1. WATCHDOG IMAGERY: BOOK II

Gadamer's belief that human beings are by nature both philosophical and spirited, and that the two are irreconcilable with one another, is derived from the watchdogs to which the guardians are compared. The passage in question to which Gadamer refers is where Plato's Socrates states, "Whoever is going to be a noble and good guardian of the city (that is, a 'gentleman') will be by nature a philosopher, spirited, swift and strong" (376c4–5). In this statement the two sides of the guardians are defined: they are both philosophical and spirited. These two dimensions are natural, as Plato says above, because for Gadamer they are exhibited in dogs (375e). Dogs are spirited in that they are aggressive toward strangers, yet also philosophical because they are friendly to what is known. Plato writes of the latter, "This subtle property of his nature shows that the dog is a philosopher, a true 'lover of wisdom'" (376b). If a dog has knowledge of friends by nature and is therefore philosophical, and if guardians are comparable to dogs, then guardians are also by nature philosophical. Gadamer concludes, just as the dog "is a friend of what is 'known,' which is to say, of 'knowledge,' so too do the guardians have knowledge, the capacity to distinguish friend from foe, truth from falsity."[3] He reiterates the truth of the analogy by stating that dogs are "quite literally philosophers,"[4] and refers to "man's philosophical nature."[5]

The question for Gadamer is to what extent the analogy between the guardians and watchdog holds (375e), and whether or not there is another way to understand the word "philosophy" when Plato attributes the latter to dogs (376b). The latter is a question proper to the virtue of temperance discussed below. Turning to the analogy, Rosen argues that while dogs and guardians are comparable, they are not identical. They are comparable in that both dogs and guardians are loyal to that which is familiar to them. But their loyalty is not natural to either of them; it is inculcated through familiarity, habit, and training. Contrary to what Plato literally says, it cannot be that the guardians are by nature philosophical, because they do not have knowledge of the Ideas; instead, like dogs, they have just enough intelligence to obey masters who could be,

---

3. Ibid., 54–56.
4. Ibid., 56.
5. Ibid., 57.

in the absence of the ability to distinguish a real from an apparent good, either tyrants or hardened criminals. That is not to say that the analogy is false. Rosen explains that the nature of dogs is "the paradigm of the military person, i.e., for purposes of guarding there is no difference between their nature."[6] The guardians and dogs are similar not because they have knowledge either of friends or of Ideas (Gadamer), but because they are loyal to what is their own.

2. EROS: BOOKS II AND III

Gadamer opposes *eros* and reason when he contrasts the philosopher with the eroticist (474c) dominated by passion and a yearning to see beauty in all things.[7] Gadamer relates what is required to educate the guardians: "Thus the guardian, which is to say man, must cultivate the philosophical nature in himself while at the same time reconciling this nature with the violent drives in himself of self-preservation and the will to power."[8] Desire is a violent drive and therefore surely opposed to gentle reason, yet in the passage above Gadamer speaks of "reconciling" the gentle to the violent side of the guardian's nature. His choice of words suggests that uneducated desire, although violent, partakes of reason. This is suggested by his use of Heidegger's term *gleichursprünglich* to indicate the concomitance of Being and non-Being, authenticity and inauthenticity, which Smith points out means that man is "always already (*je schon*) both philosophical and tyrannical." Smith concludes, "For Gadamer, the parts of the soul that are initially opposed to the gentle side are already potentially philosophical and hence, the task of *paideia* cannot be to eradicate the 'tyrannical' *eros* but to harmonize it with the 'philosophical.'"[9] While the notion "harmony" is apt, it is not quite strong enough. Harmony implies the working in tandem of distinct parts of the soul, yet Gadamer states that the just soul is at one with itself, and thereby suggests that distinctions within it are dissolved into an undifferentiated whole. Evidence of a similar propensity is his belief that, in the *Republic*, the difference between art and philosophy is removed such that the Myth of Er is not imitative, but rather a projection

---

6. *PR*, 83.
7. Gadamer cites 474c, 475d, and 403c. *DD*, 90.
8. Ibid., 56.
9. Ibid., 57 n8; see also 54.

of the order of the soul, and that it educates rather and alienates people from themselves. He says that the *Republic* is one grand dialectical myth, but also an education in philosophy that brings about a unity of the truth with political existence. This indicates that for Gadamer both *eros* (art) and spiritedness (politics) are completely rationalized by a philosophical education; otherwise there would be no unity of the soul with itself, or of art with philosophy, or truth with political existence.

But a closer examination of the dialogue suggests that Gadamer's view of *eros* is inaccurate. Like his overall depiction of human nature, it is based on Plato's description of the guardian's character (377d) rather than on how that character is formed. Gadamer's depiction of *eros* therefore presupposes a prior education from Book II.377 to roughly III.411. Stepping back to the early education of the guardians indicates that *eros* is not initially predisposed to side with philosophy, as Gadamer suggests, and is instead nonrational in the sense of loving above all self-preservation rather than impersonal ideas. Rosen supports this interpretation and relates that Plato attempts to purge *eros* of acquisitiveness (*epithumia*) with an early education in noble lies and music.[10] Noble lies are medicine for the sick soul in that they instill an identification of the guardian's own advantage with that of the city, typically by finding self-sacrifice aesthetically pleasing and the pursuit of self-interest aesthetically repulsive.[11] Music similarly instills in the youth a love for that which does not yield a good external to the soul and hence is chosen for its own sake, or for the order (mathematical order) of the soul itself.[12] Music and noble lies thus cure what Rosen calls the sickness of human beings, which is why noble lies are also said to be medicinal. By overlooking the early education of the guardian's nature, and focusing instead upon the result of that education for a portrait of their character, Gadamer overestimates them. When Plato says at 375 that the guardians are by nature spirited and philosophical (cited by Gadamer in support of his thesis), Plato is speaking about persons whose appetitive desire has already been purged by medicinal lies, and who are thus spirited, i.e., love nobility,

---

10. Rosen argues that Plato's Socrates knows that the noble lies are against human nature and are in many cases false; nevertheless, they are justified because they are good. *PR*, 87. *Republic* (377b10–c2, 378). Guardians and philosophers also know that the myths are lies, but choose to believe them because of their utility.

11. *PR*, 99, 163.

12. Music weaves a harmony of desire, spirit, and reason in that it fosters a love of beauty, which is a prediscursive knowledge of the Good.

and through a training in music have become gentle. Were it not for this basic education in myths and music, argues Rosen, the guardians would be nonrational erotic beings, because that is their nature.

The most poignant evidence in support of the guardians' nature is at the outset of Book II in the city of pigs, which Gadamer unsuccessfully attempts to discount as having any relevance to human nature. Plato states that the city is "true and healthy" (373). Gadamer dismisses Plato's words as having any bearing upon the question of human nature by arguing that the city of pigs is an ironical caricature of historical reality intended to affirm the truth of human discontent witnessed in the historical and hence, for Gadamer, "true" city of luxury. In other words, since the city of sows never has and never will exist, attributing "truth" to it, as Plato does, points in the opposite direction for truth, i.e., to historical reality, out of which Gadamer says justice arises.[13]

However, there are two ways, the historical and philosophical, in which the city might be true for Plato. First, it is possible that for Greek historians such a city was the first stage in the evolution of civilization. This seems to follow from the fact, as Rosen says, that the division of labor arising by necessity in the city of pigs produces a surplus of goods that in turn accounts for the city becoming excessive. The city of sows was therefore of explanatory significance for historians of the fifth century B.C., including Plato.[14] Second, the city of pigs may also have philosophical import for Plato. Evidence for the philosophical truth of an impossible city is that the city of excess (the historical reality) is unintelligible without a city of pigs. In the city of excess, absent either laws or religion, people amass private property without restraint. This condition would lead to a state of civil war of all against all (Hobbes) were it not for a few well-bred and self-controlled guardians. But the condition of disorder into which the city of excess plummets points back to the city of sows in the sense that the latter explains why uneducated people pursue private property to their own and other's detriment: it is human nature. The city of pigs is, as Rosen says, effectively Plato's theory about humans in a state of nature, i.e., "another paradigm in heaven." Rather than contradict Plato and argue against the "truth" of the city of pigs, it is thus possible to argue for that truth, but the result is that no one is by nature either political or philosophical (as Gadamer argues), since both are, as

13. DD, 54–55.
14. PR, 79.

Rosen says, absent from the city of sows.[15] Consequently, the guardians cannot be either spirited or philosophical by nature; on the contrary, as their early education in noble lies and music evinces, their nature is aggressively desirous.[16]

But there is considerable evidence that not even the erotic nature of the few selected to become rulers manifests a fully nonacquisitive desire. Were the guardians' erotic nature even potentially philosophical, it would not have been necessary for Plato to resort to such ruthless measures against anything that might be a catalyst for the guardians' desire; for example, denying them private property and a wife and family they could call their own, expelling poets who stir the passions, and prohibiting mourning for the loss of a friend.[17] Rosen says that Plato's measures against *eros* are so severe that they are inhuman; indeed, as he points out, the city begins to decline when the rulers break the marital laws. This suggests that irrespective of how brutal Plato is toward the desire for self-preservation, the latter is impossible to constrain or fully educate according to the dictates of reason.[18] Human nature is malleable, as Rosen says, but not completely changeable.[19]

---

15. Ibid., 79.

16. Rosen points out that the guardians "are artifacts of training, that is they are artificial and not natural." Ibid., 85, 97, 99.

17. Rosen writes, "In order to found and live within the just city, philosophers must suppress the poetical side of their nature, or what comes to the same thing, submit it to constant censorship and the degradation of poetry into political ideology. It is no empty paradox to say that the price of entrance for genuine philosophers into the just city is expulsion or purgation of their previous decadent selves." PR, 4. See also p. 129 for restrictions on the guardians' eros. In his essay "Plato's Educational State" (*DD*, 89) Gadamer glosses the part of the *Republic* dealing with the communist living arrangements of the guardians that suppresses their erotic nature. Gadamer does not think that the communist living arrangements are important, because they are unrealistic and do not pertain to how the state is a possibility, so he moves on to the question of philosopher-kings (503b). He also glosses over the communist elements in "Plato and the Poets" (*DD*, 76) arguing that they are an "ironic illusion to advertise his political program." Gadamer later develops this thought into a dialectical reading of the *Republic*, discussed below. IG, 73.

18. Rosen thus observes that Plato depreciates human existence and even humanity by stipulating that the guardians not lament the loss of a friend—witnessed, for instance, in Achilles's crying for Patroclus, Priam for Hector, Thetis for Achilles, and Zeus for Sarpedon (388a5–d1). PR, 92.

19. Ibid., 85, 97, 99.

3. TEMPERANCE-WISDOM: BOOK IV

Gadamer's belief that guardians are philosophical by nature, as mentioned, depends upon the watchdog imagery, which does not support his argument. But then what of Plato's claim that the guardians are by nature philosophical (376b-c)? Since the guardians have no knowledge of ideas, the notion that they are philosophers seems incredible. One avenue by which to explain Plato's statement consists in reading the *Republic* dialectically, or reading the earlier Books in terms of the later. This is a strategy Gadamer defends in his *Idea of the Good in Platonic-Aristotelian Philosophy*. Just as Socrates is present from the outset of the dialogue, so too is the idea of the Good, hence the guardians in Book III can be presumed to have knowledge of it. Gadamer gives formal expression to this way of reading Plato's work. However, this dialectical reading yields other questionable results in Gadamer's interpretation besides Plato's statement that the guardians are philosophers.

If wisdom is knowledge of the Good, and is identical to *sophrosyne* as stated at 443d-e, and if *sophrosyne* is distributed in every class like justice, then it makes sense to argue that everyone in a just state is a philosopher. Gadamer alludes to this when he writes, "The state is an ordering of government and populace founded upon the fact that the whole is present in each individual and his action."[20] Gadamer's attributing to every class wisdom therefore depends on (1) an understanding of what Plato means by *sophia* and *sophrosyne* in Book IV; and (2) the belief that there is a correlation between the order of the just state and the order of the soul.

With respect to the meaning of *sophia* and *sophrosyne*, the question for Gadamer is twofold. First, to what extent is justice equivalent to *sophrosyne* (temperance), and second, to what extent does Plato mean by wisdom a knowledge of the whole? Gadamer is able to reason that *sophrosyne* belongs to every part of the soul, because he conflates *sophrosyne* with justice.[21] Justice as doing that for which one is fit, and temperance as

---

20. *DD*, 84.

21. Gadamer is equivocating on justice and temperance. For example, he says that temperance (*sophrosyne*) is "an intrinsic correlation between the good constitution of the soul and *Dasein*'s self-knowledge," and continues, "The definition of justice arrived at was the sound, good constitution of the soul..." According to Gadamer, both justice and temperance are responsible for the good constitution of the soul. He thus attributes to both virtues the power to bring about unity of the soul. He explains that *ideopragein* (later, justice) "gives the state its unity" as does temperance in that it preserves the health

agreement about who should rule, seem to be implicated in one another. Justice is minding one's own business and every part of the soul agrees to do this. However, justice and temperance, although close to one another in meaning, are not the same. Rosen explains their difference as follows: temperance is "the harmonious obedience to the rule of intelligence"; justice is friendship of the parts of the soul with one another, arising after every other virtue (including temperance) has been discovered. There is then no friendship among the parts of the soul, or civic friendship between classes in the city, i.e., justice, until they all agree about the rule of intelligence. To clarify, he explains that justice is like playing an instrument (one's own part), while temperance is the acknowledgment that no one can play well without a conductor.[22] Temperance is thus the harmony that animates the soul, a sum that is greater than its parts. Given this distinction by Rosen between temperance and justice, temperance is not in every part of the soul as Gadamer presumes, and this in turn implies that not every part of the soul is "wise." (Although that is not to say that a temperate soul might not resemble wisdom, a notion that is discussed below).

Another reason Gadamer equates wisdom with the order of the soul is indirectly brought out by P.C. Smith. He argues that Gadamer projects Heidegger's understanding of Being into Plato.[23] In this case,

---

of the state and prevents it from being led astray into a condition of disunity (*amathia*). Ibid., 88–89. But unity is conferred by knowledge of the whole, which Gadamer equates with Dasein's self-understanding and *sophia*. Justice and temperance, which Gadamer considers responsible for the unity of the soul, include wisdom, and therefore so does every other part of the soul, every other virtue and class.

22. Rosen writes, "The temperate city is one in which each part does its own work in the best possible way. It is a city in which the whole and its parts all mind their own business. As we are about to see, this makes temperance hard if not impossible to distinguish from justice. We might also refer to temperance as harmony, accord, order, and measure, qualities that seem to do the work of justice and thus to make it superfluous. If this is too extreme, let us say that justice is the music of the soul, and hence of the city, which is the soul writ large." *PR*, 145.

23. P.C. Smith thus observers that on two occasions Gadamer expresses himself in Heideggerian terms. First, Smith observes that Gadamer applies Heideggerian insights to the Platonic text; for example, when Gadamer indicates that wisdom for Plato (443e) is equivalent to *Dasein*'s self-understanding (*DD*, 86 n4). Self-understanding for Heidegger is to understand the meaning of Being, the Being that belongs to human beings. If Plato's notion of *sophia* similarly is an understanding of Being, then the separate parts of the soul dissolve into wisdom and each virtue is infused with wisdom. Second, Smith reports that Gadamer uses the Heideggerian term *gleichursprünglich* to indicate the concomitance of Being and non-Being, authenticity and inauthenticity—

it makes sense to attribute *sophia* to every class because, ontologically speaking, all human beings are constitutionally the same. Assuming Smith is correct, to what extent is Plato a Heideggerian, or is his notion of the Idea of the Good coordinate with the clearing (disclosedness) that *Dasein* is? Heidegger's position is that Plato thinks of Being in terms of the self because he conflates the meaning of Being with an idea or human perspective on beings. But, as Rosen counters, it is probable that Plato does not conflate the Idea with a human perspective (or think of it in terms of the self) because "idea" is a metaphor for that which is, as Plato says, "beyond beings" (509b) (*epekeine tes ousias*), and hence at other times Socrates says simply "the Good."[24] If so, then there is a distinction between seeing and what is seen that Heidegger effaces in his criticism of Plato. There are likely other reasons to liberate Plato from the grip of Gadamer's Heideggerian *Gestell*; for example, Being is not created, nor does it come to be by either *techne* or *poiesis*. Just because we can express knowledge of Being only in speech does not mean that it is linguistic or has, as Gadamer argues, the structure of *parole*. If by Being Plato does not mean *Dasein*, then it is less probable that *sophia* enters into every part of the soul (like justice), dissolving all differences.

That is not to say that everyone in a just state might not in some sense of the word still be wise. After all, as noted by Gadamer, Plato says that the guardians are by nature philosophers (376c4-5), and that *sophia* is *sophrosyne* (433d-e). Since neither the guardians nor the dogs to whom they are compared have knowledge, as Gadamer argues, the guardians cannot be replicas of Socrates. If temperance does not belong to every class and every part of the soul because it is different from justice and wisdom, and is instead the agreement among all classes about who should rule, then it is possible that when Plato says the guardians are philosophers, he means to indicate that, like dogs, they agree to obey their superiors, the philosopher-rulers (conductors of the orchestra). In so doing, the soul and state become harmonious, i.e., peaceably coexistent, as long as there is this agreement, which depends of course on the legitimacy of the philosopher's authority. If there is no authority, there is

---

which means, for Gadamer, that man is "always already (*je schon*) both philosophical and tyrannical. Thus the task of *paideia* cannot be to eradicate the 'tyrannical' but to harmonize it with the 'philosophical'" (*DD*, 57 n8). For Gadamer, even the parts of the soul that are initially opposed to the gentle side (desire and spirit) are potentially philosophical.

24. *PR*, 401 n1.

no order, and the just state degenerates into lawlessness (where each is a law onto himself).

As if to acknowledge why Gadamer may have wrongly attributed wisdom to the guardians in Book II, Rosen explains Plato's line of reasoning and then criticizes his diction. According to Rosen, Plato says that the guardians are philosophers because he is preparing for a discussion of philosopher-rulers wherein courage and "wisdom" (i.e., temperance) are combined (as in dogs). But conveying this by equating temperance with wisdom is nevertheless misleading, as evinced by Gadamer's interpretation. Rosen thus criticizes Plato: instead of saying that dogs have a philosophical nature, Plato would have done better to say that the spirit and courage of the dog depend on the knowledge of a philosopher, that is to say, of a wise master or ruler.[25]

4. THE ORDER OF CITY-SOUL

Gadamer's belief that the class of guardians is the class of all human beings depends upon a correlation between the order of the state and that of the soul. This is a condition that Gadamer believes is characteristic of the ancient world, which, in contrast to the modern, did not distinguish between inner experience and outward action.[26] Whatever Plato says about the soul can presumably be transferred to the state, which mirrors the soul. But there are two reasons to doubt the correlation between them: (1) the education of the guardians, and (2) the relation of the person to the state.

Gadamer believes that the education of the guardians is intended to create a unity or oneness of their soul, reflected in the unity of the state. Since *eros* partakes in reason, and wisdom (temperance) belongs to every part of the soul (and thus to every class in the city), the unity of the soul seems assured. Gadamer directs the reader to this unity when he writes that the aim of education for Plato is "the unification of the

---

25. Ibid., 87.
26. P.C. Smith observes that Gadamer agrees with Hegel's criticism of the "beautiful soul" typical of the "law of the heart" in Rousseau or Kant's notion of the "good will," whereby there is an "inability to reconcile subjective thoughts with actions in the external world. *DD*, 86 n5. For Gadamer, this schism is foreign to the Greeks, a fact which agrees with both his dialectical theory of Being in Plato as well as with his prioritizing of Aristotle's *phronesis* in his interpretation of Plato's idea of the Good.

schism of the bestial and the peaceful in human beings."[27] The extremes of becoming an aggressive wolf or excessively gentle (servile) are avoided if the soul becomes not merely harmonized but, as Gadamer would put it, united or one with itself.

In reply, the dialogue teaches that while everyone has a tripartite soul, the parts are different, and neither *eros* nor spirit are completely philosophical. Rosen is in agreement with Gadamer that everyone has a tripartite soul; it would be absurd to suggest that rulers have no desire, or "to assume that money-makers are uniformly persons of uncontrollable desires."[28] However, these parts of the soul can take on differing relations to one another, reflected in different classes. The ruler is not "a large copy of the intellect in his soul; he is rather pre-eminent in intelligence; and a similar point holds for each of the other two types of person."[29] The soldier and money-maker have an intellect, but a love of knowledge is not of foremost importance to them, which is why it is just for them and everyone else that they protect the city and work the economy. Given that the variety of classes reflects variation in the soul of human beings, it is unlikely that the guardians represent, as Gadamer says, the class of "all human beings." This is just too monolithic a thought for even an alleged totalitarian like Plato, because it dissolves the diversity of lives he defends in the just state into just one, or renders harmony of different parts a monotone.

The question is, then, if Gadamer is wrong to correlate the parts of the soul with classes in the just state, why does Plato identify a person with the city (435b1–2)? Rosen's reply is that the identification is false, but nevertheless useful. He points out that persons and the city are different for the following three reasons. First, cities are not the same as persons because they are neither alive biologically nor unified organically.[30] Second, while an individual soul is courageous, the same cannot be said of the state, only the guardians are courageous.[31] Third, were there an identity between the person and the city, the city would be sick because humans by nature are ill (i.e., love things of the body and have no culture for the health of the soul). The incongruity uncovered

---

27. *DD*, 56.
28. *PR*, 150.
29. *PR*, 151.
30. Ibid., 148–149.
31. Ibid., 148–149, 192.

by Rosen between the city and a person raises the question why Plato speaks of their identification. Rosen's reply is that, by constructing a just city, Plato modifies human nature and then afterwards discovers justice in people.[32] The perfectly just state is a lie that helps educate potential philosophers.

CONCLUSION

Gadamer's focus on building a coherent theory of human nature on the basis of Plato's characterization of the guardians (375) in comparison to watchdogs is understandably limited when measured against the context and developments in the dialogue. Rather than supporting Gadamer's belief that the guardians are philosophical by nature, the watchdog imagery refutes it; rather than *eros* participating in a love of learning, *eros* by nature aims for self-preservation; rather than education consisting of a harmonizing of the parts of the soul, it is coercive and cruel above all toward the guardians chosen to become rulers; rather than the philosophical and spirited elements uniting to form one soul and state, they have contrary directions, leaving philosophers equally devoted to two jobs and thus consigned to the least happy life, if not an actually tragic life, in a just state. These results do not indicate that merely another method or approach is at work. Gadamer's hermeneutic method consistently demonstrates an underlying decision about the nature of human beings that is not borne out by the text in question. Although his phenomenology is intended to let the thing itself speak for itself, and his hermeneutic is intended to call his prejudices into question, both prongs of his approach are eclipsed by a prior decision about the meaning of being.

Just what Gadamer means by "Being" in Plato's philosophy is indicated by what his interpretation excludes: primarily, an erotic longing for wholeness or completion. In its stead, he includes moderation and self-control. When the love of wisdom is neutralized by a process of rational inquiry, it follows that the philosophical ascent beyond the city is suppressed; consequently, Gadamer takes no account of noble lies in his commentary on the *Republic*. The utility of the medicinal lie to the good of the city depends upon a knowledge of the diversity within human nature and character, the very diversity that is denied by Gadamer's rationalism. Rosen writes of "Hegel, and those thinkers for whom the

---

32. Ibid., 99.

state (= *polis*) is the highest form of human (= erotic) development" that "They must remove the noble lie and put in its place a kind of universal enlightenment, or a situation in which the laws of the state are identical with the truths of reason."[33] But the truths of reason are not fit for society at large, which is why Plato exhorts the reader not to enact a just society in the *Republic*.

---

33. Rosen, "Role of Eros," 461 n18.

16

The Politics of Inclusion

INTRODUCTION

FROM THE PREVIOUS CHAPTER it is clear that, according to Gadamer's Plato, all human beings desire self-understanding in order to be both rulers and ruled, which is to say, self-rulers. This is another way of advocating the ethics of the autonomous individual, or, in the words of Robert Sullivan, a community of "discourse rationality" that is nonetheless exclusionary of nonphilosophers.[1] In order to draw out this prejudice, this chapter contrasts Gadamer's reading of the *Republic* Book I with that of Rosen. Book I is relevant to this task because in it are presented the most varied characters in the dialogue, and whereas Gadamer repeatedly excludes the "other," Rosen finds ways of including them in a just state. Since Rosen's Plato studies defend a notion of Being transcendent to human beings, Gadamer's an immanent transcendence, it is necessary to reexamine the belief that the orthodox view of Plato advocates a closed society in contrast to Gadamer's alleged openness. The analysis of the two readings of Book I follows the order in which the characters appear in the dialogue.

1. CEPHALUS

Gadamer's discussion of Cephalus is cursory. Nevertheless, his methodological precepts are visible. He sets up a duality between Cephalus and his son Polemarchus and Thrasymachus. Whereas the latter two are sub-

---

[1]. Wachterhauser is emphatic that "our access to truth is rooted in dialogue . . . and not in the private vision of the individual who strives to conform his sight to the changeless presence of the timeless Ideas which are the true Being of reality." Wachterhauser, *Beyond Being*, 181.

sumed under the rubric of sophistry, Cephalus is a "kind of venerable, natural mirror image of philosophical life" who "praises freedom from sensuous desire and extols the joys of discussing things, and who, in conforming to cult and custom, builds his existence upon a practicable rectitude: 'telling the truth and paying one's debts.'"[2] The master of the house is a traditionalist, an unreflective philosopher whom Gadamer contrasts with the sophists. While this interpretation instantiates Gadamer's belief that there is a dynamic relationship between philosophy and its reverse image, sophistry, his interpretation falls short of Rosen's in that he neglects the relevance both of Cephalus's character and actions and of the way he functions positively within the dialogue as a whole.

Gadamer's belief that Cephalus is a "natural mirror of a philosophic life" seems to be supported by Cephalus's speech and deeds; he enjoys conversation, and his sacrificing to the gods suggests that he is concerned with something more than immediate and tangible forms of power. Gadamer seems correct, then, to have juxtaposed him with Polemarchus and Thrasymachus, the sophists, who he says embody a "tyrannical existence." Yet there is considerable evidence that Cephalus, while not a sophist, is also not merely a distorted image of a philosopher as Gadamer contends. Rosen probes Cephalus's character and finds that he has not the intelligence to be a sophist, although he is, like them, preoccupied by the satisfaction of acquisitive desire; for example, whereas Gadamer lauds Cephalus for enjoying conversations in old age, Rosen brings out that Cephalus does so only because he is liberated from the tyranny of passion (319d). Moreover, he does not sacrifice to the gods out of piety or veneration; he wants to make amends for past wrongs, something he could evidently afford (330d). Dorter concludes, "Everything about Cephalus points to a man of appetite."[3] Far from being "the mirror image of a philosophical life" as Gadamer contends, Cephalus is the least philosophical of the interlocutors, not only because he remains under the sway of his acquisitive nature, but because he is deaf to the voice of reason. After exhibiting both a contradiction between his version of justice—telling the truth and returning what is owed—and the injustice of his life, Cephalus excuses himself from the room to resume his habit of sacrificing to the gods (331d). This dramatic action, which Gadamer does not take into account, suggests that Cephalus has not

---

2. DD, 78.
3. Dorter, *Transformation of Plato's Republic*, 25.

been changed in the least by the conversation. Nevertheless, given the inclusive nature of the Good, reflected for Rosen in the structure of the dialogue, Cephalus is of decisive importance for the dialogue's positive dimension.

States at the peak of their splendor and power, as Athens was when Plato wrote the *Republic*, are inclined to become parochial, inward-looking, and averse to innovation. This is why the revolutionary conversation about a just society and persons, carried out by Socrates, Cephalus, his son Thrasymachus, and Plato's brothers, does not take place in the heart of the city. They are not conversing in either the marketplace or the assembly. Instead, as Rosen points out, they are sheltered in a domicile. Although Cephalus is therefore for Rosen a "pagan everyman" who thoughtlessly mimics tradition to the point of indifference to self-contradiction and refutation, the conservative tradition he represents is also the space in which new ideas come to fruition.[4]

Furthermore, while Gadamer is silent about Cephalus's piety and thereby suggests that religion has no place in a just city, Rosen believes that philosophy and religion, reason and faith are amiable to one another. This is indicated by the fact that Socrates is gentler with Cephalus than with any other speaker, and by Socrates's admiring respect for Homer. These indications of friendship between philosophy and religion are confirmed for Rosen by the structural unity of the dialogue. Rosen points out that the dialogue closes where it began, with a return to the issues represented by Cephalus—death and the afterlife in the Myth of Er (Book X 614a–621d),[5] a myth about reward and punishment in the afterlife. While Cephalus is the least philosophical for Rosen because he is neither spirited nor sensitive to rational argument, he nevertheless has a place (like religion) in the just city. And although no less critical of Polemarchus and Thrasymachus than Gadamer, Rosen similarly draws out positive dimensions of their character and arguments, as we shall see.

---

4. Rosen writes of the location for the dialogue, "We are detached from the city at its peak and are encouraged to a more spontaneous mode of conversation, one that is more appropriate to the shadows cast by firelight than to the splendor of political and military rhetoric . . . it also brings philosophy into a zone of freedom, privacy, and openness to what is foreign." *PR*, 20.

5. The dialogue closes where it began, with questions about immortality and religion, and thus comes full circle, except that poetry and religion have been purified by philosophy.

2. POLEMARCHUS

Rosen agrees with Gadamer that with the shift from Cephalus to Polemarchus the tone of the conversation changes. Gadamer predicts that Polemarchus will be "forced to account for what he claims to know and to justify it."[6] Rosen reiterates this when Cephalus leaves the conversation and bequeaths the argument to his son. Rosen writes, "The symbolism is obvious; at this point, the conversation leaves the dimension of social conventions and turns to argument."[7] However, whereas Gadamer emphasizes Polemarchus's latent potential for tyranny, in contrast to Cephalus being a mirror image of a philosophical life, Rosen argues that Polemarchus is a transitional figure between Cephalus and Thrasymachus, and thus plays a role in moving the discussion toward a higher level of knowledge.

Gadamer claims that Polemarchus is, unbeknownst to himself, a tyrant. Since he believes justice to be merely a *techne*, or the application of a universal rule whose validity is contingent upon predictable outcomes, his notion of justice can be refuted by demonstrating results that are not expected; for example, when Polemarchus defines justice as the art of keeping money secure, Socrates counters that the entrusted person is also in the best position to steal the money (334b); consequently, justice includes injustice. When Polemarchus argues that justice consists of harming enemies, Socrates elicits from the son of Cephalus the concession that a just man does not harm anyone (335d). What then to make of Polemarchus's views? According to Gadamer, he advocates being a thief and harming people. As a result, after outlining the argument Gadamer concludes, "what appears at first as a breakdown in the logic of his attempt to do so [i.e., justify his beliefs] is in fact the disclosure of a deeper discrepancy in his existence."[8] The "deeper discrepancy" is related by Gadamer, who writes: "There can be no doubt that the dialectical confusion into which Socrates has plunged his interlocutors discloses a latent element of the tyrannical in the latter's definition of justice, an element to which he himself remains oblivious."[9] Gadamer reasons that Polemarchus is a tyrant because his definition of justice partakes in a

---

6. DD, 78.
7. PR, 30–31.
8. DD, 78.
9. Ibid., 80.

"feeling of superiority" that justifies the deliberate harm of another. It is thus not Simonides, whom Polemarchus had initially consulted, who defends justice as helping friends and harming enemies, but rather, as Gadamer observes in the dialogue, Xerxes and Periander (336). The condemnation of Polemarchus the tyrant from the fact of Cephalus's nontyrannical nature follows the logic of contraries in Gadamer's dialectic (which would be inclusionary like Rosen's if it included an idea of what is Good or a teleology).

Rosen, however, does not find in Polemarchus solely the potential for tyranny, or a tyrannical man masking himself in the garb of traditional virtues of helping friends and harming enemies. Instead, Rosen argues that Polemarchus's definition of justice, although incomplete, is nevertheless central to the order of the just city. Rosen writes of the confusion into which Socrates has thrown him:

> Later in the discussion, this same confusion will appear as follows: Justice is minding one's own business, but one's business is not simply performing one's art, as Socrates will argue. Justice is performing one's art well, that is, to the benefit of one's friends rather than to harm them. It is entirely implausible to argue that we benefit our friends simply by doing the task that the city has assigned to us. So we are not done with Polemarchus's definition. At least half of it is correct. We still have to decide what to do with our enemies. In sum: Polemarchus is not just a curtain-raiser in the great drama of the problem of justice. He is, rather, the problem itself.[10]

Polemarchus is the problem "in the great drama of justice." By defining justice as doing one's art well, Polemarchus introduces a principle of the just city and soul that is picked up later in the dialogue, though not in the same form as he understands it. As Rosen suggests above, Polemarchus still thinks of justice as doing the task the city has assigned rather than doing a task well. Doing a task well requires self-knowledge and the ability to distinguish reality from appearance, which are not achieved for Rosen until an ascent to the Good in Book VII. Nevertheless, Polemarchus introduces the idea of justice; moreover, he is for Rosen not simply a tyrant, as Gadamer supposes, but rather a "transitional figure."

Gadamer's attention to a prior decision about the unfolding of the argument leads him to overlook the role of Polemarchus as a transitional figure between the desirous Cephalus and the spirited Thrasymachus,

10. *PR*, 37.

between their respective dispositions to pay each their due (331e) and harm people (332d). Polemarchus is essentially divided against himself. Socrates brings the two orientations into collision based upon Polemarchus's underlying belief that during peacetime money is justly saved and during war enemies are harmed. Polemarchus's problem, then, is not that he is a tyrant, but rather that he is caught between appetitive and martial dispositions. That he is not a tyrant is reinforced by the fact that he died resisting the tyranny of the Thirty. Rosen explains:

> The democratic resistance to tyranny was based in the Piraeus, and there was a decisive battle there near the temple of Bendis, at which Critias was killed. Lysias and Polemarchus, the two sons of Cephalus, participated in the resistance to the tyranny and were put to death by it, whereas Charmides died as a supporter of the Thirty.[11]

Contrary to what Gadamer asserts of him, Polemarchus is not entirely tyrannical, since he actually died defending democracy from tyranny. This is historiographical evidence; nevertheless, it suggests, as mentioned above, that Polemarchus is not only desirous like his father but spirited like a guardian. Moreover, guardians, as Rosen says, symbolize the dilemma facing philosophers; namely, how to be just to enemies (typically by means of noble lies) while also aspiring toward justice. In either case, Polemarchus moves the dialogue forward from the position his father represents.

3. THRASYMACHUS

Gadamer's thinking about Being in Plato's philosophy independently of context is reflected in his interpretation of Thrasymachus, an interpretation that is insensitive to dramatic context and conforms to the interplay of contraries (dialectic) that regulates Gadamer's reading of the dialogue. Gadamer asserts that Thrasymachus thinks that justice is to the advantage of the stronger and thus to the disadvantage of the urbane, the simpletons, the just who are ruled. Gadamer asserts twice that the conversation with Thrasymachus is fruitless: "Justice is what is to the advantage of the unjust. So the definition of justice as the advantage of the stronger provides no answer at all to the question of what justice is in essence and what justice means to the one who tries to live according to it," he writes; and "the ideal of the life of a tyrant which Thrasymachus

---

11. Ibid., 13.

develops thus contains no real answer to the question of what the essence of justice is."[12] However, what of Thrasymachus's character and the quality of his speech relative to that of Polemarchus and Cephalus?

Rosen's view of Thrasymachus parallels his interpretation of Polemarchus in that he discovers in the rhetorician a divided "nature"; but Thrasymachus is also a more promising character in some respects (in spirit and intelligence, but not desire). On the one hand, Thrasymachus's intellect is in servitude to his desires: he defends justice as the advantage of the stronger over the weaker (338c–343a), likening it to the fattening of sheep so that they might be fleeced all the better, and considers the just to be naïve simpletons because they are easily manipulated and abused. He argues that a life of injustice is best because it promises happiness and profit. Rosen comments of Thrasymachus, "In other words, if might makes right, then life is a perpetual war of each against all, as Hobbes teaches us: we are all enemies."[13] For Rosen, Thrasymachus is therefore prone to becoming a tyrant, as Gadamer emphasizes when he remarks of the rhetorician's definition of justice, "This definition says only that it is to the advantage of the tyrant, i.e., the one who violates what is just with impunity, that everybody else continue to adhere to the code of justice."[14]

On the other hand, according to Rosen, Thrasymachus takes the structure of the dialogue to a higher level than Polemarchus; though erotically uneducated like Cephalus, he displays a capacity for learning (reason) that was not evident in either of the preceding interlocutors. Rosen points out that Thrasymachus equates ruling with always achieving one's advantage and thus never making a mistake. This is Thrasymachus's reply to Cleitophon, who had suggested (in reply to Socrates) that the stronger choose what "he merely thinks" is to his advantage (340b–c).[15] By thus including knowledge in his definition, Thrasymachus moves the argument beyond Polemarchus, who did not make a distinction between what "is" and appearance.[16]

One would therefore expect Rosen to consider genuine Thrasymachus's admission that he is wrong; as, for example, when Thrasymachus

12. *DD*, 81.
13. *PR*, 39.
14. *DD*, 81.
15. Clitophon's suggestion to defend the idea of merely appearing to know rather than really having knowledge likely parrots what he had heard Socrates say in refuting Polemarchus (334–335).
16. *PR*, 44–45.

agrees with Socrates that "justice is virtue of the soul and injustice is vice, the just man will have a good life and the unjust man will have a bad one" (350d).[17] On the contrary, however, Rosen believes that Thrasymachus admits he is wrong only because he has been made to feel ashamed of himself and wants to save face, or look good in the eyes of the many. Nevertheless, as Kenneth Dorter illustrates, Thrasymachus is clearly more intelligent than anyone else in Book I; the discussion with him is more extended and complex than with either Polemarchus or Cephalus.[18] It therefore seems that although Thrasymachus takes the conversation to a higher level of reasoning and intensity, indicating a love of learning and spiritedness that Socrates deems appropriate to philosophers, he remains alienated from the Good on account of his uneducated desirous nature, a nature first introduced as an impediment to right living by Cephalus. Since it is an uneducated erotic nature that is also the ruin of Polemarchus, Book I symbolizes the ruinous forms of desire from the perspective of a philosophical *eros*.

CONCLUSION TO PART FIVE

Gadamer's tendency to focus upon a Platonic doctrine of sameness, which befits a mathematical ontology, inoculates him from taking into

---

17. Ibid., 58–59.

18. Thrasymachus is a tyrant because he is consumed by a desire for power; however, he is not intractable. More than any other speaker in Book I, Thrasymachus is a philosopher and as Kenneth Dorter observes below, his arguments are developed later in the dialogue as follows: (1) rulers serve the good of subjects (342e and later 419ab); (2) justice and knowledge have the same attributes (350c and later 442b–d and 443b; (3) virtue is performing well a function for which one is fit (352d–353c and later 433a–b, 443c–3, 608e–611a); (4) justice of groups strengthens the justice of an individual; and later, (4) what is true for the city is true for its citizens (351c–352a, 367e–372d). Dorter, *Transformation of Plato's Republic*, 4. These insights could not have been developed in conversation with either Cephalus or Polemarchus. Thrasymachus thus distinguishes himself as being more intelligent than them on account of the length, complexity, and insightfulness of his arguments. Furthermore, Thrasymachus' spiritedness had induced him to thrust himself into the conversation and exchange verbal blows with Socrates (336b–338). Yet his ambition to win the argument does not preclude a murky sense of justice. Thrasymachus' abusive language toward Socrates suggests a person who is deeply offended by sophists. He calls Socrates a shyster, swindler, "dupster," sneak, liar, and says that he is evasive (337, 338d, 341b–c). Although mistaken to attribute these qualities to Socrates, Thrasymachus' sensibilities are nevertheless philosophical: he hates liars. His capacity to be changed by the truth becomes clear during the closing stages of his conversation with Socrates.

consideration literary aspects of the dialogue he was trained to observe. As a result, he looks for a pattern of reasoning in the text that confirms his hypothesis about the dialectical structure of Being in Plato's philosophy. He contrasts the tradition, i.e., Cephalus, with the sophists Polemarchus and Thrasymachus, and remarks of Book II, "the discussion is here . . . set off from what preceded it."[19] Although the contraries exhibited in these juxtapositions might overlap in principle, in the sense of being equiprimordial, Gadamer's emphasis upon the negative character of Polemarchus and Thrasymachus to the exclusion of redeeming qualities suggests that the terms of the dialectic, as he understands it, are categorical and do not admit of opposites. The binary oppositions that characterize his reading of *Republic* I indicate that he has interpreted the dialogue according to a prior decision about Plato's theory of Being. Rosen, however, who cedes to a determinate idea of the Good that subsists independently of the process of speaking about it, demonstrates an interpretation of Book I that is inclusive of differences because he has a standard by which to gauge both the speakers' limitations and their possibilities. Allan Bloom explains, "Although the definitions of justice proposed by Cephalus, Polemarchus and Thrasymachus are all found wanting and must be abandoned, the discussions concerning them are not simply critical nor is their result only negative. From each something is learned which is of the essence of political life and which is reflected in the final definition and the regime that embodies it."[20] Even the most distorted of characters plays a positive role in contributing to the unfolding of higher degrees of intelligibility. This conclusion is not presented as a theory abstracted from the dialogue, but rather is derived from the phenomenological-existential character of the drama. In short, an investigation of Gadamer's and Rosen's differing understandings of the speeches and characters in Book I demonstrates that a transcendent idea

---

19. *DD*, 78.

20. Bloom, "Interpretive Essay," 315. Dorter reiterates Bloom's point: "The modes of thinking through which the dialogue passes during its rise and return exemplify the different levels of thought processes classified under the Divided Line." Dorter, *Transformation of Plato's Republic*, 7. Dorter summarizes that which the sequence of arguments in the *Republic* teach but which Gadamer neglects: "If the progressive changes in the character of the dialogue reflect a movement from simpler but less adequate formulations to more adequate but more difficult ones, any inadequacy in argument may be intended to reflect the limitations of the current approach, rather than being simply unsuccessful." Ibid., ix.

of the Good, rather than an immanently transcendent idea, is conducive to the formation of an open society.[21]

What are we to conclude, then? Gadamer had resisted Heidegger's interpretation of Plato on the grounds that the dialogue form belies any endeavor to reduce Plato's philosophy to a doctrine. The background to Heidegger's Plato, Gadamer suggests, is the German idealist tradition; far from undermining German idealism, Heidegger's reading of Plato perpetuates it, for by foisting upon Plato modern scientific criteria of truth, it is Heidegger, not Plato, who forgets the meaning of Being. But Gadamer does not fare any better. The Hegelian-mathematical substrate of his method inclines him to suppress in deed the other-as-other whom he lauds in speech, because the strength of mathematical reasoning is depersonalization. This has profound consequences for political theory. Mathematical notions of equality neutralize differences between people, their likes and dislikes. The result is an equality of sameness and the homogenization of the public space according to the preferences of everyone included in the conversation. For the sake of an open society, another basis for right living must be sought.

Rosen's political theory surfaces in this regard. An investigation of his interpretation of Plato demonstrates that differences between people become visible in the light of the Good. The lover of wisdom does not disdain public life, and is not a contemplative estranged from others and his own body in a flight of the alone to the alone. Rather it is precisely a love of the Good that enables a philosopher to see the worth and potential in others and act prudently in the public sphere. Without insisting upon the same standard for everyone, civic friendship finds a renewed place in establishing harmony between persons of varying occupations and desires. Instead of everyone being educated with a view to reinforcing a localized ideology couched in the language of universality, students are educated for the sake of who they are, which is to the benefit of all. No one wants Thrasymachus to become a Member of Parliament, but he can

21. In contrast to Gadamer, who emphasizes in Book I the limitations of the speakers and how they contribute to a decline in the public ethos and citizenship, Rosen explains how each of the speakers and their views are limited, yet, from another standpoint, contribute to the unity of the dialogue; for example, Rosen admits that Book I is a failure when gauged against the aim to define justice, and continues, "This may be so, but we have found considerable agreement among the main speakers with respect to the claim that justice is doing good to your friends and harm to your enemies." *PR*, 60. Whereas Gadamer juxtaposes the just philosopher (Socrates) with the unjust non-philosopher (Thrasymachus), Rosen explains how the later speeches envelop early ones into a higher sense of purpose.

still find fulfillment and serve the city in another capacity, with a degree of freedom that befits his intelligent mind but morally distorted life.

While Gadamer might recoil from the suggestion that in Plato's view not everyone desires self-understanding, his thinking does offer scope in which to elucidate Rosen's position. Referring to the "fusion of horizons" in *Truth and Method*, Rosen argues that Gadamer's negotiation of the past and present through dialogue attests to a third possibility:

> I hold, in other words, that *Verstehen*, or the act of coming to a mutual understanding, is not simply the production of a new sense through the fusion of two horizons, my own and that of the producer of the work I am inspecting, but that the fusion of horizons is intrinsically the opening of a single horizon thanks to the union of my understanding with that of the producer in the universal sense that the work exhibits. This suggestion, incidentally, is not offered as a criticism of Gadamer but rather as my own "interpretation" of the truth of his doctrine of *Horizontverschmelzung*. I therefore claim to have entered into the universal sense of his doctrine, but not to have thought his thoughts as he himself thought them.[22]

According to Rosen, mutual understanding does not produce a new sense, but rather opens up a third sense, a single horizon implicit to the past and the present.[23] This is the eternal idea available, in however partial a way, "to any competent thinker."[24]

---

22. Rosen, "Horizontverschmelzung," 211.

23. Consider the following words by Gadamer: "Now the moral example which we have used makes clear at once what is meant when the text says that he who is himself supposed to get a vision of the thing itself or he who would engender that vision in another must have an 'affinity' for the thing besides having the intellectual gifts of comprehension and memory." Also, "The best that can be hoped for is a meager 'indication' which could illumine the thing only for someone who has the prerequisite nature to understand it" (*DD*, 116–118). What is this affinity to which Gadamer is referring? Is it the prerequisite nature for understanding? Is it a vision of the thing itself and an interpretation that is true to Plato's intent? It would seem that Gadamer is referring to pure thought (reason) thinking itself, that this is a gift of nature to the few and that Plato's motivations or intentions are knowable because they are grounded in a desire for the universal and unchanging idea to which Gadamer himself is drawn. Rosen might well make this argument against Gadamer; however, it depends upon imposing a judgment about the nature of existence upon Gadamer's thought that Gadamer does not share. The "fusion of horizons" construed by Rosen as a universal idea presumes that Gadamer's phenomenological descriptions are metaphysical claims, that when Gadamer relates an experience he is making an objective statement about the nature of reality.

24. Rosen thus announces a criticism that resembles Derrida's; namely, that the "fu-

It might be countered that this third way is impossible to distinguish from a human way of looking without insisting upon human finitude, an argument that undermines the ontological status of the ground to which Rosen is pointing. However, mutual understanding transpires in the realm of genesis. There is no knowledge of the Ideas that is not mediated by the contingencies of human existence. Yet this does not mean that the Ideas are themselves historical any more than the alternative, Rosen's, means that they are tantamount to an objective doctrine. This either/or reasoning is but a reversion to a mathematical-logical rationalism that prevents Gadamer from discerning the universal in the particular. In other words, there is no *logos* of the whole without a desire for completion that responds to the creative impulse to express it. Truth is linguistically mediated, but is not reducible to language. In fact, it is the conviction that language and object are the same that inclines Gadamer to counter with a dialectical relationship between word and thing. But this kind of "dialectic" is a reverse image of a logical identity, and thus it is yet another kind of logic nevertheless. If we might then part from Gadamer's rationalism, and argue that there is no "method" required to understand the Good because it is revealed to us (and not by us), then we might quell the quarrel between poetry and philosophy and educate people for the sake of a more just and inclusive society.

---

sion of horizons" is a "rationalism of the world." Derrida writes: "Does not the 'good will' presupposed by the attempt to come to a mutual understanding, agreement, or 'fusion of horizons' reveal a form of will, indeed will to power, asks Gadamer." Quoted in Lammi, "Zuckert's Postmodern Platos," 228. The phrase "will to power" refers to a Kantian metaphysics of the will.

Appendix

THE EARLY GREEK NOTION OF TRUTH

ACCORDING TO HEIDEGGER, THE early Greeks understood truth as *aletheia* and the region in which truth appears (or what he calls the "essence of Being") as *physis*.[1] Both *aletheia* and *physis* are represented during the first stage of the ascent toward the idea of all ideas in "The Allegory of the Cave" (*Republic*, 514a–521b). P. Christopher Smith speaks for Heidegger: ". . . this existence in-the-world, this 'dwelling' of the inhabitants of the 'cave,' is indeed closer to the original, earlier truth of things. The inhabitants of the cave live trustingly within a world as it first presents itself."[2] Heidegger observes that the entrance to the cave is both hidden from the light of the sun and illumined or unconcealed by it, and writes, "The enclosure of the cave, open in itself, and what it surrounds and thus hides, indicate together an outer part, the unhidden, which by day extends in the light."[3] The cave is an enclosure that is open. What is revealed is thus gradually concealed, and what is concealed is gradually revealed, such that shadows become enlightened and the enlightened falls within a shadow. The movement Heidegger suggests is symbolic of the Heraclitean essence of Being, as appearing (*physis*) is not something that sometimes happens to beings. He states, "Appearing is the very essence of Being."[4] That is, Being as *physis* is an emerging-withdrawal.

---

1. Heidegger defines Being (*Sein*) as follows: "In the question which we are to work out, what is asked about is Being—that which determines entities as entities, that on the basis of which [*woraufhin*] entities are already understood, however we may discuss them in detail. The Being of entities 'is' not an entity." Heidegger draws a distinction between Being and beings (*seiend*). Being is the context or prior understanding in which beings are understood, and hence is not itself a being. *BT*, 25–26.

2. Smith, "Gadamer's Heideggerian Interpretation of Plato," 211.

3. *PDT*, 261.

4. *IM*, 101.

In Heidegger's interpretation then, appearing in the sense of coming to be visible, or ontologically present, precedes and makes possible the derivative sense of "appear" meaning "seem" or "have a semblance."

> The essence of Being is physis. Appearing is the power that emerges. Appearing makes manifest. Already we know then that Being, appearing, causes to emerge from concealment. Since the being as such is, it places itself in and stands in unconcealment, "*aletheia*."[5]

While *physis*, or the essence of Being, is the power of appearing-disappearing that makes it possible for beings to come to be, the open region within that dynamic power of *physis* in which beings come to stand is called *aletheia*. In other words, in the early Greek understanding of Being, beings (entities) become visible or appear within and out of Being or, as Heidegger says, "out of themselves."[6] This standing in itself is called presence. He writes, "Something is present to us. It stands steadily by itself and thus manifests itself. It is. For the Greeks 'being' basically meant this standing presence."[7] More specifically, Heidegger equates presence with the German *Anwesen*, which designates a homestead or an estate.[8] The metaphor suggests that beings that come to be under their own power establish a home and therein feel like themselves, glowing radiantly in the entrance to the cave.

PLATO'S DOCTRINE OF TRUTH

In the "Allegory of the Cave" Plato initiates a different way of thinking about Being. Whereas Being, for the early Greeks, was constituted in a manner that enabled the power of *physis* to manifest itself in appearances, Plato founds a relationship to Being that is subjective and hence conceals the ground of beings. He shifts from thinking of beings from a position within the entrance of the cave to determining them to be from the perspective of the sun, which symbolizes a human-centered position because it is fixed on sight. By thinking of beings solely in terms of what is visible, Plato determines them to be according to an idea (*eidos, Ausehen*) that belongs not to beings, but to human beings. The ramification of this shift toward truth as correctness of sight is that

5. Ibid., 102.
6. Ibid., 100.
7. Ibid., 61.
8. Ibid.

Being is divested of non-Being. This, Heidegger says, is tantamount to the forgetfulness of Being that subsequently came to define the history of western philosophy.

In "Plato's Doctrine of Truth" Heidegger maps the stages through which Plato increases the magnification of light upon one aspect of an appearance, the outward appearance of whatever is seen (*eidos*). In so doing, the showing-forth in unconcealment is "wrested from, and sustained within surrounding obscurity (*lethe*)."[9] The magnification of light is signaled in the "Allegory" by pauses during the ascent, at which times the vision of the prisoners, already painful after having been liberated from the cave, grows accustomed to the brightness. The transitions from the cave into the light of day, and from there back into the cave, always demand a reorientation of the eyes from the darkness to the light and from the light to the darkness. But the pain is not simply due to the adjustment of vision. Heidegger explains that the gradual shift in the orientation of seeing is symbolic of a change in the "Being of man" (*paideia*). Just as the eyes are corrected in order to fix the gaze according to the radiance of a permanent light, there is also a gradual reorientation of the soul toward an unchanging position *vis à vis* beings.[10] Heidegger, therefore, denies that the sun is beyond being with a character all its own, and instead believes that it is coordinate with a human relation toward Being.

The ascent from the cave to the sun centers upon correct seeing (*idein*). Heidegger writes, "If, in every attitude towards beings there is, we are concerned with the *idein* of *idea*, with catching sight of 'outward appearance,' then every effort must be gathered into the possibility of such a 'seeing.'"[11] The correctness of seeing is determined by a permanent and unchanging light (*idea*), but this light, as Plato says of the sun, is what makes beings visible in their outward appearance (*eidos*). The intensification of light magnifies one aspect of the outward appearance until it is brought into alignment, or made to correspond, with the idea. The Idea of all ideas is thus the first cause, as Plato says, of everything coming to be and is "the yoke between recognizing and what is recognized."[12] But as such it makes what is seen (*eidos*) correspond to the permanent

9. Smith, "Gadamer's Heideggerian Interpretation of Plato," 212.
10. *PDT*, 256.
11. Ibid., 265.
12. Ibid., 266.

seeing (*idein*) of the *idea*. Heidegger explains, "In consequence of this assimilation of perceiving as an *idein* into an *idea*, an *omoiosis* subsists, an agreement between recognizing and the thing itself."[13] At the height of the ascent, when the sunlike mind's eye is assimilated to the sun, the *eidos* of the appearing has similarly been brought into conformity with the thing itself. The thing itself is the first cause of all that is visible, responsible for its coming to be; but for Heidegger it is above all identical to the human intellect.[14]

The First Cause or Being of beings, therefore, does not let beings come from out of a region of obscurity (non-Being). Instead, by intensifying the focus upon one aspect of "the individual things themselves" (*eide*), by increasing their exposure to the light, Smith says, "the privation 'a' of 'aletheia' is lost sight of . . . ."[15] At the highest stage of the ascent, the way in which the outward appearance (*eidos*) becomes visible has shifted to a permanent and unchanging idea of the intellect. Heidegger concludes:

> When Plato says that the idea is the master permitting unhiddenness, he banishes to something left unsaid the fact that henceforth the essence of truth does not unfold out of its own essential fullness as the essence of unhiddenness, but shifts its abode to the essence of the idea. The essence of truth relinquishes the basic feature of unhiddenness.[16]

The abode of the idea that masters *aletheia* or places it under a yoke is a human perspective (intellectual) upon beings. Truth as correctness that consists in achieving the "right look" with respect to what is seen is thus ultimately "the label of the human attitude towards beings."[17] More specifically, since *idea* is both what is seen (*eidos*) and a human way of seeing (*idein*), Plato conflates what he takes to be Being (whatness) with a subjective perspective. For Heidegger, this in turn launches a pattern of thinking that reaches its consummation in Nietzsche's will to power, where "all truth is fabrication, an invention of the human subject."[18]

13. Ibid., 265.

14. Heidegger states, "[C]onsciousness, properly speaking, has to do with the way outward appearance manifests itself and is preserved in the brightness of its steady appearance . . . Consciousness, properly speaking, applies to the idea." Ibid., 261.

15. Smith, "Gadamer's Heideggerian Interpretation of Plato," 212.

16. *PDT*, 265.

17. Ibid.

18. Smith "Gadamer's Heideggerian Interpretation of Plato," 212.

Bibliography

Ambrosio, Francis, J. "Dawn and Dusk: Gadamer and Heidegger on Truth." *Man and World* 19 (1986) 21–53.

———. "The Figure of Socrates in Gadamer's Philosophical Hermeneutics." In *The Philosophy of Hans-Georg Gadamer*, edited by Lewis Edwin Halan, 259–73. Chicago: Open Court, 1997.

———. "Gadamer and Aristotle: Hermeneutics as Participation in Tradition." *Proceedings of the ACPA* 62 (1988) 174–82.

———. "Gadamer, Plato and the Discipline of Dialogue." *International Philosophical Quarterly* 27:1 (1987) 17–32.

Aristotle. *The Complete Works of Aristotle*. Translated by Jonathon Barnes. Princeton, New Jersey: Princeton University Press, 1995.

Bambach, Charles. *Heidegger's Roots: Nietzsche, National Socialism and the Greeks*. Ithaca, New York: Cornell University Press, 2003.

Bernasconi, Robert. "Bridging the Abyss: Heidegger and Gadamer." *Research in Phenomenology* XVI (1986) 1–24.

Bloom, Allan. *Love and Friendship*. New York: Simon and Schuster, 1993.

———. "Interpretive Essay." In *The Republic of Plato*. Translated by Allan Bloom, 307–436. New York: Basic Books, 1968.

Bluck, R. S. "The View of Stenzel" Appendix Eight. In *Plato's Phaedo*, 184–85. Translated by R. S. Bluck. New York: The Liberal Arts Press, 1955.

Carman, Taylor. *Heidegger's Analytic*. Cambridge: Cambridge University Press, 2003.

Dahlstrom, Daniel, O. *Heidegger's Concept of Truth*. Cambridge: Cambridge University Press, 2001.

Dallmayr, Fred. "Hermeneutics and Justice." In *Festivals of Interpretation: Essays on Hans-Georg Gadamer*, edited by Kathleen Wright, 90–110. Albany, New York: State University of New York Press, 1990.

De Paulo, Craig, editor. *Augustine's Influence on Heidegger: The Emergence of an Augustinian Phenomenology*. New York: Edwin Mellen, 2006.

Decker, Kevin. "The Limits of Radical Openness: Gadamer on Socratic Dialectic and Plato's Idea of the Good." *Symposium* IV:1 (2000) 5–32.

Dorter, Kenneth. *The Transformation of Plato's Republic*. Toronto: Lexington, 2006.

Dostal, Robert. "Beyond Being: Heidegger's Plato." *The Journal of the History of Philosophy* 23:1 (January 1985) 71–98.

———. "Gadamer's Continuous Challenge." In *The Philosophy of Hans-Georg Gadamer*, edited by Lewis Edwin Hahn, 289–307. Chicago: Open Court, 1997.

———. "Gadamer: The Man and His Work." In *The Cambridge Companion to Gadamer*, edited by Robert Dostal, 13–33. New York: Cambridge University Press, 2002.

———. "Gadamer's Relation to Heidegger and Phenomenology." In *The Cambridge Companion to Gadamer*, edited by Robert Dostal, 247–66. New York: Cambridge University Press, 2002.

Dreyfus, H. and H. Hall. *Heidegger: A Critical Reader*. Oxford: Blackwell, 1992.

Fried, Gregory. "Back to the Cave: A Platonic Rejoinder to Heideggerian Postmodernism." In *Heidegger and the Greeks: Interpretive Essays*, edited by Drew A. Hyland and John Panteleimon Manoussakis, 157–76. Bloomington: Indiana University Press, 2006.

Friedlander, Paul. *Plato: An Introduction*. Translated by Hans Meyerhoff. New York: Harper Torchbooks, 1964.

Fritsche, Johannes. "With Plato into Kairos before the Kehre: On Heidegger's Different Interpretations of Plato." In *Heidegger and Plato: Toward Dialogue*, edited by Catalin Partenie and Tom Rockmore, 140–77. Evanston: Northwestern University Press, 2005.

Gadamer, Hans-Georg. *Dialogue and Dialectic: Eight Hermeneutical Studies on Plato*. Translated by P. Christopher Smith. New Haven, Connecticut: Yale University Press, 1980.

———. *The Gadamer Reader: A Bouquet of Later Writings*, edited by Richard E. Palmer. Evanston: Northwestern University Press, 2007.

———. "The Greeks (1979)." In *Heidegger's Ways*. Translated by John W. Stanley, 139–152. New York: State University of New York Press, 1994.

———. *Hegel's Dialectic*. Translated by P. Christopher Smith. New Haven: Yale University Press, 1971.

———. "Hermeneutics as Practical Philosophy." In *Philosophy: End or Transformation?* edited by Kenneth Baynes, 319–350. Cambridge: MIT Press, 1987.

———. *The Idea of the Good in Platonic-Aristotelian Philosophy*. Translated by P. Christopher Smith. New Haven: Yale University Press, 1986.

———. *Philosophical Apprenticeships*. Translated by Robert Sullivan. London: MIT Press, 1985.

———. *Philosophical Hermeneutics*, edited by David E. Linge. Berkeley: University of California Press, 1976.

———. "Plato (1976)." In *Heidegger's Ways*. Translated by John W. Stanley, 81–93. New York: State University of New York Press, 1994.

———. *Plato's Dialectical Ethics*. Translated by Robert Wallace. New Haven: Yale University Press, 1991.

———. "Reflections on My Philosophical Journey." In *The Philosophy of Hans-Georg Gadamer*, edited by Lewis Hahn. Chicago: Open Court, 1997.

———. *The Relevance of the Beautiful and Other Essays*. Edited by Robert Bernasconi. Cambridge: Cambridge University Press, 1977.

———. "Reply to Robert J. Dostal." In *The Philosophy of Hans-Georg Gadamer*, edited by Lewis Edwin Kahn, 308. Chicago: Open Court, 1997.

———. "Reply to Robert R. Sullivan." In *The Philosophy of Hans-Georg Gadamer*, edited by Lewis Edwin Kahn, 256–58. Chicago: Open Court, 1997.

———. *Truth and Method*. New York: Crossroad Publishing, 1988.

Gonzalez, Francisco. "Dialectic as 'Philosophical Embarrassment': Heidegger's Critique of Plato's Method." In *Journal of the History of Philosophy* 40:3 (2002) 361–89.

Graeser, Andreas. "Does Philosophical Hermeneutics Rest Upon a Mistake? Some Quarrels with Truth and Method." In *Issues in the Philosophy of Language Past and Present*, 169–78. Bern: Peter Lang, 1999.

Grondin, Jean. "Gadamer and the Tubingen School." In *Hermeneutic Philosophy and Plato: Gadamer's Response to the* Philebus, Collection "Studies in Ancient Philosophy." Edited by C. J. Gill and F. Renaud. Academia Verlag: Sankt Augustin (Germany), 2009.

———. *Hans-Georg Gadamer: A Biography*. Translated by Joel Weinsheimer. New Haven: Yale University Press, 2003.

———. *The Philosophy of Hans-Georg Gadamer*. Translated by Kathryn Plant. Montreal: McGill-Queen's University Press, 2003.

———. "The Universality of Hermeneutics and Rhetoric in the Thought of Gadamer." *Symposium: Journal of the Society for Hermeneutics and Postmodern Thought* 8:2 (2004) 325-38.

Heidegger, Martin. *The Basic Problems of Phenomenology*. Translated by Albert Hofstadter. Bloomington, Indiana: Indiana University Press, 1988.

———. *Being and Time*. Translated by Joan Stambaugh. New York: State University of New York Press, 1996.

———. *The Essence of Truth: On Plato's Allegory of the Cave and Theaetetus*. Translated by Ted Sadler. New York: Continuum Books, 2002.

———. *Identity and Difference*. Translated by Joan Stambraugh. New York: Harper & Row, 1957.

———. *An Introduction to Metaphysics*. Translated by Ralph Manheim. New Haven: Yale University Press, 1974.

———. "Letter on Humanism." In *Martin Heidegger: Basic Writings*, edited by David Farrell Krell, 189-242. New York: Harper & Row, 1977.

———. *Nietzsche: The Will to Power as Art*. Translated by David Farrel Krell. New York: Harper and Row, 1961.

———. "Plato's Doctrine of Truth." In *Philosophy in the Twentieth Century* 3, edited by W. Barnett and H. Aiken, 250-70. New York: Random House, 1962.

———. *The Question Concerning Technology and Other Essays*. Translated by William Lovitt. New York: Harper Torchbooks, 1977,

———. "Self-Assertion of the German University." In *The Heidegger Controversy: A Critical Reader*, edited by Richard Wolin, 29-39. Cambridge, Massachusetts: MIT Press, 1993.

———. *Supplements: From the Earliest Essays to Being and Time and Beyond*, edited by John Van Buren. Albany: State University Press, 2002.

———. *Time and Being*. Translated by Joan Stanbaugh. Evanston: Harper and Row, 1972.

Hölderlin, Friedrich. "Germania." In *Hyperion and Selected Poems*, edited by Eric Santner, 210-11. New York: Continuum, 1990.

Hopkins, Burt C. "Klein and Gadamer on the Arithmos-Structure of Platonic Eidetic Numbers." In *Philosophy Today* 52 (2008) 151-57.

Jeager, Werner. *Aristotle's Fundamentals of the History of His Development*. Translated by Richard Robinson. London: Oxford University Press, 1948.

Kant, Immanuel. *Critique of Pure Reason*. Translated by Norman Kemp Smith. New York: Palgrave Macmillan, 2007.

Kidder, Paulette. "Gadamer and the Platonic Eidos." *Philosophy Today* Spring (1995) 83-92.

Kisiel, Theodore. *The Genesis of Heidegger's Being and Time*. Berkeley: University of California Press, 1995.

———. *Heidegger's Way of Thought*. New York: Continuum, 2002.
Kisiel, Theodore and Thomas Sheehan, editors. *Becoming Heidegger: On the Trial of His Early Occasional Writings, 1910-1927*. Evanston: Northwestern University Press, 2007.
Korab-Karpowicz, W. J. "Heidegger's Hidden Path: From Philosophy to Politics." *Review of Metaphysics* December (2007) 295-315.
Kramer, H. J. *Plato and the Foundations of Metaphysics: A Work on the Theory of the Principles and Unwritten Doctrines of Plato with a Collection of Fundamental Documents*, edited and translated by John R. Catan. Albany: State University of New York Press, 1990.
Lammi, Walter. "On Catherine Zuckert's Postmodern Platos and the Strauss-Gadamer Debate." *Interpretation* 25:2 (1998) 223-48.
Linge, David E. "Editor's Introduction." In *Philosophical Hermeneutics*. Translated by David E. Linge, xi-xvii. Los Angeles: University of California Press, 1976.
Mitscherling, Jeff. "Gadamer's Legacy in Aesthetics and Plato Studies: Play and Participation in the Work of Art." *Symposium: Journal of the Society for Hermeneutics and Postmodern Thought* 6:2 (2002) 149-65.
Mulhall, Stephen. *Philosophical Myths of the Fall*. Princeton: Princeton University Press, 2005.
Newell, Waller. *Ruling Passion: The Erotics of Statescraft in Platonic Political Philosophy*. New York: Rowan and Littlefield, 2000.
Nietzsche, Friedrich. "How the 'Real World' at Last Became a Myth." In *Twilight of the Idols*. Translated by R. J. Hollingdale, 40-41. New York: Penguin Books, 1968.
———. "The Madman." In *The Gay Science*. Translated by Walter Kaufmann, 181-82. New York: Vintage Books, 1974.
Orozco, Teresa. "The Art of Allusion: Hans-Georg Gadamer's Philosophical Interventions under National Socialism." In *Gadamer's Repercussions: Reconsidering Philosophical Hermeneutics*, edited by Bruce Krajewski, 212-28. Berkeley: University of California Press, 2004.
Palmer, Richard. *Hermeneutics*. Evanston, Illinois: Northwestern University Press, 1969.
Partenie, Catalin and Tom Rockmore. "Introduction." In *Heidegger and Plato: Toward Dialogue*, edited by Partenie and Rockmore, xix-xxviii. Evanston: Northwestern University Press, 2005.
Passmore, John. *A Hundred Years of Philosophy*. New York: Penguin, 1980.
Peperzak, Adriaan. "Heidegger and Plato's Idea of the Good." In *Reading Heidegger: Commemorations*, edited by John Sallis, 259-85. Bloomington, Indiana: Indiana University Press, 1993.
Plato. *Plato: The Complete Works*, edited by John Cooper. Indianapolis: Hackett, 1997.
Poggeler, Otto. *Martin Heidegger's Path of Thinking*. Translated by Daniel Magurshak. New Jersey: Humanities Press International, 1963.
Politis, Vasilis. *Paul Natorp: Plato's Theory of Ideas*. Germany: Academia Verlag Sankt Augustin, 2004.
Richardson, William. *Heidegger: Through Phenomenology to Thought*. The Hague: Martinus Nijhoff, 1967.
Rockmore, Tom. "Heidegger's Uses of Plato and the History of Philosophy." In *Heidegger and Plato: Toward Dialogue*, edited by Catalin Partenie and Tom Rockmore, 192-212. Evanston: Northwestern University Press, 2005.

Rosen, Stanley. "Are We Such Stuff as Dreams are Made On? Against Reductionism." In *Gadamer's Century: Essays in Honour of Hans-Georg Gadamer*, edited by Jeff Malpas, Ulrich Arnswald and Jens Kertscher, 257–77. London, England: MIT Press, 2002.
———. "Heidegger's Interpretation of Plato." In *Essays in Metaphysics*, edited by Carl G. Vaught, 51–77. University Park: Pennsylvania State University Press, 1970.
———. *Hermeneutics as Politics*. Oxford: Oxford University Press, 1987.
———. "Horizontverschmelzung." In *The Cambridge Companion to Gadamer*, edited by Robert Dostal. New York: Cambridge University Press, 2002.
———. "Ideas." *Review of Metaphysics* 16 (1963) 407–41.
———. "Leo Strauss and the Quarrel Between the Ancients and the Moderns." In *Leo Strauss's Thought: Toward a Critical Engagement*, edited by Alan Udoff, 155–68. Boulder, Colorado: Cynne Rienner, 1991.
———. *Nihilism: A Philosophical Essay*. New Haven: Yale University Press, 1969.
———. "Plato's Myth of the Reversed Cosmos." *Review of Metaphysics* 33:1 (1979) 59–85.
———. *Plato's Republic: A Study*. New Haven: Yale University Press, 2005.
———. *Plato's Symposium*. New Haven: Yale University Press, 1987.
———. *The Question of Being: A Reversal of Heidegger*. New Haven: Yale University Press, 1993.
———. "Remarks on Heidegger's Plato." In *Heidegger and Plato: Toward Dialogue*, edited by Catalin Partenie and Tom Rockmore, 178–91. Evanston, Illinois: Northwestern University Press, 2005.
———. "The Role of Eros in Plato's *Republic*." *Review of Metaphysics* 18 (March 1965) 452–475.
Schmid, Thomas. *Plato's Charmides and the Socratic Ideal of Rationality*. Albany: New York Press, 1998.
Schmidt, Dennis, J. "Poetry and Political: Gadamer, Plato, and Heidegger on the Politics of Language." In *Festivals of Interpretation*, edited by Kathleen Wright, 209–27. New York: State University of New York Press, 1996.
Sheehan, Thomas. "Heidegger and the Nazis." *The New York Review of Books* 25:10 (June 16, 1988) 38–47.
Smith, P. Christopher. "Between the Audible Word and the Envisionable Concept: Re-Reading Plato's Theaetetus after Gadamer." *Continental Philosophy Review* 33 (2000) 327–44.
———. "The Ethical Dimensions of Gadamer's Hermeneutical Theory." *Research and Phenomenology* 18 (1988) 75–91.
———. "H. G. Gadamer's Heideggerian Interpretation of Plato." *Journal of the British Society for Phenomenology* 12:3 (October 1981) 211–30.
———. "Plato as Impulse and Obstacle in Gadamer's Development of a Hermeneutical Theory." In *Gadamer and Hermeneutics*, edited by Hugh Silverman, 23–41. New York: Routledge, 1991.
———. "Translator's Introduction." In *The Idea of the Good in Platonic-Aristotelian Philosophy*, by Hans-Georg Gadamer. Translated by Christopher Smith, vii–xxxi. New Haven: Yale University Press, 1986.
Strauss, Leo. *The City and Man*. Chicago: University of Chicago Press, 1964.
———. *Natural Right and History*. Chicago: University of Chicago Press, 1950.
———. *Persecution and the Art of Writing*. Chicago: University of Chicago Press, 1980.

Sullivan, Robert. "Gadamer's Early and Distinctively Political Hermeneutics." In *The Philosophy of Hans-Georg Gadamer*, edited by Lewis Edwin Kahn, 237–55. Chicago: Open Court, 1997.

———. *Political Hermeneutics: The Early Thinking of Hans-Georg Gadamer*, London: Pennsylvania State University Press, 1980.

———. "Translator's Introduction." In *Philosophical Apprenticeships*, by Hans-Georg Gadamer. Translated by Robert Sullivan, ii–xiii. London: MIT Press, 1985.

Tigerstedt, E. N. *Interpreting Plato*. Stockholm: Almqvist & Wiksell International, 1977.

Van Buren, John. "Martin Heidegger, Martin Luther." In *Reading Heidegger from the Start*, edited by Theodore Kisiel and John van Buren, 159–74. Albany: State University of New York Press, 1994.

———. *The Young Heidegger: Rumor of the Hidden King*. Bloomington, Indiana: Indiana University Press, 1994.

Wachterhauser, Brice R. *Beyond Being: Gadamer's Post-Platonic Hermeneutic Ontology*. Evanston, Illinois: Northwestern University Press, 1999.

White, Carol, J. "Heidegger and the Greeks." In *A Companion to Heidegger*, edited by Herbert L. Dreyfus, 121–40. New York: Blackwell, 2005.

White, Nicholas. "Observations and Questions about Hans-Georg Gadamer's Interpretation of Plato." In *Platonic Writings, Platonic Readings*, edited by Charles L. Griswold, 247–57. New York: Routledge, 1988.

Zarander, Marlene. "The Mirror and Triple Reflection." In *Critical Heidegger*, edited by Christopher Macann, 7–26. New York: Routledge, 1996.

Zuckert, Catherine. "Hermeneutics in Practice: Gadamer on Ancient Philosophy." In *The Cambridge Companion to Gadamer*, edited by Robert J. Dostal, 201–24. New York: Cambridge University Press, 2002.

———. "On the Politics of Hermeneutics: A Response to Orozco and Waite." In *Gadamer's Repercussions: Reconsidering Philosophical Hermeneutics*, edited by Bruce Krajewski, 229–43. Berkeley: University of California Press, 2004.

———. *Postmodern Platos*. Chicago: University of Chicago Press, 1996.

———. *The Truth About Leo Strauss: Political Philosophy and American Democracy*. Chicago: University of Chicago Press, 2006.